POOR JOSHUA

POOR JOSHUA

THE *DeSHANEY* CASE AND CHILD ABUSE IN AMERICA

John R. Howard

SUNY
PRESS

Published by State University of New York Press, Albany

Printed in the United States of America

For information, contact State University of New York Press, Albany, NY
www.sunypress.edu

Library of Congress Cataloging-in-Publication Data

Names: Howard, John R., 1933- author.
Title: Poor Joshua : the DeShaney case and child abuse in America / John R. Howard
Description: Albany : State University of New York Press, 2018. | "Appendix: DeShaney v. Winnebago County Department of Social Services, 489 U.S., 189 (1989)." | Includes bibliographical references and index.
Identifiers: LCCN 2017038440 | ISBN 9781438470498 (hardcover : alk. paper) | ISBN 9781438470504 (ebook)
Subjects: LCSH: DeShaney, Joshua, 1979—Trials, litigation, etc. | DeShaney, Melody—Trials, litigation, etc. | Winnebago County (Wis.). Department of Social Services—Trials, litigation, etc. | Child abuse—Law and legislation—United States—Cases. | Social service—Malpractice—United States—Cases. | Government liability—United States—Cases.
Classification: LCC KF228.D464 H69 2018 | DDC 345.73/025554—dc23
LC record available at https://lccn.loc.gov/2017038440

10 9 8 7 6 5 4 3 2 1

CONTENTS

Acknowledgments ix

PART ONE: JOURNEY TO A DISTANT LAND

Chapter One An American Story / 3

Chapter Two Background to Judgment Day / 11

Chapter Three Things Unseen / 27

Chapter Four Into the Night / 41

Chapter Five A Light Too Late / 47

PART TWO: THE LAW'S MAJESTY

Chapter Six Prologue to Armageddon / 67

Chapter Seven In a Distant Place / 85

Chapter Eight The Supreme Court Decides / 99

Chapter Nine The Crying Game / 127

Chapter Ten Rearguing *DeShaney* / 141

Appendix 159

Notes 183

Bibliography 193

Index 199

"Poor Joshua . . . It is a sad commentary on American life . . .
that this child . . . and his mother . . . are denied . . .
the opportunity to have the facts of their case considered . . ."

—Justice Harry Blackmun, in his dissenting opinion,
DeShaney v. Winnebago County Department of Social Services

ACKNOWLEDGMENTS

In the course of doing research for *Poor Joshua*, I met with Judge John Reynolds, who wrote the first decision in *DeShaney*. I also interviewed Donald Sullivan and Curry First, the attorneys who carried Joshua's cause to the Supreme Court. I owe all three more than words can express for their candor, their intellect, their passion, and their insights. The interviews were conducted several years after the Supreme Court decision was handed down, the passage of time allowing the three men to reflect even more deeply on the meaning of the case and their involvement in it. This book has been completed years after the interviews, allowing me to draw on a wider array of resources in analyzing the decision and exploring its social consequences. I also want to thank the librarians at the National Archives and the Supreme Court Library for their assistance in making available files that allowed for a day-to-day recounting of *DeShaney*'s tragic events, and Purchase College for providing a grant that afforded an opportunity to journey to Wisconsin and visit the places where many of the events in the case unfolded. Finally, I owe a debt of gratitude to Karen Leahy, Leigh Howard, Robert Smith, Joseph Fashing, Barrington Wright, and Douglas Sheff, who read various versions of the manuscript and provided valuable suggestions as to how to make it better.

PART ONE

JOURNEY TO A DISTANT LAND

CHAPTER ONE

AN AMERICAN STORY

This Is How It Began

January 22, 1983

In emergency rooms, the week has a rhythm as predictable as the ocean's tides. On Friday night a wave begins to wash in: the knife wounds, the busted noses, the fractured ribs. And then around three a.m., Saturday morning, the tide recedes as the bars close, the parties end, and the bruised but not broken make their way home. But by Saturday night a stronger, more furious tide sweeps in and crests in the hours around midnight with the gunshot wounds, the slashed faces, the mangled limbs, and the cracked skulls. And then, again, the tide recedes as Saturday night turns into Sunday morning and the kitchen fights end, the barroom brawlers pass out, and the drunk drivers reach home, jail, the hospital, or the morgue. By Monday, the wreckage has swept through the emergency room to other wards, and a relative calm returns. The weekend's carpeted battlefield gives way to the single body in distress. The crowded waiting room gives way to the huddled relatives waiting in fearful silence to hear news of the heart attack victim, the breadwinner monstrously injured on the job, the badly damaged child.

Marie DeShaney brought the three-year-old into the Theda Clark Medical Center emergency room early Saturday afternoon during a lull in the weekend's drama. He had been playing, she claimed, and had accidentally been struck across the forehead with a metal truck by a two-year-old playmate. His name was Joshua DeShaney and she was his caretaker. His father was away ice fishing. The three-inch-long bruise on the boy's forehead was clearly evident to the doctor, Robert Gehringer, but there was also a blue bruise on Joshua's right cheek, an abrasion on the back of his head, and a bruise the size of a half dollar on the left side of his scalp.

As Gehringer moved to examine Joshua further, there might have been pause, a gesture, something suggesting hesitation on Marie's part, but the nurses moved swiftly to remove the boy's clothing. There were bruises on his spine and on his arms, several with dotted, textured patterns. There were also bruises across his buttocks, his thighs, his ankles, and his heels.[1]

An emergency room nurse placed a call to Thomas Hoare, a medical social worker on duty that afternoon. Unlikely accidents, unexplained injuries, the scars and bruises of old injuries on children brought in for treatment triggered suspicion. The parent or the guardian always had an innocent explanation, but the law mandated that inquiry be made. The nurse ". . . indicated to me that they had a child there who was approximately three years old and they suspected that the child had been physically abused," Hoare later recounted; ". . . there were a number of bruises on the child and the child was brought in by an aunt."

He went down to the emergency room, and after taking a look at Joshua spoke with Gehringer and with Marie. The doctor's view was unequivocal. The boy had multiple contusions and there was no satisfactory explanation. He believed that this might be a case of child abuse and recommended that Joshua be admitted to the hospital.[2]

Hoare's craft often took him into the netherworld of an uncertain reality. At first glance, the evidence of abuse was rarely unequivocal. The unlikely injury could have an innocent explanation. Bizarre accidents do occur. But, on the other hand, the law demanded that the uncertainties attending possible abuse be resolved, that the authorities make an effort to determine where responsibility lay when confronted with an injured child and an improbable story, or no story at all. He was no stranger to this shadow world. He had taken in-service training courses on child abuse and child neglect detection and had come face-to-face over the years with the grim realities of child abuse. He had also given talks on the matter, seeking to increase public awareness of a problem that played out behind closed doors, away from witnesses, with victims seldom able to give voice to their hurt.

Ordinarily, an adult bringing a child to an emergency room has a right to take the child home following treatment, except for those occasions when emergency room medical staff become concerned that returning home might not be in the child's best interest. Joshua had recent injuries and showed signs of possible past abuse. It was not clear, however, that Marie could be compelled to leave the boy in the hospital's custody. The hospital would need a court order granting it temporary custody to admit him, or the permission of the parent, but the boy's father was not available to give permission. If Joshua were to remain in the hospital, the machinery necessary to turn suspicion into intervention had to be quickly put in motion.

Hoare left the emergency room and set about translating concern into action. It was the weekend. Offices were closed. The mechanics of seeking-custody would be more complicated. He made two calls: one to the police department, the other to Ann Kemmeter, a social worker at the Winnebago County Department of Social Services. Although a social worker himself, Hoare knew that County Social Services should play a role in the unfolding case from the outset, given questions about the source of the boy's injuries and the possibility of foster care placement should one of his caretakers be found to have caused them.

The police dispatcher contacted Keith Nelson, the officer on duty that afternoon. If there was abuse rising to the level of criminal assault, there would have to be an investigation, suspects would have to be questioned, evidence gathered, and the district attorney would have to become involved. Nelson would spearhead the immediate inquiry to determine how far suspicion moved in the direction of certainty.

Nelson arrived at the hospital just before four in the afternoon and went to the emergency room to get a firsthand look at the injured boy. Having children of his own, he believed he knew what normal childhood scrapes and bruises looked like. In his view, whatever had happened to Joshua was beyond the likelihood of run-of-the-mill bumps and falls. The circumstances demanded investigation and the gathering of evidence for the two agencies that would have ultimate responsibility for deciding Joshua's fate: the District Attorney's Office and the Winnebago County, Wisconsin, Department of Social Services.[3]

Had it not been the weekend and had she not lived in Neenah, Ann Kemmeter might never have become involved in the case. But, it was the weekend, and the Department of Social Services did not have anyone on call. The police or the hospital could have gone through Helpline, a crisis intervention service that would have provided assistance, but because she lived not that far from the hospital, from time to time they called her in for cases like this.[4]

Sometime toward late afternoon, an hour and a half or so after Marie had brought Joshua to the emergency room, Hoare reached Kemmeter by phone. Could she come to the Medical Center immediately? The Social Service Department might have to become involved in the case, should it be necessary to seek a court order transferring custody of Joshua to the hospital. If he were the victim of abuse, the department would have to find placement for him outside the home. If an investigation determined that there was no abuse, the department might still wish to monitor the home situation and offer a range of services to his caretakers to help them cope with child-rearing problems.

Kemmeter arrived at the hospital in late afternoon and, along with Keith Nelson, was apprised of the situation by Hoare. He asked her to contact Juvenile Court Intake in order to secure formal authorization for Theda Clark Medical Center to assume temporary custody of Joshua DeShaney, pending an effort to determine the origin of the immediate injury that brought him to the emergency room on a cold winter afternoon and the other injuries the examination revealed. "I did not have a history as to what really happened to this child," he would explain later, ". . . and the father was not available to . . . get a history."

Hoare went up to the pediatric unit and spoke to the staff. Given that this was a case of possible child abuse, it was his feeling that Joshua was going to be admitted to the protective custody of the hospital. They were to be particularly sensitive to the interaction between Joshua and any adults coming to see him.

Outside a light snow had fallen, leaving a shimmering silver mist on the ground. The trees in Riverside Park shivered in the brisk wind sweeping in off the lake. The early evening streets were rapidly becoming deserted, save for the few souls compelled by duty or driven by need to face the looming night away from home: here and there a shopkeeper waited for the last customer, the policeman on lonely patrol passed through darkening streets, the traveler huddled against the cold in the dim glow of a streetlight, and the child in distress, newly admitted to the hospital, lay still, comforted by the warmth of strangers.

At 4:15 p.m., just under three hours after Joshua DeShaney had been brought into the emergency room, Dan Venne, intake worker with the Winnebago County Circuit Court, acting on a request by the County Department of Social Services, granted temporary custody ". . . pending a complete investigation of the numerous and unexplained bruises that appeared on Joshua' s body." The County Department of Social Services was alleging that Joshua was a child, ". . . in need of protection . . . who has been the victim of physical abuse . . . inflicted by another." His father and Marie were to be queried, as well as anyone else who might have information about what had happened to him.

Randy DeShaney, Joshua's father, arrived at Theda Clarke while the social worker and the policeman were still there. With Ann Kemmeter present, Keith Nelson questioned Randy and Marie regarding the circumstances that brought the four of them together at the hospital late on a winter day in January. They were very cooperative. They denied abusing Joshua and expressed concern regarding the bruises he had. Given that the bruises did not seem to be healing, they intended, they said, to make an appointment to bring him to the Nicolet Clinic that coming Monday for a full, head-to-toe examination. They were in accord with regard to their expectations of Joshua and their methods of disciplining him.

As evening passed into night, the interrogation broke off. The couple agreed to make itself available for further questioning if necessary. Nelson intended, in any event, to pursue the investigation the next day, and the next, if need be. Randy and Marie lived nearby. Neenah was a small town. There were neighbors to be queried as to what they had seen or heard. What remained out of sight could not long be hidden.

The settlers who founded the community had named it Neenah, the Indian word for water. It lay fifteen miles north of Oshkosh, which in turn lay 70 miles north of Milwaukee. The train from Chicago stopped in Milwaukee, but did not run to Oshkosh. The bus from Milwaukee stopped in Oshkosh, but did not run to Neenah.

Nestled on the edge of the Wisconsin North Country, Neenah was the sunlit, small town of the American imagination, shaped in its early decades by American dreams and American passions. The American dream of owning a small business and being one's own boss was reflected in Elwer's Drugstore, old Fred inside behind the counter, serving customers who had been coming in since the place opened, while American passion, the quest for fair treatment and a decent life, echoed in repeated strikes by Neenah Boot and Shoe company workers seeking better working conditions, their struggle inspired by the fierce rhetoric of William Jennings Bryan, the nineteenth-century populist who railed against the malefactors of great wealth, and for whom the town bridge across the Fox River was named.

But the region had also been shaped by great wealth concentrated in a small number of hands. From the time of its founding in 1872, the Kimberly-Clark Corporation, manufacturer of paper products, had dominated the area. Symbols of the sway of the founding families marked the local landscape: a village to the north named Kimberly, land given to Neenah, called Kimberly Point Park, and in 1909 a hospital named Theda Clark Medical Center.[5]

The hospital's beginning lay in tragedy, and it had been founded to prevent future tragedy. Theda Clark Peters, ". . . a bright princess . . . of wealth and refinement," died at home in childbirth in 1903. She had been devoted to good works during her life, hence her family, following her death, financed the building of a hospital in her memory so that future mothers in crisis and children in danger would have a place to which they could be brought for care and comfort.

The hospital's very location spoke of haven and refuge. There were parks and gracious green spaces nearby—Wilderness, Doty, Riverside—offering peace and solitude to the husband, the father, the anxious mother waiting to learn the fate of a loved one. It sat on a point of land overlooking the Fox River, at once distant from the tragedies that brought the distressed to its doors, yet near enough for them to swiftly find shelter. Marie had been able to rush Joshua quickly from whatever world yielded his injuries to Theda Clark Peter's sanctuary.

At some point, as afternoon became evening and events became more complicated, Hoare found time to sit down and begin assembling his notes, "putting everything in chronological order." There was no telling where the unfolding situation would take the increasing number of professionals charged with addressing it. At some point it might be vital to know where they had been.

On Monday, January 25, Randy came to the hospital again to see his son, as did Marie and his ex-wife, Christine. All three were interviewed by Kemmeter and Thomas Hoare and, again, were very cooperative, conveying information freely and easily. Christine had been Randy's second wife. His first wife, Melody, was Joshua's mother. She lived in another state and he had custody of his son. He and Marie had lived together since the breakup of his marriage to Christine. In addition to taking care of Joshua, Marie looked after her own son, Rusty, a year younger than Joshua.

As the conversation progressed, Kemmeter began to form the impression that Randy and Marie lacked parenting skills. Perhaps they failed to provide adequate supervision for Joshua while at the same time having unrealistic expectations of him. They felt that Joshua's behavior had deteriorated in recent weeks. They reported that he was wetting his bed, playing rougher with other kids, and biting and pinching himself. Randy seemed to want to do the right thing as a father, but neither he nor Marie exhibited knowledge of what the right thing might be. Their behavior did not suggest the bad conscience and fumbling fabrications of abusers. But, on the other hand, a three-year-old lay in a nearby hospital bed with multiple, unexplained bruises and abrasions.[6]

About a decade earlier federal funds had been used in schools around the state to support a series of pilot programs intended to increase awareness of the growing problem of child abuse. Randy would have been in high school at the time they were being offered and may or may not have participated.

But whatever his exposure or Marie's to prior guidance on the challenges of child rearing, the basic fact remained that parents did not "own" their children to do with as they pleased, but it was also true that the state could not take a child away from a parent without just cause established by fair procedures. There was evidence that Joshua had been abused, but at that point, no clear evidence that either his parent or his guardian had abused him. Randy and Marie left Theda Clarke, crossed over the bridge and returned to their Wright Avenue apartment, two miles and a few minutes away, far enough away to yield respite, yet near enough to respond quickly if summoned. There was nothing to do but await the decision of those who would determine whether Joshua would remain in the custody of caring strangers or leave the hospital with his father and Marie.

Randy was in his early twenties. He was part of a vast army that occupied no territory in the American imagination: young white men with no particular skills, no advantages of name or money. A high school graduate, he had a spotty job history. He had been briefly in the military. He had two failed marriages. And he was not yet twenty-six. The American imagination did not celebrate his style: neither the music, nor the mode of dress, nor the way of walking and talking. He had no personal accomplishments that thrust him into American consciousness. He could not hit a baseball with uncommon power. He could not throw a football with force and accuracy. He could not sing or dance in a manner attracting the adoring attention of an enraptured public. Even the misdeeds of his class lacked glamour: the barroom brawls on Saturday night, the "disorderly conduct" episodes with law enforcement, the police called by neighbors to pull a warring couple apart, merchants seeking payment for small amounts still owed, landlords demanding overdue rent.

If the Kimberlys and the Clarkes were the shining mountains above, Randy and his brethren were the shrub below, trying to survive in barren soil, seldom enjoying the warmth of the sun, often bent by driving rain.

The law mandated a prompt hearing to determine Joshua's immediate fate. It fell to Thomas Hoare to convene a meeting of a Child Protection Team to sort through the evidence and make a decision as to whether to keep Joshua in state protection or return him to the custody of his father. The team was, in Hoare's words, ". . . a conglomerate of people that are called together to help determine if we feel that we have a child abuse situation and to determine if it's safe for the child to return home . . ." And if the child were to return home they made recommendations ". . . as to what can be done to . . . improve the family situation."

The team would include hospital staff and others who had been involved with Joshua or with the adults responsible for his care, perhaps a dozen or so people. The County Social Service Department would be represented, and legal counsel would be present to advise the team as to whether the situation justified retaining custody of Joshua beyond his stay in the hospital.

The law set forth criteria for reaching a decision, but that language—seemingly precise and directive—masked a contradiction in two long-term trends regarding child protection. Evidence of possible child abuse—the bruises, the broken bones—yielded a strong rationale for removing a child from a potentially harmful home environment, the error to be guarded against by childcare professionals being leaving a children in dangerous homes too long, subjecting them to their abusers malevolent caprice, with inevitably tragic consequences.

On the other hand, the profession encouraged preservation of the family by keeping a child in a problematic home while providing services to help the family cope with its problems: mandated classes in parenting, regular clinic visits for the child, periodic home visits by childcare professionals. The error to be guarded against was taking a child from a home too quickly, subjecting a child not in danger to the trauma of being wrenched from the only shelter that child has known and placed with strangers.

This contradiction hung in the air, as Hoare made phone calls, searching for a time when all of the parties could meet and decide where Joshua would be taken when he left the hospital. On the one hand, the dilemma posed by the ambiguous evidence of abuse might be resolved by removing him from Randy's home; on the other hand, the uncertain evidence might support an argument favoring family preservation, returning him to Randy's care while providing help to Randy in meeting the challenges of parenthood.

These conflicting considerations informed the team's debate as it struggled to decide what was in Joshua's best interest. A grasp of the evolution of these opposing options is crucial to understanding the Child Protection Team's ultimate decision about Joshua, and the decision other teams, similarly situated, make about other Joshuas.

CHAPTER TWO

BACKGROUND TO JUDGMENT DAY

Child abuse as a social problem first gained a national spotlight in the last quarter of the nineteenth century and remained a focus of concern for lawmakers and social reformers through the 1920s. As other issues and passions came to the fore, it faded from view until being rediscovered in the early 1960s. Removal of the child from the home was the preferred, but not exclusive, approach to the problem during the first era of national concern. Preservation of the family has been the preferred, but not exclusive, approach during the second.

The specific horrors that first awakened the national conscience to child abuse came to light on Christmas Eve, 1873. A light snow had fallen in New York City, adding color to the hustle and bustle in Washington Market. "Young and old, rich and poor, good women and bad, honest men and thieves, gentlemen and blackguards, were all there on a common errand," one celebrant remarked, "that of procuring the materials for the best and jolliest Christmas they could each and several afford." A happy youngster was noted in the throng, ". . . arms and pockets full of all the almost impossible things he had ever and never dreamed of." Farther south in Manhattan, dozens of children gathered at Trinity Church for a Christmas festival. Palms and lighted candles graced the altar, and after service a Christmas tree festooned with gifts was unveiled, bringing much delight and wonderment.

Elsewhere plans proceeded apace to provide a happy Christmas for youngsters not so fortunate as to be laden down with presents in Washington Market or blessed with the promise of a tree laden with delights "ever and never dreamed of." The Newsboys Lodging House and St. Ann's in Brooklyn offered shelter, donated presents, and a holiday feast to destitute and orphaned youngsters. Other organizations such as St. John's Guild sent volunteers out to work among the poor trapped in the city's slums. Hence, it was in the spirit of doing good work among the poor during this happiest of seasons that Etta Angell Wheeler, a church visitor, climbed the stairs of a tenement on West Forty-First Street on a mission of mercy to comfort a dying woman. The ailing woman told of loud noises coming from an adjacent flat; beatings; a child crying. Her dying days would be easier if she knew that something was being done.

Inquiry by Wheeler confirmed the dying woman's claim and lent urgency to her plea. She later recounted what transpired when she knocked on the door of the flat and was reluctantly admitted by a surly woman. "I was an unbidden guest and stopped only long enough to note the conditions. I saw a pale, thin child, barefoot, in a thin scanty dress, so tattered I could see she wore only one garment under the dress. She appeared to be . . . 5 years of age, but it was afterwards found that she was 9 years old. It was winter and the room was bitterly cold. From a pan set upon a low stool she was washing dishes, struggling with pots about as heavy as herself. Across the table lay a whip of twisted leather, and the child's pinched face, and meager arms and legs bore many marks of its use, but the saddest part was the look . . . of a child . . . who had seen only the fearsome side of life."

"Little Mary Ellen" was a nine-year-old orphan. She had been taken in by Mary Connolly, a demonic woman who had beaten, burned, and slashed her, and kept her in a closet. The sum of Little Mary Ellen's life was a chronicle of horrors, but rescuing her proved more difficult and elusive than Etta Wheeler anticipated. She sought help from her church and from the police, but to no avail, both offering the same excuse. Mary Ellen was neither homeless nor abandoned. Her home life was unduly hard but there was nothing church or state could do. They had no authority under the law to remove her from "mama's" harsh care.

In despair, Wheeler turned to Henry Bergh, an acquaintance, born to wealth, a pillar of society, and a former diplomat. A decade or so earlier, affronted by a street vendor's mistreatment of a horse, he had formed the Society for Prevention of Cruelty to Animals. He used his political power to secure passage of a law giving the organization quasi-police powers, its agents being able to take animals from abusive owners, arrest them, and pursue prosecution in court. He was appalled by the Mary Ellen story and the failed effort to get her out of Mary Connolly's horrific home. The law allowed rescue of an abused animal from its owner but not rescue of an abused child from a vicious parent or guardian.

Bergh moved swiftly. Through an influential friend he secured a court order to have Mary Ellen removed from Mary Connolly's home pending a hearing. The newspapers caught wind of the unfolding drama and the story broke in the *New York Times* on April 10, 1874, immediately creating a sensation. "She is a bright little girl," the *Times* reported, ". . . but with a care-worn, stunted, and prematurely old look. Her apparent condition of health, as well as her scanty wardrobe, indicated that no change of custody or condition could be much for the worse." Mary Ellen knew that her mother and father were dead but she did not know how old she was nor could she recall a time that she had not lived with Mrs. Connolly. She had never been allowed to go outside, except at night, and then only to the yard of the tenement. She slept on the floor at night and toiled in Mary Connolly's dark apartment by day. She could not recall being kissed or caressed or sitting on Mrs. Connolly's lap. Her body was a tapestry of bruises inflicted by the whip Mrs. Connolly used to discipline her, and there was a gash on the left side of her forehead, made by a pair of scissors.

Mary Connolly's trial, three weeks after Mary Ellen's removal from her home, brought out ". . . a number of persons . . . all of them evidently deeply sympathetic with the little, neglected waif, whose cause had been espoused by Mr. Bergh . . . ," wrote Jacob Riis, whose classic work, *How the Other Half Lives* would later provide a graphic portrait of the city's poor. "I was in a courtroom full of men with pale, stern looks. I saw a child brought in . . . at the sight of which men wept aloud. And as I looked, I knew I was where the first chapter of children's rights was (being) written." The testimony was heart-wrenching: neighbors spoke of having seen the little girl out in cold weather, barely dressed, one side of her body ". . . all black and blue." Her crying had pained their days and tormented their nights.

Bergh built on the widespread sympathy for the abused child and with fellow influential socialite Eldridge Gerry formed a new organization in December of 1874, its mission being to "rescue little children from the cruelty and disorganization which neglect, abandonment and improper treatment engender. . . ." The Society for the Prevention of Cruelty to Children was patterned after the Society for the Prevention of Cruelty to Animals. Its agents could secure court orders to remove children from abusive homes and could bring court proceedings against abusive parents, based on a seemingly unassailable premise: if a suffering animal could be taken away from an abusive owner, surely a suffering child could be removed from an abusive home.[1]

The Society for the Prevention of Cruelty to Children dominated the field of child protection services for the next four decades, eventually spreading to other cities and becoming a behemoth with its own shelters and training schools. Its 1918 annual report boasted of having rescued children ". . . from lives of vice, or cruelty of various forms and from destitution."[2] In 1920, the forty-fifth anniversary of its founding, a prominent member articulated the Society for the Prevention of Cruelty to Children's view of its history and reason for being, stating that over nearly half a century it had ". . . worked against . . . obstacles . . . where man and law recognized the need for protection of . . . animals from cruelty but insisted that a parent's rights over his child was absolute . . . (but) through the efforts of the Society . . . in Manhattan alone . . . more than 300,000 (children) have . . . been rescued . . . and in all parts of the world 500 sister Societies have been formed."

But the Society for the Prevention of Cruelty to Children's zealousness also bred fear and resentment in the impoverished immigrant ranks swelling New York's population, generating the perception that they were "child snatchers" whose patrician sponsors mistook old-country methods of child rearing for abuse or neglect. And even though the organization embraced offering social services, its defining mission and principal approach reflected the "rescue" story that inspired its founding.

The rise of social work as a profession in the first two decades of the twentieth century, along with the shift of public attention to other matters, promoted a decline in the influence of the Society for the Prevention of Cruelty to Children.[3] The field of social work brought a different orientation to the issue, focusing more on support for the family and improvements in community conditions rather than the punitive, quick removal of the child from the home. As with all social changes, the evolution to a "family support" model rather than a "rescue and remove" model was gradual and complex. *The Social Work Yearbook* of 1929 described a trend then underway. While the approach of the Society for the Prevention of Cruelty to Children was ". . . legalistic . . . employing rescue work and the punishment of offenders . . ." dependent almost entirely on police methods, Massachusetts and other states had begun to bring social service professionals into child protective services and to measure success ". . . by the number of rehabilitations brought about by means of which children remained in their own homes."[4]

As the issues and concerns attending the Great Depression, World War II, and postwar adjustment came to dominate the national agenda and occupy the attention of the helping professions, child abuse ceased to be a matter of great concern. Not until the early 1960s was it again a major focus of attention for social service professionals. From its inception in 1955 through the early 1960s, *Social Work*, the journal of the National Association of Social Workers, did not carry a single article on child abuse. Neither did other professional journals such as *Child Welfare* or the *Psychological Bulletin*. The absence of attention in the professional journals was mirrored in the popular media. Neither the *New York Times Index* nor the *Readers Guide to Periodical Literature* carried "child abuse" or "cruelty to children" as categories during the decade of the 1950s.

The rediscovery of child abuse occurred rapidly. In 1962 the *Journal of the American Medical Association* introduced the helping professions and the public to the term *the battered child syndrome*, yielded by a study of 302 children in seventy-two hospitals. Based on the work of Denver pediatrician C. Henry Kempe and his colleagues, the article reflected the convergence of a growing awareness in both the medical and social work professions of child abuse as a problem. A year before the publication of the Kempe article, *Social Work* had published a piece called "Abused Young Children Seen in Hospitals," recounting a grim reality out of Los Angeles Children's Hospital involving children seen on multiple occasions for unexplained injuries. And in the same year, 1961, the *New England Journal of Medicine* published a pathologist's study called "The Slaughter of the Innocents," on child homicides resulting from adult abuse, a catalog of contusions and abrasions, burns on genitalia and buttocks, scalding, broken bones, and fractured skulls.[5]

As early as 1946 pediatric radiologists had recognized and written about unexplained injuries among children, but had been reluctant to infer a cause. The 1962 Kempe study gave the horror a name and the name helped draw public attention. The press quickly picked up on the story, the *New York Times* asserted that, ". . . there has been a sudden increase in the brutality of the attacks—mostly on very young children and infants . . . an estimated 10,000 children a year are battered, maimed, burned, and starved and broken in body, mind and spirit by the people who should care most for them."[6]

Other mass circulation publications such as *Today's Health* and the *Christian Century* soon followed, as did *Time* magazine in an article called "The Battered Child Syndrome," and the *Saturday Evening Post*, with a piece called "Parents Who Beat Children." Public television also raised public consciousness, airing a documentary in which, according to one critic, ". . . the tragedy of child abuse was intelligently and movingly studied." In addition, scholarly publications such as the *Harvard Educational Review* lent credibility to the escalating alarm, asserting that, ". . . approximately one child in every one hundred in America is physically abused, sexually molested, or severely neglected."[7] And Kempe added to the accumulating body of material on the subject with the publication of *The Battered Child*, a work lauded as a ". . . pioneering, multidisciplinary study." A number of public service organizations also spoke to the issue, including the American Humane Association, dedicated to the welfare of children, which accused the country of "failing in its obligations to mistreated and neglected children . . ." and of being ". . . years behind . . . in giving (children) the right kind of care and protection. . . ." Soon the courts were allowing expert testimony against parents charged with abuse as the medical profession developed indicants of the battered child syndrome. The language used by medical professionals constituted an inventory of the horrors yielding evidence of abuse: multiple asymmetrical fractures, the isolated spiral fracture, separation of distal epiphyses, subdural hematoma, diffuse axonal injury. To the layperson the language spoke of bones snapped by sudden twisting or heavy blows, of breaks in the walls of blood vessels causing blood to collect under the skull, of ligaments torn loose from their mooring, of bleeding in the back of the eyes, of a ripping or shearing of the brain under a sudden impact.

Policy makers in government were also drawn to the problem. The key figures in the Kennedy administration, Hubert Humphrey and Lyndon Johnson, men whose formative political years in the 1930s saw the formulation of New Deal policies to cope with the Great Depression, were oriented to activist government as an instrument of social reform. Thus, in 1962 the Children's Bureau sponsored a conference ". . . to consider the challenge of child abuse" from which emerged a proposal for a model statute mandating the reporting of suspected cases of child abuse.

Between 1963 and 1967 the District of Columbia and every state in the Union passed laws requiring persons such as teachers and emergency room personnel to report possible child abuse. These laws rested on the assumption that abusive parents will not voluntarily seek help.[8] Mandatory reporting of possible abuse was necessary to bring troubled families to the attention of helping agencies that could determine what was in the best interest of the child. Most of these laws also provided immunity from being sued for defamation if the report of possible abuse was made in good faith but turned out to be wrong.

In 1974 Congress passed the Child Abuse Prevention and Treatment Act, creating the National Center for Child Abuse and Neglect, a federal agency charged with working with the states on program development, evaluation, and data gathering. This complex piece of legislation reflected public and political concern with the plight of children in danger and the implicit belief—reflective of the impulse that drove the Society for Prevention of Cruelty to Children for decades—that they should be removed from homes threatening their safety. But the new law also reflected the intellectual framework of social work, centered on the provision of services in the interest of family preservation.

A half dozen years later, an equally complex piece of legislation, the Adoption Assistance and Child Welfare Act, mandated a "reasonable effort" to preserve the family unit before removing a child from a threatening home environment, the concern being the rising number of children in foster care and a perceived slighting of parental rights.

Concurrent with the growing legislative concern with child abuse, a growing body of social work research literature strongly supported family preservation as policy. Articles appeared in *Child Welfare, Child Abuse and Neglect*, and *Social Work*, offering data suggesting that children who were quickly removed from potentially threatening home environments suffered psychological harm.[9] Child protection workers and other professionals were warned that unwarranted intervention was most likely to occur in borderline cases where the evidence of abuse was not conclusive. An article in the *New York Times* observed that "keeping a child in his or her home had been increasingly emphasized as the primary goal of social services in Federal and State laws, in regulations, in funding and monitoring or auditing local child-care agencies . . . In a home when a child is at risk of injury, there usually are pros as well as cons for leaving the child there."

The profession was divided over how best to explain parental behavior in troubled homes. There were, ". . . many popular theories that (made) assumptions about the *pathology* of abusing adults." But, on the other hand, there were those who argued that abusive adults simply lacked the skills necessary to function with competence in the parental role. These parents knew little or nothing about child development. They lived under stressful conditions, economically and socially, and in order to ease the demands on their own already overburdened lives they expected too much of their children, placing demands on them beyond their years. And when frustrated, they relied on punishment to control and shape the behavior of their children, in the absence of being aware of and comfortable with less punitive techniques. "Abusive parents have few skills," a *Social Work* article argued, ". . . They gain little satisfaction from their role as parents . . . They control their children's behavior almost exclusively through punishment, because they lack knowledge of alternative means of controlling them."

But abusive parents were responsive to "therapeutic personnel" willing to work with them in their own homes. One member of the profession observed that the social worker adopting this model becomes a "nurturer-cum-educator," strengthening the client's feelings of competence.[10]

From this perspective the abusing parent was viewed as an incompetent adult who needed instruction in how to be a responsible parent and assistance with some of the practical problems that attend everyday life. Something akin to this approach would later come into play as the DeShaney drama unfolded.

A catalog of horrors catapulting child abuse back into the national consciousness and spurring a spate of protective legislation formed the background against which the Child Protection Team met to decide the fate of Joshua DeShaney. There had been a significant rise in the number of reported cases of child abuse in Winnebago County about a decade prior to Joshua coming to the attention of the child welfare professionals, and it was around that time that Theda Clark Medical Center's Child Protection Team came into existence.

The heightened sense of public responsibility for the welfare of the innocent generated the law under which Dr. Gehringer reported his suspicion that Joshua might be the victim of abuse. The new sense of public concern rested on an understanding that damage was being done to children behind closed doors. The privacy of the home was a sanctuary for the torturer. No protector, no agent of the state could be present twenty-four hours a day. Inevitably the child was in the hands of the abuser, inevitably at the abuser's mercy.

Contradictory imperatives were implicit in the laws that created the committee charged with determining whether Joshua had been abused. Four- and five-year-old lives, enduring constant torture, a nightmare of burns and beatings, spoke to removing a child from the home when in doubt. But equally strong cross-cutting themes in the law and the professional literature emphasized resolving doubts about the safety of the child in favor of family preservation and against removal, except in obvious and outrageous cases of mistreatment.

The Child Protection Team deliberated within a framework shaped by complex and inconsistent laws and a set of theoretical propositions yielded by limited and contradictory research studies. But in the end it would have to make a decision, stark in its simplicity: Joshua would leave the hospital with his father Randy, or he would not.

The Child Protection Team

Early Tuesday morning, January 26, Thomas Hoare placed a number of phone calls. The Child Protection Team would meet at noon at the hospital because that was when Gehringer, the pediatrician, and DeRozier, the psychologist, could attend. The emergency room nurses who had been on duty when Joshua was brought in were asked to attend also, as were the pediatric ward nurses who had seen Randy and Joshua together.[11] Ann Kemmeter and her supervisor, Cheryl Stelse, were also asked to be there. Whatever the outcome of the meeting, whether Joshua was kept under the protection of the court or returned to Randy, the Department of Social Services would most likely be involved. Given her happenstance early involvement, Ann Kemmeter would most likely be the caseworker with whom the family would meet should the Team recommend ongoing counseling and guidance. A phone call from Kemmeter advised Keith Nelson as to the time and place of the meeting.

In the end a decision would have to be made as to whether the facts were sufficiently compelling as to justify court proceedings to take Joshua away from Randy, at least temporarily, on the grounds that he would be in danger in his father's home. That was a legal question beyond the competence of the medical people or the social workers, hence, John Bodnar, assistant corporation counsel, several years out of the University of Pittsburgh Law School, would advise them on the meaning of the facts from the perspective of the law. Would a recommendation to remove Joshua from his home withstand court challenge by Randy, or would it fail?

As coordinator of the team it was Thomas Hoare's responsibility to guide the assembled doctors, nurses, social workers, and law enforcement personnel through the rough terrain ahead. He was a long-term employee of the hospital and was familiar with the personnel assembled to make the decision in this difficult case. He knew most of them and had worked with them over the years and thus was equipped, in a bureaucratic sense, to handle the differing points of view and strong feelings that might emerge as the team sought to reach a decision. He would also be looked to by the team to contribute substantively to the discussion. He was working toward his master's degree in social work, but more importantly brought prior involvement with the issue to the table. Several years earlier the local newspaper had carried a story reporting that the Department of Social Services was ". . . becoming increasingly concerned by the number of child abuse cases . . . being reported. . . ." He had been quoted as saying that "There is something more to the problem than . . . first meets the eye." In some cases, he suggested, the abusive parent had an unconscious antipathy toward the child, having never wanted a child in the first place.

The practice of convening a team to examine possible cases of child abuse had been in existence at the hospital for about a decade, but the mandate did not, and perhaps could not, offer clear directives as to how to move from inference to conclusion in a way that was sensitive to the needs of the child but respectful of the legal rights of the parents. Physicians tended to focus on the medical needs of the child, not being equipped by training or inclination to assess whether the provision of social services to a distressed family might be a reasonable alternative to removing the child from the home. The other team members operated from similar, limited professional perspectives. The collective effort, entailing a sharing of professional perspectives, seemed to offer a chance of moving from inference to conclusion with at least some degree of confidence that both the welfare of the child and the rights of the parent had been honored.

The questions confronting the team were specific: What evidence suggested Joshua might have been abused? How could that evidence be explained? What recommendation followed from the most plausible explanation for the evidence?

Hoare was a conscientious and diligent note-taker. Three days earlier he had drafted notes outlining the events leading to the hospital's decision to seek temporary custody of Joshua. He would now try to make sense of the many voices that would determine whether that temporary custody was to be surrendered. Under his direction, the meeting began with a review of the physical facts as they emerged in the course of Joshua's examination.

The injuries were numerous and not immediately subject to innocent explanation. He had not been rescued from a terrible automobile accident or a collapsed building, yet his body was a tapestry of injuries. The bruises on his buttocks, thighs, ankles, and heels suggested he had been struck, as did the textured patterned bruises on his arms; that they might have been self-inflicted or incurred as the result of accidents strained belief. He did not show the fractures and internal bleeding of the classic battered child syndrome, but his body spoke of ordeal beyond the ordinary.

Marie's explanation for bringing Joshua into the emergency room fell short of accounting for the multiple injuries, and, indeed an emergency room nurse thought that she seemed hesitant as they moved to undress Joshua. In addition, neither Randy nor Marie, in later questioning, satisfactorily accounted for the boy's numerous bruises and abrasions.

In the course of the back and forth, someone on the team might have suggested that the skin abrasions could be carpet burns, the result of a fall that caused searing and bruising. But then, of course, there would be the question of what caused the fall.

Keith Nelson recounted going the previous day to Randy and Marie's apartment across the bridge, a short distance from the hospital. He had seen the toy truck Marie alleged caused the gash across Joshua's forehead. It was not likely. Whatever the source of the injury, it was not the little metal truck. Nor was it clear what else could have caused the injury.

Evidence was on the table supporting an inference of abuse. The boy was injured and the adult's explanation for those injuries was implausible. But, any move to deprive Randy of Joshua's custody would most likely be contested, and a decision recommending removal of Joshua from his father's home would probably have to be defended in court in an adversarial proceeding.

Nelson's further comments mirrored some of the arguments one might expect from any attorney Randy might hire to contest losing custody of his son. In the course of his investigation he had questioned Randy's neighbors, even the postman, but turned up nothing of an incriminating nature. They had not heard the awful sounds of persistent abuse: constant crying, blows punctuated by a child's pleading promises to "be good." Randy and Marie fought noisily on occasion, but the telltale sounds of a child being endlessly punished had not disturbed their neighbors' sleep nor troubled their days.

In addition, any lawyer representing Randy would surely argue that no bad inference could be drawn from Keith Nelson's doubts as to whether the toy truck could have caused the gash on Joshua's forehead. Did Marie deliberately mislead the emergency room staff, or was it just as likely that, anxious and upset, she thought the truck had caused the gash?

Observations about the demeanor of Randy and Marie over two days of questioning further undermined the case for removal. Thomas Hoare, Ann Kemmeter, and Keith Nelson had interrogated them separately and together several times. They had not shown signs of bad conscience. There had been no crack in the voice, no guilty shifting of the eyes, no fumbling to remember the vague details of a hastily manufactured story. Both had been cooperative in every encounter. Both seemed to strain to answer every question fully and truthfully. Both denied abusing Joshua. They had not had the opportunity in the initial questioning to coordinate their stories, yet their stories meshed. They claimed that the boy's behavior had deteriorated over the preceding four or five months. He wet himself involuntarily. He was rougher in play. He bit and pinched himself. He pulled out patches of his own hair.

The team was told that Randy and Marie's description of Joshua's behavior had led to consultation with Doctor DeRozier, a psychologist. DeRozier told the team that he had done a partial work up on Joshua and had met with Randy. In his view, Joshua did have behavioral problems, whatever their source. He believed that the boy showed separation anxiety relative to Randy, and that, perhaps, he tore out hair when he feared his father was about to depart. Joshua had lived with his birth mother during early infancy, before coming under the care of his father, and that, perhaps, was a factor in his separation anxiety. There seemed to be a bond between father and son. DeRozier believed they should remain together, but felt that they should receive professional help. He also believed all parties might benefit from Marie's leaving the household.

In addition, it appeared from some of the background information on Randy, that he might have had a drinking problem in the past and appeared himself to have come from a difficult home situation.

Mary Armbruster's contribution to the accumulating pool of information was consistent with DeRozier's remarks. As a licensed practical nurse in pediatrics she had witnessed Randy's visits with Joshua. Given the circumstances of Joshua's admission to the hospital, a particularly close eye had been kept on the father when he came to see his son. She told the team that Joshua ran to Randy whenever he entered the room. The boy seemed very attached to his father. Her words connoted nothing suggestive of abuse, nothing suggesting a victim shrinking from the false embrace of his tormentor. This did not mean that Joshua had not been abused, but complicated the question of whether Randy was the abuser.

Perhaps seeking a way out of the thicket, legal counsel, John Bodnar, put a question to the doctors. Beyond the injuries that generated suspicion of abuse, what otherwise could be said about Joshua's general medical condition? The answer pushed them further along an uncertain road. Joshua's immunizations were up to date according to the pediatrician. His medical history otherwise seemed normal. There was nothing that could flatly be said to be a sign of neglect.

And after input from all of the participants, Hoare posed the question they had been convened to answer: Can we say abuse has taken place?

The evidence pointed in two directions. There were unexplained injuries, some of which could not have been self-inflicted. But, on the other hand, there were few signs, if any, of abuse in terms of the way Joshua related to his father or the demeanor of Randy and Marie under questioning. Unspoken but ever present in such deliberations was the conflict between the older Society for Prevention of Cruelty to Children's impulse to remove the endangered child from the home and the more contemporary impulse to preserve the family, treating it as a distressed unit in need of services.

The consensus emerging from the discussion reflected the ambiguous nature of the evidence. They could not say whether Joshua DeShaney had been physically abused at the hands of his caretakers. John Bodnar's legal conclusion followed. In the end, a court would want clear and convincing evidence that removing Joshua from his father's custody was in his best interest. The team was not prepared to say that there was enough evidence to make that argument. Uncertainty as to whether abuse had or had not occurred was not likely to yield success in a court contest for custody of Joshua.

But the ambiguous nature of the evidence also yielded a consensus that the situation could not be left entirely unattended. There were unexplained injuries. The DeShaney household did appear to be in need of professional help and Randy had expressed the wish for help in coping with his parental responsibilities. This reality provided the basis for a plan of action. Randy would be asked to enter into an agreement with the Department of Social Services, under the terms of which he would

- allow regular visits from a caseworker to monitor the household and help with obtaining needed services,
- enroll Joshua in Head Start for the opportunity it would provide him to enhance his social skills and experience an intellectually stimulating environment,
- continue to work with the Department of Social Services for purposes of increasing his knowledge of child development and in order to enhance his parenting skills,
- bring Joshua in on a regularly scheduled basis over the next several months for pediatric examination at Nicolet Clinic, and
- ask Marie to leave the household.

It was believed that the household would be more stable were Marie to move, but it was understood that there was no legal way in which the Department of Social Services or the Neenah Police Department could force her to leave. It would be up to Randy to ask her to go.

Later a memo was sent to Juvenile Court reviewing the case, providing details on the Child Protective Team meeting, and recommending dismissal of the temporary protective order. The memo outlined the follow-up program involving Randy, Joshua and the Department of Social Services, and noted that "Should there be any further injuries to this child of an unexplained origin . . ." the matter would be brought back before the court. The memo also specified Kemmeter's role in the follow-up process in greater detail. "I will advocate full-time employment for Randy in having him explore possible job opportunities. . . . I will advocate sound health care practices for Joshua and monitor to be sure that he gets in for his bi-monthly exams with Dr. Gehringer. . . . I will continue to provide counseling services to Randy to improve his knowledge of child development and parental skills."

It was an outcome that seemed to satisfy only on the surface. Something was wrong, but no one could say exactly what. Conscience and professional responsibility did not allow for simply walking away from the situation, returning Joshua to his home with no stipulations on Randy. But, on the other hand, neither did horror seem imminent, justifying removing him from the home.

In the background was the question of what to do with Joshua in the event that a permanent order of protection was sought from the Juvenile Court. Presumably the option was foster care placement, but a growing body of writing in social service journals suggested that foster care presented its own emotional and psychological problems for the child placed with strangers, even those who were deeply caring. There was no quick, easy, sure answer as to what to do.

Epilogue

The team had sifted through sheaths of notes, charts, memos, and reports on Randy and Joshua but could find no hint or clue clearing away the fog of ambiguity. Their decision seemed to bear the weight of the evidence and meet the demands of conscience. They were presented with a condition without a history, injuries whose genesis was unknown. Efforts by Keith Nelson, Ann Kemmeter, and the other professionals to attach a history to the condition had failed. Viewed without context or background, the moral meaning of a child's distress may almost always be ambiguous. Tears in an infant's eyes may have been preceded by an angry slap or medicine lovingly administered. The team was unwilling to make pessimistic assumptions about Joshua's future in his parent's home in the absence of evidence about a past that suggested malevolent causes for his present distressed condition. And that evidence was just not there.

Or was it?

There was at least one crucial item missing from the sheaths of notes, charts, memos, and reports available to the team. It had not been on the table and no one on the team seemed to be aware of it. Had they known of it, the discussion might have taken a different direction. The outcome of their deliberations might have been different.

A year earlier, virtually to the day, the Neenah Police Department had received a call from an attorney. His client, Christine DeShaney, was preparing to file divorce papers against her husband, Randy, in a few days. Randy had a two-year-old son from a previous marriage with him named Joshua. She claimed that Randy had struck the boy in the past, causing marks. She was afraid that when she left Randy in a few days and the boy was left with his father that "something may happen." They wanted this information on record with the police. They also intended to contact the Department of Social Services.

A copy of the Police Complaint report, date stamped January 27, 1982, was in Winnebago County Social Service Department files.[12]

Four days had passed. Joshua had enjoyed the comfort and protection of strangers. The Child Protection Team meeting ended in the early afternoon, and the participants scattered to their appointed tasks—home, work, play. Later that day Joshua was released from Theda Clark Medical Center into the care of his father. The bleak, sunlit day turned cold. Darkness came early.

CHAPTER THREE

THINGS UNSEEN

This Is What Happened

February 4, 1983

A week had passed since Randy had taken Joshua home. He had met with Ann Kemmeter at the Social Service offices and had readily agreed to lend himself to the plan designed to create a better environment for son and father. Kemmeter's memo to the Juvenile Court recommending suspension of the temporary custody order and dismissing any further allegations regarding child abuse had been sent the day after the Child Protective Team meeting. The proviso regarding referring the matter back to the Court in the event of any further injuries to Joshua of unexplained origin reflected the balance between hope and caution that drove the team's decision.

And now, on the fourth day of February, a cold day in midwinter, Kemmeter was to make her first home visit to see the setting within which the family drama was playing out. Neenah averaged four feet of snow during the winter months. In a warmer climate frustration might be taken out with a walk around the block, a jog in the park, a stroll down to the corner store. In Neenah, in the winter, family dramas played out indoors, whatever the tensions, however shackling the frustrations. February could pose a sterner test than June ever did.

But when she got to the apartment on Wright Avenue for the scheduled meeting, Randy was not there. He had gone out of town to help a relative relocate. Joshua was in Marie's care and appeared no worse for it. The lump on his forehead was less visible and the discoloration around the eyes had nearly disappeared. He appeared to be on his way back from the injury that had brought him to the emergency room nearly two weeks earlier. All seemed to be in order. There was no present sign of physical abuse. But Randy was not there and Marie was. Although the team had thought it to be in Joshua's best interest were she to move out, the present circumstance did not present a basis for pressing the matter. An appointment was made to return a month later for a second home visit.[1]

Native to the area, Kemmeter had been with the Department of Social Services for a number of years. Her initial interests in college had been in elementary education, but had then shifted. She had graduate credits in social work and had attended a number of in-service workshops and training sessions dealing with family problems, including child abuse. After a brief stint out of state she had returned to Wisconsin and the Fox River Valley area that she knew. She had applied to social service departments in Fond du Lac County and Outagamie County, but was hired by the Winnebago County Department of Social Services. In 1981, she came to work primarily out of the Winnebago County Department office in the Neenah-Menasha area. This placed her close to her Neenah home and made her available to receive a call on a cold weekend in January that might otherwise have gone to a different caseworker.[2]

On February 14, a week-and-a-half after the abbreviated first home visit, the Juvenile Court, pursuant to recommendation, formally closed its file on Joshua DeShaney. The responsibility for monitoring his welfare passed to the Winnebago County Department of Social Services. The County Department's handling of to the case reflected the consensus in the profession as reflected in a number of articles that had appeared in *Social Work* arguing for an approach emphasizing the provision of services intended to help the marginal parent acquire better skills. The parent suspected of abuse was seen as deficient in understanding how to play a nurturing role and unaware of community resources available to help those feeling overwhelmed by the challenges of parenthood.[3] There was little consensus in the profession, however, as to what signs and portents might suggest that a nurturing approach to under-resourced parents was not working.

March 15, 1983

Thomas Hoare phoned Kemmeter. He had not discussed the *DeShaney* case with her since chairing the Child Protection Team meeting six weeks earlier, but circumstances now demanded that he contact her. Joshua had been brought to the Theda Clarke emergency room the day before with a laceration on his head. Allegedly he had fallen and cut himself. The history surrounding the case rather than the immediate injury prompted his concern and the phone call to Social Services. Scrapes and cuts are the price children pay for playground fun. Joshua's scrape did not itself indicate abuse, but prudent concern required that Kemmeter be notified.

She had made a home visit a week earlier and had noted nothing amiss. Perhaps Joshua, like other children his age had merely had an accident, or perhaps not. A week and a half after the call from Hoare, she made a second March visit to the Wright Avenue apartment. Again, she saw nothing untoward. Joshua appeared to be any four-year-old concerned with play and fun.

The basic treatment plan had not changed. The visits allowed her to monitor Joshua's well-being and encourage Randy to keep the regularly scheduled Nicolet Clinic appointments with Dr. Gehringer. The visits also allowed her to counsel him with regard to his parenting skills and the expectations he had of Joshua. There had been the matter of Marie moving out, but this did not come to the fore.[4]

Had the matter been pressed and had Marie departed the household, Randy would have been left a single parent raising a son, and there was nothing in his background to suggest that he was prepared for such a role. His parents divorced when he was very young, and he had been raised for a time by his father. He graduated from a high school in the Fox River area in 1976, and entered the military. In 1978, while still in the air force, he met and married Melody Bridgewater in Wyoming after a brief courtship. Their son, and only child, Joshua, was born on March 21, 1979. In December of that year divorce papers were filed, and in January of 1981 a modified divorce decree was signed, transferring ". . . sole care, custody, and control of the minor child . . . Joshua Eli" from Melody to Randy. On assuming custody of his son, Randy left Wyoming and returned to Wisconsin and the Fox River area where he had family. Soon thereafter he married Christine, only to see that union quickly dissolve.

In his report to the Child Protection Team the psychologist, Dr. DeRozier, had spoken of Joshua's brief tenure with his birth mother and his transfer from his mother to the custody of his father. He believed that this experience was a factor in the separation anxiety that Joshua seemed to show whenever Randy appeared to be about to leave the hospital room. Later events would pose the question of whether the anxiety sprang from infant experience or had more immediate causes. Although the modified decree granted Randy custody of Joshua, Melody was not shut out of her son's life. She had refused to sign the original decree because it denied her all visitation rights. The modified decree granted her ". . . the right of reasonable visitation . . . ," with reasonable notice to be provided to Randy as to the time of any proposed visit. But she had not come to see the boy in the months that had elapsed since signing the decree. Custody had been surrendered by dropping Joshua off at her uncle's home in Cheyenne, Wyoming. She had stayed for a while then left before Randy arrived to pick the boy up.[5]

In later years she would confront the common view that a mother surrendering her child to the father in a divorce situation must be a morally wanton person. She would also encounter suspicion about her motives when she sought to reenter Joshua's life. She would claim, however, that surrendering her son on that cold winter day had been a bitter, wrenching experience, saying that, ". . . giving up Joshua was a vulnerable point with me." Surrendering her son was also a factor in her later experiencing something akin to "survivor's guilt."[6]

The economic burden of single parenthood on Randy was intended to be eased by the court order directing Melody to make child support payments, the money to be sent on a monthly basis to the clerk of the District Court, Winnebago County. The emotional and physical toll of parenthood was fully his, however, and contributed to a difficult life. He was a single parent in his early twenties. His uncertain skills led to a constant search for steady employment. He had moved immediately from a failed marriage into a new, troubled relationship, and from that into yet a third difficult relationship. Now, as he sought to cope with multiple demands, his struggle was subject to scrutiny and evaluation lest he fail the test of adequate care for his infant son.

May 2, 1983

A scheduled April meeting had been canceled because Randy was out of town. He was sometimes away for days at a time working as a truck driver, leaving Marie to tend to Joshua and her son, Rusty. He had also unsuccessfully sought work out-of-state. Kemmeter had not seen Joshua since late March. In the weeks that had passed, the North Country winter had given way to verdant spring. May brought renewal to Neenah, Menasha, Appleton, Kimberly, Little Chute, and the other towns clustered in the Fox River valley or strung out along the lakefront. Plamann Park, just north of Appleton, offered a setting for picnics, and foot races, and kite flying, and skimming stones along the water's surface. Golf courses, museums, a state park, and two nature preserves also graced the area which, according to the Chamber of Commerce, offered ". . . residents and visitors . . . big city dynamism and small town spirit."

A century earlier madness in this North Country Eden had been open. "Tramps packed guns and overran towns. Old women threw themselves down wells. Hypnotists flourished. Railway men saw ghosts along the tracks. Farmers saw monsters pull squealing pigs into lakes. The living received messages from the dead in their dreams (and) mothers carried their children into rivers."[7]

But that spring, as the North Country came to life after a long winter, the madness lay below, out of sight—a muffled cry, a pleading glance, a horrific thing barely seen until the bruised child's body draws the frantic attention of emergency room personnel or, as the case may be, the more measured attention of the coroner.

The warm weather brought children out doors to play, to run about, ride their bicycles, and have a good time. Sometimes they got hurt. Kemmeter could not say with certainty that the bump on Joshua's head had not been caused by a fall from his bicycle. That is what she was told, and she could not state that it had not happened. Four-year-olds fall from bicycles. But the accumulation of incidents was becoming troubling.[8]

A communication the next day, May 3, brought further cause for concern. Robert Gehringer phoned Social Services from his office at Nicolet Clinic. Joshua had been brought into the Theda Clarke emergency room and had been sent from there over to the Clinic. The boy had a laceration on his upper lip caused, allegedly, by a fall from a toy wagon while playing at home. He put sutures in the wound and scheduled an appointment for Joshua to be brought to Theda Clarke four days later to have them removed. He also indicated that Randy and Marie had missed previously scheduled appointments to bring Joshua in for general check-ups.

Following Gehringer's call Kemmeter made a second May visit to the Wright Avenue apartment. Joshua did not appear to be a child in distress. He had no apparent new scrapes, bruises, or lacerations. It was a strange situation. She was like the pilot at the helm of a boat traversing a lake. Various observers from afar radioed warning messages. The seas were choppy, angry waves had dashed a fragile boat against jagged rocks. There was danger about, every reason to fear the worst. But her own observations were of a sea that seemed to be placid as often as it was choppy and when she saw the fragile boat it had a few scrapes but did not seem in danger of sinking. There seemed to be no need to radio for help, no need to have the fragile craft towed immediately to a safe harbor.

When queried years later about this period and what came next, she stressed that Randy's cooperation was voluntary. He was not under a court order to work with the Department of Social Services. At any point he could have refused to accommodate her visits. Implicitly, she seemed to be asking whether it would have been in Joshua's interest to press for court intervention on ambiguous evidence and risk being shut out entirely by Randy or continue to visit and press for changes in his expectations of his son and the way in which he raised him.

On the other hand, Joshua had twice been brought to the Theda Clark emergency room since having been released back into Randy's care. It would be bitterly debated in coming years, once the *DeShaney* case reached the United States Supreme Court, and knowledge of what happened later went beyond Neenah, Oshkosh, and the Fox River area, as to whether that was not enough to reopen the question of custody. In the meantime, spring, and its bright companion, hope, had come to the Fox River valley. Winter in the North Country was always difficult. The Memorial Day weekend loomed and with it the summer months beyond. There might be better days ahead.

A meeting scheduled for June 10 was canceled, and one month later, on July 13, Randy and Marie and the children left Neenah and moved to Oshkosh, fifteen miles to the south. Relocation did not change matters at all. The main County Social Service office was in Oshkosh. Ann Kemmeter would continue to meet with the family. And, indeed, Oshkosh being a larger community than Neenah, the opportunity to find work might be better and needed social services more accessible. The move could be seen in a positive light.

July 25, 1983

Ann Kemmeter sat down to dictate a Service Plan review examining what had transpired over the preceding six months, and to formulate a new service plan based on that review. She had seen the family a week-and-a-half earlier and there were no visible signs of mistreatment or disorder. Still the situation had troubling elements.

Her narrative indicated that little had changed since January. At one point Randy had expressed thoughts about leaving Marie, but then changed his mind. They seemed to feel that the move to Oshkosh had been good for their relationship and that they had gotten Joshua away from a neighbor's child whom they believed had caused many of his injuries. Randy had been looking for full-time employment without success. In his spare time he did a lot of fishing, and had lately taken Joshua with him on these happy forays.

She indicated her concern, however, that Randy and Marie held expectations of Joshua that exceeded his chronological age. Joshua made his own bed in the morning and went to the kitchen to make himself a peanut butter sandwich. Randy insisted that Joshua wanted to do more demanding tasks rather than being forced to do them. The review stated that at the last home visit there had been discussion of Joshua being put in Head Start. She had indicated that it would improve Joshua's social skills and provide a stimulating learning environment and Randy promised to contact the Oshkosh program in order to enroll him.

The review also expressed concern about the number of injuries Joshua had suffered. The March visit to the emergency room was noted, as well as the bump seen on Joshua's head in May. She noted that some of the explanations given by Randy and Marie for the injuries were feasible, but there was enough unsettling in the situation to warrant continuing to follow the family.

The narrative, dictated in late July and transcribed in early August, allowed that the DeShaney's had been cooperative during the preceding six months, and appeared to be open and forthright in discussing Joshua. She concluded that she would continue to monitor the family for another six months with particular attention being given to Joshua's frequent accidents, and she would suggest specific services that might help the family address its problems more effectively.[9]

In accordance with Social Service Department policy, Cheryl Stelse as immediate supervisor of Ann Kemmeter sat down with her on a regular basis to review her ongoing cases, including DeShaney. The Service Plan review represented consensus on the state of the family and the needs of the boy six months after Marie had brought him to the Theda Clarke Medical Center emergency room.[10]

September 21, 1983

Weeks had passed since the last home visit. Summer's golden haze had given way to fall's darker hues. Children no longer played in Plamann Park. The wetland hiking trails were deserted. Even now there was a hint of frost in the air and the cold days that were to come. Kemmeter was brought face to face again with the ambiguity of the situation and the ever-present troubling questions.

It could have happened the way they said it did. Kemmeter could not say with certainty that it had not. They had rushed Joshua to Mercy Medical Center emergency room, closer than Theda Clark, had returned home, and now offered an explanation. They told her that they were in the kitchen. Joshua had grabbed and squeezed a plastic dish detergent bottle, squirting the stinging soap liquid into his eyes. Their frantic efforts to wash the liquid from his eyes and rush him to the emergency room as he screamed and writhed in pain caused the scratched cornea and the laceration on his forehead.

Kemmeter added a record of the unsettling occurrence to the growing Social Service Department DeShaney file, and also noted a phone call from the Oshkosh Police Department a week earlier. A worried citizen had called them to report that a woman was slapping a little boy named Joshua to the ground repeatedly.

November 9, 1983

There had been two home visits during October. The first, on October12, had been without incident or note. The second, a week later, had occasioned concern on Kemmeter's part. Joshua had a lump on the left side of his forehead. And now, two weeks later, the first November home visit, brought additional reason for worry. Joshua had marks on his chin that might be cigarette burns. Kemmeter asked Marie what had happened, were there cigarette burns on the boy's face? Marie issued a denial and instructed Joshua to tell the caseworker what had occurred. He had scraped his chin while outside playing, Marie claimed, and Joshua got down on his hands and knees to demonstrate how it had happened, apparently to the social worker's satisfaction.

In the two decades that passed between the reemergence of child abuse and the initiation of Ann Kemmeter's visits to the DeShaney household, an enormous body of writing on the subject had appeared. Many points of view could be found in the journals and books available to social work professionals. Psychologists, psychiatrists, social workers, physicians, and lawyers had declaimed on the subject, often with great eloquence and compassion. As would be expected, there was one voice not heard, one type of commentator whose inner thoughts were not available for scrutiny, the abused child.

Understandably, professionals attempted to penetrate the inner world of the child, possibly subject to abuse, by making inferences based on the child's behavior. The Child Protection Team inferred that Joshua was not being abused by Randy because he seemed to be drawn to his father rather than shrinking from him when his father visited him at Theda Clark Medical Center. Later, it was inferred that there was a possible benign explanation for what might have been a cigarette burn on Joshua's face, because when asked to demonstrate how a mishap had caused the mark, he did so.

Meditation on the inner world of the child, possibly being subjected to abuse, suggests a different way of interpreting that child's behavior. On the day Joshua was queried about the mark on his chin he was four years and eight months old. The world he knew was the world constructed by the adults who took care of him. In his world those adults, Randy and Marie, were the all-powerful sources of whatever comfort he enjoyed or whatever pain he experienced. At four years and eight months he was unaware of others who could intervene decisively in his life, or of a moral universe different from the one in which he lived. Whoever this nice lady was who appeared every now and then, after the door closed behind her, the world would be as it had always been. Those who were omnipotent in that world would still be omnipotent. Whatever the source of the scrape, if Marie asked him to get down and demonstrate that it had been caused by a fall, he would get down and demonstrate that it had been caused by a fall.

One week later, Kemmeter visited the Tennessee Avenue apartment again. There were no new signs of distress. At her own request she was now accompanied by a second caseworker. The situation was increasingly troubling. She felt the need for a second pair of eyes, a second voice, a second opinion as to what was going on.

In early December the local paper published an article about a ruling of the Wisconsin Supreme Court empowering authorities to enter a home without a search warrant when they believed children to be in danger. Cheryl Stelse, identified as supervisor of the Winnebago County Child Protective Unit, was quoted as stating that she supported the law but that it would have little effect in the county. "Even if a child is in danger," she observed, "the Department would normally get a search warrant through the district attorney. That can take from one hour to several days."

The observation lent itself to any number of inferences. At one level it could be taken as reflecting appreciation of personal privacy and the rights of the parents, a position well respected in both the legal and social work professions. But in a universe that often did not offer morally unambiguous alternatives, the exercise of virtue might also carry significant costs—it was only a question of who would bear those costs. Much damage could be done to a child in "several days."

January 10, 1984

Kemmeter's conference with Ruth Davis, who was associated with Headstart, addressed the now year-old recommendation that Joshua be enrolled in that program. On several occasions Davis had attempted to make contact with the family in order to initiate the enrollment process, but they had been out of town or otherwise unavailable. Finally, a meeting with Randy and Marie yielded their agreement to Joshua's participation in the program. Then matters changed. Davis had stopped by the Tennessee Avenue apartment, found Joshua alone, and had so notified the Department of Social Services in writing.

Perhaps frightened, perhaps resentful, Randy and Marie withdrew consent for Joshua to enter Head Start. They claimed that it was happenstance that he had been found home alone. Because they had no telephone, making a phone call required walking about three blocks to the nearest public phone. That day, they had just left the apartment to go call Randy's father. Joshua preferred to stay at home and take a nap while everyone else, Randy, Marie, and Rusty, strolled up to Main Street and New York Avenue where the phone was located. They claimed that it was chance that the Headstart worker had shown up during the fifteen minutes that they were gone; no bad meaning should have been attached to their absence.

Ruth Davis assured Kemmeter that she would continue to press the matter with the DeShaneys in the hope of reversing their decision. Strongly believing that Headstart participation would provide Joshua with intellectual stimulation and a setting in which his social skills would improve, Kemmeter supported Ruth Davis's intention to continue to try to be in contact with the family.[11]

January 25, 1984

Six months had passed since the first review and a year since Joshua had first been rushed to the emergency room of Theda Clarke Medical Center. It was now time for another Service Plan assessment. Ann Kemmeter set forth her concerns in writing in this second review of the case.

The tone was more somber. She was worried for Joshua's welfare. She believed that Randy and Marie continued to have high expectations of the boy and that they might be subjecting him to verbal threats for falling short. She expressed suspicion regarding the numerous accidents Joshua had had, and noted that on her last visit a week earlier she had not seen him because he was in bed, allegedly, with the flu.

She had learned and now recorded in the report that November had been a particularly brutal month. The Oshkosh police had been contacted on the November 11 and 12 regarding violence between Randy and Marie. Words had become blows and Marie had wound up with a black eye. They had separated for a time but were now back together.[12]

But the most disturbing event had occurred at the end of November. Joshua had been brought to the emergency room at Mercy Medical

Center for a laceration on his forehead. Examination revealed that there was blood in his left nostril. His left ear was red and swollen, and there were bruises on his shoulders. According to Randy, he had fallen in the bathroom and hit his head on the toilet. Dr. Bowers, the examining physician, did not believe it. Randy denied abuse and insisted that there had been an accident.

Pursuant to law, Dr. Bowers reported suspected child abuse to the hospital's Social Service department. Kemmeter in turn had been called on the phone and apprised of the situation, including the right-side forehead laceration. The internal hospital form generated by the circumstance signaled the possibility of abuse but did not itself constitute a judgment that abuse had occurred. These suspicions and the evidence on which they rested became part of the growing file on which Kemmeter based her second Service Plan review.

She concluded the written assessment of the year-old case by expressing concern about the "innumerable accidents" that Joshua seemed to suffer. She also expressed doubt that the serial injuries were simply a matter of an accident-prone child. She was concerned about the fighting between Randy and Marie, and speculated that it might be related to a dynamic that led to abuse of Joshua. Perhaps anger and frustration were displaced on Joshua. She concluded, however, that ". . . none of this could be proven, and none of it was serious enough to warrant court intervention."[13]

She also noted that Randy and Marie had become more resistant to having Joshua's welfare monitored. Although they had again agreed to lend themselves to a treatment plan, increasingly they failed to be home for scheduled visits. She expressed the intention to stop by unannounced and to continue to work toward helping them acquire better parenting skills and more age-appropriate expectations of Joshua.

Over the course of the year there had been occasions when she had sat Joshua on her lap and read stories to him. She was fond of him and believed he was fond of her. She could make one of two kinds of mistakes regarding his fate. Court intervention and placement away from Randy could be recommended even though, in reality, he was not in danger; or, on the other hand, she could fail to recommend court intervention when, in reality, he was in danger. The law commended sensitivity to the danger of child abuse but, at the same time, honored the integrity of the family. The service plan reflected both pressures. The contradictory impulses resided comfortably in the language of statutes but might generate tragedy in the hospitals, hallways, offices, clinics, playgrounds, and morgues where the desperate dramas attending child battery were actually played out.

The second review was completed approximately a year after the Child Protection Team had met at Theda Clarke to determine whether the available evidence suggested that Joshua DeShaney was the victim of abuse. That evidence was comprised, in part, of Keith Nelson's report that Marie and Randy's neighbors had neither seen nor heard anything that would suggest that the boy was being mistreated. Had a similar investigation taken place one year later in Oshkosh, pursuant to a new request for temporary custody of Joshua, at least three citizens having relevant information could have been found.

One of these citizens would have indicated that on December 8 or 9, an adult, seemingly in charge of Joshua, had stated to her that she could not stand him and was afraid she would hurt or kill him someday. Later that evening, she encountered Randy, accompanied by Joshua who had stitches in his head. On inquiry Randy indicated that Joshua had defecated in his pants, had been ordered by Marie to clean it up, and when he refused had been struck, causing his head to hit the bathroom sink.[14]

Another citizen would have indicated that in the summer of 1983 she had seen Joshua being bodily thrown in the air.[15] And had the investigation continued, a third citizen would have been found who would have indicated that in February of 1984, Joshua had informed her that his penis hurt due to having been kicked in that area, and that he was having trouble urinating.

But there was no renewed request to the court to take custody of the boy. If the 1983 Child Protection Team had before it the record that had accumulated by 1984, would it have recommended that the Juvenile Justice Court be petitioned to remove Joshua from Randy's custody? More visits to emergency rooms had occurred. There were now bystanders who testified to having seen what might have been mistreatment. Why not another meeting to assess Joshua's situation? That question eventually perplexed child advocates, defenders of public agencies, lawyers, judges, and members of the public in a debate driven by passion as well as intellect, but not yielding a clear answer.

February 1984

Contact was attempted but no one was home.

March 7, 1984

The midweek home visit was unannounced, but neither Randy nor Marie was upset. Indeed, it seemed to be a festive occasion. It was Rusty's second birthday, and Randy and Marie were in the kitchen decorating his birthday cake. Kemmeter joined in, writing, "Happy Birthday, Rusty" on the cake; then Randy finished the decorating. Rusty and Joshua were napping, and when Joshua woke up, Kemmeter remained in the kitchen while Marie went back to his bedroom, quieted him, and then rejoined the two adults. Randy and Marie seemed at ease with each other, and told her that they were getting along much better and that, indeed, things were looking up. Randy was being called back for a third interview with a security company and might soon have full-time employment.

As they talked Randy began to clean and fillet more than two dozen perch that he had caught. Friends with children were coming over for dinner that night to celebrate Rusty's birthday. Filleting, he explained, would allow the children to enjoy the fish without fear of choking on bones. It was a good time, a happy household anticipating the laughter of children and the warmth of friends.

As the visit approached an hour in length she decided to take her leave. The atmosphere appeared to be relaxed. Nothing appeared amiss. Two adults were preparing a child's birthday party. Joshua's fifth birthday was two weeks away. It was now more than a year since she had first seen him, a three-year-old in bandages in a hospital room. In the fourteen months that had passed since those January days, she had seen him often and had come to like him. She would later wonder why on that happy evening she did not ask to see him.[16]

CHAPTER FOUR

INTO THE NIGHT

Twenty-four hours later Joshua was rushed comatose to the Mercy Medical Center emergency room by Randy and Marie. His breathing was labored and resuscitation was necessary with a hand respirator. As the medical team struggled to reverse failing vital signs, Randy became increasingly frantic. Marie, unable to comfort him, had to tend to her son, Rusty. Someone urged calling Ann Kemmeter as the scene spiraled toward chaos.

About 7:00 p.m. on Thursday, March 8, 1984, Kemmeter received a call from Helpline asking her to contact Judy, a nurse in the emergency room at Mercy Medical. Kemmeter asked whether an Oshkosh Child Protective Service caseworker, someone else, might be available, but was told that she was being asked for. She had been working with the DeShaney family for fourteen months, with particular concern for the welfare of Joshua. There was urgent need now for her presence.

Kemmeter arrived at the hospital around eight in the evening and was met by Sister Joanne Hein, a hospital chaplain, accompanied by a nurse who explained that Joshua had been unconscious at the time of arrival. A hand respirator had been rushed into use as his breathing became labored, and a CAT scan had been ordered against the possibility of severe head injury. There was now nothing to do but await its results.

She was told of the desperate and difficult scene that had unfolded before her arrival. Randy had pounded on the walls and lashed out verbally at the medical team as it struggled to save his son's life, panic preventing awareness of the team's need to concentrate on the fight to keep Joshua's vital signs from falling further toward a point of no return.

It was quiet now as all parties awaited the results of the tests. Kemmeter encountered a distraught Randy in the hospital hallway and spoke to him, trying to calm him down. He was crying and shaking. His voice was loud and unsteady. He insisted that Joshua was his whole life; if anything happened to his son he would have no reason to go on living. He mentioned the possibility of suicide.

Kemmeter was able to get him back to the small lounge area, and while he was sitting there sobbing and shaking uncontrollably, she spoke with the nursing staff to see if the emergency room physician could give him some sort of sedative. At approximately 9:30 p.m., Dr. Plueddeman ordered Randy be given five milligrams of Haldol by injection.

From the earliest moments of the crisis and periodically throughout the evening, the medical staff asked Randy and Marie what had happened. It was important that they know in order to be able to respond quickly and effectively in the struggle to save Joshua's life. Ann Kemmeter also pressed them to learn what had happened.

The catastrophe had occurred in a matter of minutes according to the pair. They were doing home repairs, fixing a clock, repairing a table, and found that they needed a screwdriver and a hammer, both of which were in the basement. When Joshua volunteered to go down and get them, Randy walked out into the kitchen and opened the door for him. Joshua, wearing pajamas with feet that were too big, started down the basement stairs. They heard loud bumping sounds and called out to him. And, when there was no answer, Randy ran down the stairs.

He found his son at the foot of the stairs, he said, curled up in a ball and limp. He carried him back up to the kitchen where he and Marie tried mouth-to-mouth resuscitation, slapped his cheeks, and cried repeatedly for him to wake up. When there was no response, they rushed him to Mercy Medical Center, hoping against hope that there would be some sign or flicker before they got there, but there was none.

Following the CAT scan, Randy, Marie, and Ann Kemmeter got their first glimpse of Joshua. His eyelids were taped shut, there were tubes attached to him, and a nurse was holding a hand respirator to assist his breathing. The CAT scan indicated the enormity of the crisis. There was massive bleeding under the skull, making a brain operation an immediate necessity in order to relieve the pressure. The odds were steep. Joshua had a 25 percent chance of pulling through surgery that evening, but he would surely die without surgery.

The full nature of the catastrophe would not be known until probing in the operating room, but the surgeons faced a daunting array of possibilities: the bleeding might be the result of a shard or fragment of skull bone slicing through a blood vessel and causing blood to accumulate between Joshua's skull and the surface of his brain; or the result of a tearing of the blood vessels carrying blood away from his brain; or it might be caused by bruises and tears in the brain itself. The medical lexicon had various names for these and other grim possibilities, epidural hematoma and subdural hematoma, but whatever the appropriate vocabulary, the language bespoke a frightful struggle throughout the course of a very long night. "When I came to the emergency room Joshua was on a cart, unconscious," one of the doctors later recalled. "His pupils were dilated. He had multiple bruises, and he was unresponsive to verbal stimuli."

As preparations for the operation were being made, Randy sat with Joshua, crying softly and stroking his tousled, blond hair.

He was with his son when the police arrived.

The life of a four-year-old was in the balance. The Winnebago County Department of Social Services had been involved with the family for more than a year. This might be an accident as Randy and Marie claimed, or it might be child abuse rising to the level of criminal assault. Against the chance that the worst had occurred, Ann Kemmeter had phoned the Oshkosh Police Department after Randy had been sedated. Detective Novotny and Officer Kronenwetter arrived after the grim results of the CAT scan had been made known but before Joshua was wheeled in for brain surgery.

Randy had no objection to meeting with them, but expressed surprise at the need to do so given that he had already explained that the injury was caused by an accident. Joshua had fallen down the basement steps. He expressed bewilderment that anyone might think otherwise. He sought assurances for the police from Kemmeter. "Ann, you know that Joshua bruises easily."

Kemmeter also called her supervisor Cheryl Stelse, who said that she would get to the hospital quickly. After meeting with detective Novotny, Kemmeter called Stelse back to ask that she bring Joshua's Social Service file for the detective to study. If there was a record of possible abuse, the detective wanted to know about it. Given that a child was suspended between life and death, possibly as the result of a criminal act, Novotny phoned the district attorney, Dee Dyer. Kemmeter also spoke with Dyer, providing background information. If an arrest was imminent, there was the matter of a charge and an arraignment. The evidence was not yet in, but all possibilities were open. While they were on the phone with the district attorney, Cheryl Stelse arrived with the DeShaney file.

Thursday night turned into Friday morning. Randy, Marie, and Rusty had been at Mercy Medical Center for hours. Joshua was still in surgery. Following their meeting with Novotny and Kronenwetter, Randy and Marie asked if they might return to their Tennessee Avenue apartment to see if anyone at that late hour could take Rusty in. No one objected

In a crisis, as the mind plays with infinite, awful possibilities, activity is its own balm. Randy and Marie disappeared into the cool Wisconsin night, away from the contagious tension, the slow passage of time.

Eventually they returned, the two-year-old still with them. Their neighbor had not been home, but the trek had provided the opportunity to get fresh air and a pack of cigarettes. Randy and Rusty returned to the small lounge area and fell asleep while Marie went to another area and watched television. Meanwhile the surgeons labored on.

Fourteen months had passed since the cold January afternoon that first brought them together, a struggling young couple with two small children, social workers, medical staff, and law enforcement. There had been ongoing contact with this troubled family, more than a dozen home visits from social work staff over the course of a year, some pleasant and uneventful, some disturbing, but Joshua had also been seen by doctors over that period of time for various bruises and abrasions, beyond what would be expected for a young child. There had been staff reports and phone calls about the family, questions raised and suggestions made, but in the end, nothing had been done. And now they were all assembling again in this fearful place, unable to go back in time and make the call or advance the recommendation that might have made a difference. And the "what ifs" would loom larger as events unfolded.

The bleeding under Joshua's skull connoted damage to his brain, but with consequences yet to be determined. The brain has the consistency of molded and shaped jelly and is made up of more than 100 billion nerve cells. Different parts of the brain—the cerebral sphere, the stem, and the pituitary—relate to different functions, ranging from thinking and speaking to breathing, smelling, and tasting.

If Joshua had suffered brain damage there could be greater or lesser consequences for shorter or longer periods of time: there might be cognitive damage, including loss of memory and spatial disorientation; there could be physical consequences, including seizures and impairment of vision or hearing loss; there might be psychosocial trauma involving anxiety and agitation, or depression and withdrawal.

Joshua was four years old and his brain had probably reached 80 percent of its adult weight. Ordinarily, the intellectual and motor skills of a four-year-old unfold rapidly. A four-year-old can pedal and steer a tricycle skillfully; jump over objects five and six inches high; walk a straight line; and run, jump, hop and skip around obstacles with ease. In the absence of trauma, the intellectual skills of the four-year-old encompass being able to sing simple songs, place objects in a line from largest to smallest, recognize familiar words in children's books, name six to eight colors and three shapes, and make up nonsense words. Barring serious head injury, the four-year-old understands the passage of time in the short run, as in what happened yesterday and what might happen tomorrow. The four-year-old also enjoys playing with other children, understands the idea of taking turns but does not always want to, seeks the approval of adults, and is afraid of the dark and of monsters.

But Joshua had suffered serious head injury, and whether he would run, jump, skip, or hop; be able to name six to eight colors; seek the approval of adults; or be afraid of the dark and of monsters depended on what sections of his brain had been damaged. As with every human being, many of his physical and intellectual skills were related to specific regions of the brain. A section of the frontal lobes influenced voluntary movement, cognition, and learning. The capacity to appreciate language and speak coherently was influenced by a different frontal lobe area, while the occipital lobes near the rear of the brain processed visual stimuli.

Joshua had a birthday coming up in two weeks. A serious brain injury would rob him of next year's possibilities at an age when he was too young to realize that next year had possibilities. And the life lost could not be resurrected. Brain cells once destroyed do not regenerate. A portion of the brain, once removed, does not grow back again. The adult suffering a brain injury may compensate by building on stored experience; the child has little or nothing on which to rebuild. An assault causing brain damage dims the light on the child's humanity, and the more severe the assault, the closer the child comes to eternal stillness in an endless night.

And finally the surgery was over.

Randy and Marie were joined by the others as the neurosurgeon recounted the results and the prognosis. A large part of Joshua's skull had been removed to relieve the pressure on his brain. His brain had been depressed causing him to be comatose. The hemorrhage had been on the right side, mainly toward the rear, the occipital area. There had been major brain damage. He was in intensive care now; "it would be a week before he would wake up if he did at all." The news was not good, but it could have been worse. Joshua might live, but the quality of his life would be deeply compromised due to the massive head injury.

The news drained emotional wells dry. Joshua had not died in the operating room even though the future was uncertain.

In the short run, the news seemed to change a number of agendas. There was not a death and, hence, whatever suspicions the detectives might have had need not translate into immediate detention of Randy.

For the social workers, Joshua's immediate problems seemed to be in the medical realm. What happened next depended on what the doctors could do to sustain Joshua and bring about his recovery.

For Randy, in a certain sense, the worst was over. Whatever there was to face when dawn came, it would not be arrangements for a funeral. There was nothing that could be done now but hope. They were emotionally exhausted. He and Marie and Rusty had been at the hospital for hours. He could return now to their Tennessee Avenue apartment for whatever sleep that lingering fear and anxiety would allow. The police had questioned him, but Joshua would live. Perhaps, the police had no further role in the matter.

And after Randy, Marie, and Rusty left, Dr. Letellier, the surgeon, and other staff people met with the social workers, Kemmeter and Stelse, and with the detectives, Novotny and Kronenwetter. His message was direct and unequivocal. Joshua's injuries were not consistent with the story about his falling down basement stairs. There was neither a skull fracture nor the kind of cranial injury that would have been sustained had he tumbled down a flight of stairs and hit the floor. When the boy's head had been shaved preparatory to surgery, several old bruises were revealed, but there was no fresh injury consistent with a fall. His current injuries were akin to those that would be seen in a high-speed automobile crash when the head snaps violently back and forth. Joshua's cranial bleeding was more consistent with having been shaken violently or hit repeatedly and hard with an open hand. Shaking or hitting would result in the tearing of blood vessels in the skull, and torn blood vessels would yield the kind of cranial bleeding discovered when the operation commenced.

At 9:27 Marie was advised by detective Novotny of her Miranda rights to remain silent and that anything she said might be offered in evidence against her in any later proceeding. Sometime later Randy was also advised of his Miranda rights.

At approximately 12:40 a.m., Gladys Farr, Juvenile Court intake worker, was contacted to authorize custody being taken of Joshua DeShaney.[1]

Fourteen months after Marie brought Joshua into the emergency room of Theda Clarke Medical Center, and twenty-six months after the Department of Social Service received, date stamped, and filed a warning as to his dangerous circumstance, the state assumed responsibility for his care and safety.

Four years later *DeShaney v. Winnebago County Department of Social Services* was argued before the United States Supreme Court, but being severely disabled and profoundly retarded as a result of the injuries that brought him to Mercy Medical Center, Joshua DeShaney would never know.

CHAPTER FIVE

A LIGHT TOO LATE

This Is What Followed

Ten hours had passed since the surgeon's predawn briefing. Assault rather than accident was the more likely cause of the injuries threatening Joshua DeShaney's survival. As dawn turned to morning, various government offices opened. Machinery to extend the state's guardianship over the battered child and pursue the batterer had to be set in motion.

Ann Kemmeter met in midmorning with Juvenile Court intake worker, John Juknialis, to apprise him of the circumstances attending the court's introduction into the case. She indicated that Randy had left the Mercy Medical Center prior to the Social Service Department having taken custody of Joshua, and thus had to be made aware of his status in relation to his son. She informed him further that a police investigation was underway to determine if Joshua had been the victim of a criminal assault. Later they met with Randy, who indicated understanding that he could not remove Joshua from Mercy Medical Center without authorization from the court.

Shortly thereafter they spoke with corporation counsel John Bodnar, whose opinion at the Child Protection Team meeting fourteen months earlier yielded the conclusion that there were insufficient legal grounds for denying Randy the right to remove Joshua from Theda Clarke Medical Center. They all agreed that Randy should not be allowed to have contact with Joshua. He would be confined to seeing his son only through an intensive care unit window, and, in any event, the police were now asking whether his fury had wreaked such havoc on this child.

In the early afternoon she returned to Mercy Medical Center for a meeting with Ann Marshall, the hospital social worker, and with the nurses tending to Joshua. The nurses were told that civil and criminal proceedings were moving forward in the case and that two courts were now involved.

It was important that they understand that Joshua could not be removed from the premises without a court order. They were asked whether they felt comfortable with the restrictions to be placed on Randy when he visited his son. They had no problem with them.

Kemmeter then asked to see Joshua and was brought into his room. The light played off the elaborate instruments marshaled to overcome catastrophe. He was on life support. A machine maintained and regulated his breathing. Drainage tubes ran from the right side of his head where the surgery had been performed. His head and face were encased in bandages. He was being fed intravenously. She asked to see the marks on his body and a nurse drew away the clothing. There was extensive bruising on both thighs. There were bruises in the groin area. There were two bruises on his left arm. But the nurses did have news that gave reason for hope. There was some involuntary movement, a good sign. The swelling and pressure in the brain seemed to be under control.

And then she left the hospital for a short trip across town.

Tell Me Again What Happened

Randy was asleep on a sofa when she arrived. Rusty was in his bedroom taking a nap and Marie was at a neighbor's house across the street. Only a few days had passed since the last visit to a household seemingly so full of hope and promise. Joshua had been asleep in a bedroom on that occasion as Randy and Marie completed preparations for Rusty's birthday party. Joshua had awoken, made noise, and Marie had gone to quiet him. Kemmeter had not seen him on that last visit, but all had seemed well. There had been nothing in that visit hinting that their lives as they understood them were in their waning hours.

Randy summoned her in and she told him she had just come from the hospital to bring him up to date on Joshua's condition. She explained the visitation procedure, but couched the matter in terms that were not accusatory. Joshua was still barely on the edge of survival. Round-the-clock care and sophisticated machinery were sustaining his life. It was best that the medical staff be left to do their job without the intrusion of anxious relatives. It would be best if he viewed Joshua from behind the glass partition in the intensive care unit. Randy indicated that he understood. And then she asked him to tell her again what had happened.

Tragedy once told must often be told again as the listener strains to find meaning in the grim facts of bodies shattered or lives destroyed.

Tell me again what happened. Tales of catastrophe must be repeated as the listener struggles to understand the "why" in addition to the "how." Tell me again what happened. And maybe this telling will yield reason to believe that it was an accident rather than something more dreadful.

Randy again recounted the story. He and Marie were doing repairs on a clock and a coffee table. They needed a hammer and a screwdriver and Joshua volunteered to go down to the basement to get them. Randy and Marie followed him out into the kitchen where he pulled open the door from the kitchen to the back hall by the night lock chain, because the door did not have a doorknob. Joshua went past them and proceeded down the stairs to the basement. At that point Marie returned home and Randy broke off his narrative, going back to lie down on the sofa while Marie continued the grim chronicle. She and Randy had remained in the kitchen. They heard thumps, called out, and when there was no answer, Randy ran downstairs.

Kemmeter asked Randy to rejoin them as she took a look at the stairs. Six very steep steps covered with worn, green linoleum led down to the basement. At the bottom to the right was a workbench with tools on it. They claimed that Joshua lay crumpled on the floor at the foot of the stairs, his head toward the workbench. They stated that anxiety turned to fear as he remained unresponsive to their efforts to revive him, and fear for his welfare brought them to the Mercy Medical Center that Thursday evening, less than twenty-four hours earlier, but seemingly an eternity ago.

Their story brought no more closure on retelling than it had when first related in the hospital. It explained too little and left too many questions unanswered. There was no point in asking again.

She said good-bye to Randy and Marie. It was Friday, late afternoon. The sun was still high in the sky on this cold, crystal-clear winter day. There was no breeze. The streets were slowly emptying, becoming solitary and lonely. Here and there a car seemed to huddle against the curb. Ordinarily there was a caseload to which to tend, and the week was organized to accomplish that task. In the hours since Joshua had been brought into the emergency room at Mercy Medical Center there had been only one case, and it promised to occupy ever more space.

Melody DeShaney: ". . . too alone, too poor, too young"

The distance overland from Cheyenne, Wyoming to Oshkosh, Wisconsin is one thousand four hundred and sixty miles. By car the trip takes twenty hours; by train, twenty-four hours; by air, two hours to Milwaukee and another hour by car. But time and distance are elastic no matter how the traveler makes the trip. They expand or contract according to the claim circumstance makes on the traveler's emotions. A child's graduation, a friend's wedding speed the traveler to the destination. The anticipation of tragedy extends time and distance into an infinite arc as the mind plays with the awful possibilities at journey's end: no survivors have been found, no one has been rescued, the child will not recover.

Melody DeShaney reached Randy by phone at Mercy Medical Center late Sunday afternoon. His story was short, uncomplicated, and alarming. Joshua had fallen down a flight of stairs. He was in the hospital in very critical condition. His survival was uncertain. And after the conversation, Melody and her mother left Cheyenne to make the one-thousand-mile trip to Oshkosh.

Mercy Medical Center, where Joshua lay bandaged and hooked up to machinery, had been founded by an order of nuns early in the twentieth century. Over the decades it had expanded, adding a nursing school and a pediatric unit of great renown. Its small staff had increased in number and now included practitioners across the spectrum of medical and health-care professions. Leadership, however, remained in the hand of the order that created it, The Sisters of the Sorrowful Mother.

Randy had been at the hospital almost continuously since Joshua had been brought in three days earlier. Ann Kemmeter had also maintained continuous contact with the hospital staff, and with the police and Juvenile Court. She arrived at the hospital just before three o'clock that Sunday afternoon and found Randy, Marie, and Rusty in the intensive care visiting area. The outlook was grim. The nurses reported brain pressure rising into the danger area. The call from Melody came while she was there and she heard Randy's end of the conversation. Afterward he gave her a Cheyenne number where Melody could be reached. But his ex-wife was already on her way to Wisconsin.

On Monday and Tuesday Ann Kemmeter met again with hospital social worker, Ann Marshall, and with the hospital intensive care staff to discuss finding a facility able to care for someone with Joshua's severe disabilities, should he survive. She also met with John Juknialis, the court intake worker, and Detective Novotny as matters moved forward on the criminal investigation, and with Kim DeShaney, Randy's sister, and Tom, his father, as well as with Randy and Marie. And later she had her first meeting with Myrna Bridgewater, Joshua's grandmother, and with his mother, Melody DeShaney.[1]

As the social worker responsible for Joshua's case she had known of Melody DeShaney. She knew that she was a mother who had surrendered custody of her child pursuant to a divorce decree, and that she was under court order to provide child support. The Temporary Physical Custody Request form submitted to the court a year earlier, following Joshua's admission to the Theda Clarke Medical Center, had indicated that Melody's whereabouts were "unknown" to the Department of Social Services.

As a mother living at a distance from the ex-husband who had custody of their child, Melody had not known of Ann Kemmeter and the circumstance that had brought her into her son's life. There was much to learn as she and her mother arrived in town and made their first contact with the major players in Joshua's life.

In the course of the day Melody and Myrna Bridgewater went with Kemmeter to her office. There they learned that there was a file on Joshua chronicling a year or more of possible child abuse. They learned of the numerous emergency room visits and of the injuries that prompted them. They would later both say that the social worker told them that she feared one day getting a phone call that Joshua was dead.[2]

Melody would also say later that surrendering custody of Joshua was a "point of vulnerability" in her life. And indeed, giving up her son had colored relations with relatives and touched many aspects of her life. She and Randy, both very young, had married after a two-month courtship. By the time the custody battle started after dissolution of their brief marriage, Melody had departed Cheyenne. She had refused to sign an initial divorce decree that denied her any visitation rights.

Shortly after turning Joshua over to her uncle to be picked up by Randy and his second wife, Christine, she went on the road. A modified decree allowing visitation had been forwarded to her in Phoenix, Arizona. Although Randy and her mother were occasionally in touch, her own contact with him had been sporadic and difficult. She did not have a phone number for him, and his address seemed to change frequently. She recounted receiving verbal abuse from Randy's mother when she made efforts to reach him, and the situation was made worse when Randy sued her for child support and she responded by having an attorney send him a letter demanding a phone number where she could call Joshua on Sunday afternoons.

She believed that Randy was attempting to prevent her from having contact with Joshua, and for months stretching into years, from December 1980 through March 1984, there had been little contact. When last seen he was an infant, seemingly in good health. When next seen he was in a hospital, a battered child, encased in bandages, sustained by medical machinery, constantly tended to by an intensive care staff. She would later say that she thought in the years she did not see him that he was "having a nice kid life." The kind of life that she felt ". . . too alone, too poor, and too young, to give him."[3]

Perhaps she understood the widely held assumption that it is the mother who is given custody of a child in a divorce proceeding, not the father. And if the mother does not get custody, there must be something wrong with her, she must, in some way, be a bad person, uncaring, unfit, unable to shoulder the responsibilities of parenthood. The initial documents filed a year earlier entrusting the Winnebago County Department of Social Services with looking out for Joshua's welfare following the Theda Clark emergency room visit listed her address as "unknown." It seemed to her that, in some sense, she was being dealt with as if her address was still "unknown," as if she was not there, on the scene, asking questions, a mother desperately anxious about the fate of her child.

As March turned to April she was also beginning to struggle with deep and growing feelings of grief and remorse, saying of herself, "somehow I should have known," feelings of guilt welling up that would eventually push her emotionally to the edge.

In the third week in April, Patrick Suebert, a local attorney, was appointed guardian ad litem, by the court to represent Joshua's interests. As various agencies made decisions concerning his care and treatment, Melody remained bereft of information and powerless in making decisions concerning his fate. Responsibility for her son had passed from Randy to the court, to a stranger. Joshua was, it seemed, being passed around hand to hand in a circle that excluded her. The social workers, doctors, court officers, and lawyers handing him among themselves all seemed to know more about what had happened than she did, but no one offered to tell her the full story. But until she knew what had happened she could not sort out her own emotions or figure out how to cope with a future holding out the promise of more hospitals, more institutions, and more operations for Joshua. Each passing week brought evidence that the end of his rehabilitation was not in sight. Indeed it began to appear that he might never, in any meaningful sense, be rehabilitated.

Joshua's Story

Two weeks after the all-night operation that saved Joshua's life, Dr. Letellier, the surgeon, sat down with the Mercy Medical Center medical team. They were driving along a treacherous road, at night, with no map.

Joshua would live, but with severe brain damage. The journey from the night of the operation to this point a fortnight later had been perilous. Two days after the operation pressure on his damaged brain had challenged the skill and nerve of the medical staff as they fought to keep him alive. Zero pressure was normal. Thirty was in the danger zone. Joshua's brain pressure fluctuated between twenty-eight and thirty. His prognosis was poor but over the next week or so the situation improved. Were he to die it would be due either to massive infection or to upper respiratory failure, but should he survive it would be with severe brain damage. In any event there was no longer need to keep him in the intensive care unit, raising the question of where he would be sent for the long run, given that the hospital could not be his permanent home.[4]

In early April, several weeks before Joshua's move from the ICU to Pediatrics, Wisconsin Governor Anthony Earl signed a proclamation informing the citizenry of Child Abuse Prevention Month, the intent being to bring attention to a widespread problem that had escaped public attention. Ann Kemmeter's supervisor with the Winnebago County Department of Social Services, Cheryl Stelse, commented on the proclamation for the local press, asserting that it would help educate the public and make the reporting of suspected child abuse more likely. Reports received by Social Services were followed up on to determine if the abuse was actually occurring, she opined. "Once problems are pinpointed and the family shows motivation then the social worker begins to work with them . . . For the most part we want to help parents deal with problems and overcome them."

On April 16, one day after Stelse's comments appeared in the newspaper, the Oshkosh Police Department investigation of Joshua's case brought detectives to neighbors and others who might have knowledge of the circumstances of his life in the months preceding the final battering. Various accounts emerged. Joshua had complained of having problems urinating after having been kicked in the penis. He had been seen with stitches in his head after having been struck, causing his head to hit a bathroom sink. He had been seen being manhandled on the street.

In early May the Mercy Medical Center team invited professionals from the Central Wisconsin Center for the Developmentally Disabled to come down from Madison to evaluate Joshua for placement. A state-run residential facility that had admitted its first patients in 1959, the Center specialized in offering care, treatment, and training for the mentally retarded and disabled. Joshua had virtually no control over movement of his limbs or head. Scans suggested minimal activity on the right side of the brain. The Central Wisconsin professionals offered a hopeful prognosis, however. It was possible that he might regain memory and speech and, with intensive physical therapy, might regain use of his limbs. But, on the other hand, there was no certainty.

The traumatic brain injury Joshua had suffered impacted patterns of development that would normally extend through adolescence. It was believed at one time that younger children overcame brain injury more easily than adults, given that the organ was still growing. Later judgment reversed that view. The less developed the brain the more vulnerable it was to injuries, having unknown consequences for later physical and intellectual development. Trauma of the sort Joshua had suffered, violent shaking and blows to the head, caused diffuse damage as the brain slammed back and forth inside the skull, and the frontal and temporal lobes often sustained major bruising. Depending on the extent of the damage, problems involving speech, motor control, and digestion could occur. Joshua was five years old. Some of the consequences of the trauma were immediately evident. Others could become manifest over time.

On the fifth of June, just short of two months after having been rushed into the Mercy Medical Center emergency room, Joshua was transferred to the Central Wisconsin Center—a new setting that denoted new hope. But it did not quite work out. A few weeks into their effort, the Wisconsin Center began to fear that he would regress if not placed in a setting capable of providing more appropriate, ongoing stimulation. Hence, in the last week of June, the Mercy Medical Center team met to discuss the possibility of moving Joshua from the Central Wisconsin Center to the Gillette Rehabilitation Center in St. Paul, Minnesota.

These shifts reflected the difficulty inherent in attempting to find the appropriate match between the brain-damaged child's needs and an institution's capabilities. The immediate consequences of severe brain damage in a child were generally evident in the days immediately following injury, swelling, and contusions effecting breathing and coordination. The long-term consequences might not be evident for weeks, months, or years. The Gillette Center, in business since 1897, seemed to offer a program and facilities that could promote a degree of physical and mental rehabilitation and deter further deterioration. Every new effort offered hope, but not a promise.

Melody DeShaney: ". . . if I had only known . . ."

There had been hints of a story more complicated than the simple narrative of a child assaulted by a vicious adult, suggestions of a story more nuanced and subtle and involving other actors, but Melody did not know that story.

She had picked up bits and pieces, pages torn at random from a book, giving glimpses of a more complicated narrative and a wider range of characters, but without the connecting details that yield a coherent story. And then legal proceedings were initiated against Randy, and a different, more disturbing story than the "bad parent beats child" narrative began to emerge.

Randy had been arrested on May 30, following an extensive police investigation, and brought before Judge Robert Haase for a preliminary hearing. Three weeks later he appeared before Judge William Carter to determine whether there was probable cause to arraign him on criminal charges for the injuries suffered by Joshua. He vehemently and emotionally denied having hurt his child. His attorney moved to exclude television coverage of the proceedings, arguing that the interests of his client would be prejudiced by the inflammatory nature of the details of the case. The court denied this motion. At least a part of the story would now be widely broadcast.

The first witness, Dr. Basher Kayali, made the desperate efforts of the medical staff on the part of the story about the night Joshua was rushed to the hospital, laying before Melody and the public the full extent of the horror as it unfolded. He recounted coming into the emergency room and seeing Joshua bruised, battered, and unresponsive to any kind of stimuli. He had asked Randy about the extensive bruising and believed that the response was that Joshua was the kind of child who needed spanking.

Defense counsel sought to reshape the story by soliciting testimony from Kayali to the effect that Randy had not stated that he personally spanked Joshua.

Letellier, the surgeon, followed Kayali to the stand and amplified the story of what had happened that terrible night. He explained that the brain is gelatinous matter inside a fixed box, the skull. When it is massively vibrated within that box, the only things that can give are veins and the gray matter itself. Joshua's brain was bruised and depressed. Hemorrhaging had occurred, mainly toward the back of the skull area. Joshua was comatose.

Defense counsel again attempted to reshape the story by asking whether the injuries could have been self-inflicted, but this was quickly brushed aside.

At the close of testimony Randy's attorney moved to have the charges against his client dismissed, arguing that although Joshua had injuries there was no evidence that Randy had inflicted them. "We have an injury . . . so we need a scapegoat."[5.]

But the court concluded that there was no plausible alternative explanation for Joshua's massive injuries. The motion was dismissed and Randy was held for further proceedings.

But as testimony was heard and evidence examined, an unsettling story began to emerge. Joshua had been the victim of numerous assaults, not just one. The beatings seemed to have gone on over a period of months, leaving graphic evidence in the form of bruises and scars. And it also seemed that the Department of Social Services had assumed some kind of oversight in his case, some kind of responsibility to see to his welfare. It was not entirely clear how much they knew or what they had done over the long year of Joshua's torment. Somebody had administered the beatings, the hearing suggested, but would whoever was involved have had the opportunity to inflict serial damage on the boy if the professionals had stepped in before it was too late? The question was out there, for the public, and for Melody.

As spring turned to summer, Melody moved to claim a formal role in Joshua's life. She hired a local attorney, George Curtis, hoping to gain custody and bring Joshua back to Cheyenne for whatever ongoing care was needed, supported by the county. Curtis contacted the Department of Social Services in Cheyenne, requesting a review of Melody's home circumstances to determine the feasibility of Joshua being relocated to be cared for by her. And on July 5, he filed a claim with local government that was taken up by its Personnel and Finances Committee. Six weeks later, on August 21, this Committee rapidly disposed of the matter in language that was formal and dismissive. "NOW, THEREFORE, BE IT RESOLVED, by the Winnebago County Board of Supervisors, that the claim of Melody DeShaney and Joshua E. DeShaney . . . related to an incident which occurred on March 8, 1984, be the same is hereby disallowed for the reason that there is no basis for liability on the part of Winnebago County."

A century earlier desperate poverty in a half-settled land yielded tragedy, as mothers roamed villages and towns mad with grief over a child dead or on death's doorstep. In Eau Clair, a destitute woman from Chippewa County ". . . was found wandering . . . the streets . . . with a dead baby in her arms." And whereas the child had not yet died, desperate bitterness attended helplessness in the face of the child's suffering. In another town a woman carrying a sick child came up on the sidewalk in front of a grocery store, and when the grocer offered her a chair, "She sat for a quarter of an hour almost without moving . . . rose and went out on the street, carrying the baby . . . desolately homeless . . ."[6]

A century later, a mother's grief in the face of tragedy was met by the casual, summary indifference of bureaucratic language, ". . . Therefore, be it resolved . . . related to the incident that occurred on . . . there is no basis for liability . . ."

Shutting the door on her, from a bureaucratic point of view, might end the matter. Letting her in the door held unknown risks. The bureaucratic impulse would be to shut the door.

And for her, no matter how often she felt ". . . I should have known," the past could not be relived. No rescue of Joshua could be affected. Whatever feelings of guilt existed had to be dealt with in the here and now, and in a shaping of the future. The matter could have been dropped after the Board of Supervisor's dismissal of the claim. This case was no longer a part of their lives, but it remained deeply a part of her life. Continued struggle held out the possibility of learning what had happened, and the struggle was itself a way of coping with grief.

She was not a lawyer but she believed wrong might have been done. Things did not add up. Something bad might have happened and no one wanted to look back. No one wanted to stop and tell the full story. She did not "know" and she wanted to find out, for Joshua's sake, and for her own.

Cheyenne Autumn

Melody had probably passed his law office many times when she lived in Cheyenne. The capital of the state, it was a big city by Wyoming standards but small by the standards of most other places. An hour or so walk north to south along Central Avenue or east to west along Pershing Boulevard took one through the business district and the good and bad neighborhoods to the city's limits. Chamber of Commerce literature indicated that it took the average commuter less than thirteen minutes to get to work. The city was manageable. Distances were not great, either physical or social.

Months had passed since the phone call from Wisconsin. Joshua remained a child broken into pieces who could not be put together again. Randy had been arraigned on criminal charges but had not yet faced trial, and the Department of Social Services had not been open about where they had been and what they had been doing as the beatings and abuse were being administered. Melody had an attorney in Wisconsin, George Curtis, but Wisconsin was like another country. She needed advice, someone to talk to close to home who might know what to do. Maybe there was nothing to do. But if someone beyond Randy was responsible, they should not be allowed to walk away without looking back. Putting her life back together, dealing with the grief and feeling of guilt depended on knowing what had happened. If she was going to go any further she needed help.

Sometime in the fall she came into his office.

Don Sullivan was a transplant to Cheyenne from the East, a 1970 graduate of Syracuse Law School; he practiced in New York for five years then moved, looking for a better place to raise his children. The western town, on the edge of the Great Plains, seemed to be the place. He and his family lived in an impressive, large, old house with a colorful past within walking distance of his office and downtown Cheyenne. Built in the late nineteenth century by an eccentric millionaire, the mansion had an imposing stone facade reminiscent of medieval castles and topped by a tower. It stood out in a town of one- and two-story buildings with names like "the Wrangler" and "the Plains Hotel." It had long since fallen on hard times when he acquired it, including having been a social service shelter. It required a certain sensibility, a certain flair, both to conceive of it as again being a place to live, and to envision its restored elegance.

Intellectual restlessness and an ambition to perform on many stages had characterized his career. He had been on the editorial board of the *Syracuse Law Review* in his last year of law school. Just prior to moving to Cheyenne he had served in the Onondaga County Legislature. He was a member of the Board of Directors of the Wyoming Trial lawyers Association and would, a year later, become its president. On the eve of oral argument before the Supreme Court years later a crisis would occur as Melody raised a charge that political ambition had interfered with his pursuit of the case.

It was not clear who had given her his name. He was a successful lawyer. It could have been any of a number of clients or former clients; as with many of the people who carne through the door seeking his counsel, she knew a little bit about a terrible story and wanted to find out more about what had happened. In that respect she was like many of his clients. The grieving parent, the distraught spouse did not come to him with a legal theory, they came in with a terrible story—a car accident and the loved one was taken to the hospital and died even though the injuries did not seem that bad, a child had been hit by a car despite parental complaints for months to City Hall that a light should be installed at the intersection.

They showed up saying, "This bad thing happened to me; can I find out something about it?" Part of the lawyer's job, as he conceived of it, was to find out what happened.

He did not think that she was looking to sue anyone at the outset. He was sensitive to client motives. Money was almost always at stake. The possibility of the big score might vie with grief in driving the client onward. He did not feel that Melody was a lady looking to score. She was distraught. Her manner spoke more of a silent cry: "Something terrible has happened. I need somebody with experience to tell me what I'm supposed to do—what it all means."

Melody had come to talk and he listened. There was a child, her son, and he had suffered devastating injuries. It was her understanding that social services had been actively involved with him for some time and had neither taken action to safeguard him nor contacted her. It appeared that they might be moving to claim that she was an uncaring mother and that they did not know where she was, yet when she needed to be contacted one phone call had done it. And preying on her, coming back to her, was the comment she believed she heard the social worker utter, "I'll get a phone call and he'll be dead."

There was every reason not to take the case. Melody DeShaney was not a person of means. The case would have to be litigated a thousand miles away. Expenses would have to be borne out of pocket with no hope of recovery unless the case was won. He was making a good living. And if he took Melody's case his family would also pay a price in terms of his time away from home and the claim it would make on his time, his mood, and his capacity to be a husband and father when he was at home.[7]

As he looked into Melody's story, autumn came to Cheyenne. Outside his office window leaves on the trees turned gold and deep red. On some mornings a silver mist covered the leaves, all that remained of light, overnight snow, and patches of ice crinkled underfoot.

Cheyenne sat out on the high plains in a kind of lonely majesty. Denver, the big city, lay nearly a hundred miles to the south. It began as a railroad town a few years after the end of the Civil War, a rough place that gave birth to the term the *Wild West.* Cowboys, soldiers, bar girls, drifters, and bandits crowded the muddy streets, and every other building was a saloon or a burlesque theater. As a key railhead on the way west and a center for shipping cattle east, it began in the 1870s to attract a stable population interested in home, family, making money, and the sense of possibility in this growing city on the edge of the plains. In 1882 an opera house was built and popular performers such as Lilly Langtry made Cheyenne a stop on national tours. A century later the Cheyenne of the "Wild West" remained only in myth and fancy, in the annual "Frontier Days" rodeo and the Cheyenne Gunslingers Club, formed to "promote tourism and business."

Chamber of Commerce figures indicated less crime in Laramie County than in single blocks in the big cities back east. The schools were good. There was no shortage of business. Cheyenne was a good place to live and raise a family for the children of homesteaders who had put down stakes a century earlier and for lawyers from the east who had moved there barely a decade earlier.

Beyond the city limits the Great Plains stretched out to the horizons, a vast expanse, fiat and barren, beyond which lay hope or maybe despair.

In late autumn he set out for Wisconsin to determine whether Melody and Joshua might have a case against the Winnebago County Department of Social Services.

Into the Valley

Curry First was in his Milwaukee office when Don Sullivan called in the fall of 1984. The Wyoming attorney indicated that he was looking for a good civil rights attorney with experience in litigating in federal court. He had called a prominent Wisconsin attorney and had been given two names.

Sullivan outlined the dimensions of the case that led him to make the phone call. A woman named Melody DeShaney had come to see him some weeks earlier regarding a terrible event that had taken place in Oshkosh and in a small town named Neenah a hundred miles north of Milwaukee. His preliminary investigation indicated that there was something to her story. It appeared that the Winnebago County Department of Social Services, having undertaken to monitor the welfare of her son Joshua, knew for a year that he was being subjected to ferocious abuse, but failed to intervene. As would be expected, no one was talking, but a public record was beginning to emerge. Randy DeShaney, Melody's ex-husband, was being prosecuted for violence inflicted on Joshua. The newspapers had picked up the story and printed summaries of the testimony. In addition, a local attorney Melody had hired to represent her in seeking custody of Joshua had filed a suit against the Social Service Department that had been quickly dismissed.

As a seasoned attorney First understood Sullivan's approach. A client comes into the office with a story about a possible wrong having been done to them or a loved one. The client may sincerely believe the story but may be unaware of crucial facts that determine whether there are grounds for legal action. The lawyer's first task is to test the client's story against information available from other sources, other parties to the events, and the public record. That investigation allows the attorney to decide whether the client does or does not have a basis for going into court.

Discussion between the two attorneys quickly yielded agreement that there was a case. Agreement was also reached that the case had to be pursued in federal court. They did not doubt that they could prove in state court that the Department of Social Services had been negligent, but the maximum damages a plaintiff could receive for this kind of grievance under Wisconsin law was fifty thousand dollars. They agreed that fifty thousand dollars was not meaningful in terms of the costs Melody would bear for Joshua's care should she obtain custody, nor was it responsive to the magnitude of the monstrous harm that had been done.

Pursuing the case in federal court meant advancing the argument that Joshua or Melody had been injured in the enjoyment of a right conferred by the United States Constitution. It meant arguing that the civil rights of one or both had, in one form or another, been violated by the action or inaction of the Department of Social Services. It meant, potentially, extending the protection of the United States Constitution to children in more sweeping terms than previously articulated.

First was no stranger to civil rights litigation. As a law student he had been a summer intern with the New York Civil Liberties Union. He had started practicing in Philadelphia in 1969, and had been involved in public interest law for almost two decades. In 1983, a year before Sullivan called regarding a terrible incident in a small town north of Milwaukee, he had been a candidate for the national board of the American Civil Liberties Union. As he consulted with Sullivan in the fall of 1984, facts were unfolding in another case involving official negligence that he would argue up to the Supreme Court.[8]

Litigation is warfare without as much blood. Sullivan and First were about to become combatants attempting to take a hill under heavy enemy fire. They would have to depend on each other. Cover for each other. Watch each other's back. Use each other's strengths and abide each other's weaknesses. Or try to.

They brought different backgrounds and different styles to a high-stakes case that might take them through the corridors of justice to the Supreme Court itself. They were first-rate attorneys, but first rate in different ways. They complimented each other. Don Sullivan brought a sense of drama to the promised litigation, a strong sense of the story, a strong feel for how the details of Joshua's torment would reach the core of humanity in the most callous juror. Curry First, the somewhat more formal of the two, brought a keen professorial mind to the issues presented by the case. Through the early stages of the litigation a rough division of labor developed—Sullivan was involved more in the taking of depositions and in trial preparation, and First was responsible for preparing the various briefs and written legal arguments submitted to the court.

Their first task was to shape the facts as they knew them into a complaint to be filed in federal court, and even as they strove to find the right words it became clear that they spoke for other Joshuas.

> *In Everett, Washington, three-year-old Eli Creekmore died after being kicked in the stomach by his father and beaten with a belt in a final assault. "It was a tragedy that happened in front of everybody," according to one commentator. The daycare center Eli attended had called child protective services on numerous occasions. His parents denied abusing him, saying his clumsiness caused his bruises, and a state-appointed psychiatrist who examined Eli said he was lying when he said his father beat him. But when a waitress in a diner alerted police to the wretched condition of the boy at one her tables they took him to the hospital "where doctors noted . . . 'raccoon eyes' . . . circular facial bruises that can indicate a skull fracture." The doctors urged social services to assume custody, but to no avail. Shortly thereafter, Eli was dead.*[9]

There was only one plaintiff in this case, but there could have been many.

Work on the complaint continued into the New Year 1985, as Sullivan and First crafted an argument that Joshua's rights under the United States Constitution had been violated. That Joshua had suffered grievous injury was undeniable. That he had a claim under the United States Constitution against those responsible for allowing him to remain in the circumstance in which he was being abused was not at all obvious. Presumably state law afforded an injured party the opportunity to seek damages for harm done to interests not protected by the Constitution. And if state law was inadequate, or even nonexistent, it did not follow that redress could be sought under the Constitution. Wisconsin law did not afford reasonable redress. It did not follow that he therefore could seek justice in the federal court under the United States Constitution. Sullivan and First would have to make that argument beginning in the district court.

A blizzard swept down from Canada on Sunday evening, March 3. On Monday schools and shops were closed in Oshkosh, as citizens sought to dig out from under snowdrifts three feet high. Milwaukee was also hit by the storm, but public buildings remained open, including the United States District Court for the Eastern District of Wisconsin.

The complaint was filed with the clerk of the court just before 10:00 on Monday morning, two days short of a year since Ann Kemmeter had stopped at Randy's apartment but had not seen Joshua, and three days short of a year since Joshua had been rushed to the emergency room of Mercy Medical Center. Accompanying it were Notices of Appearance by Donald Sullivan and Curry First establishing them as the attorneys of record. The language was spare: Joshua DeShaney, a minor, represented by his guardian ad litem, Curry First, and Melody DeShaney, plaintiffs, were bringing suit against the Winnebago County Department of Social Services, various related agencies, and particular named parties including Cheryl Stelse, Ann Kemmeter, and Randy DeShaney.

On Tuesday, March 5, the Oshkosh newspaper sought out the principles. John Bodnar, the assistant corporation counsel present at the initial Theda Clark team meeting that returned Joshua to Randy, denied the Social Service Department's liability and indicated that the matter was being referred to the insurance company representing them.

Cheryl Stelse indicated wishing she could talk, ". . . but we have to keep everything confidential." Melody DeShaney said she wanted ". . . to get enough money to put Joshua somewhere so I can be with him . . . he's had so many brain surgeries, it's unreal. I hope he can get well enough to live with me someday, but I guess that's . . . optimistic."

Henceforth the matter would be in the courts, subject to the law's majesty.

PART TWO

THE LAW'S MAJESTY

CHAPTER SIX

PROLOGUE TO ARMAGEDDON

This Is How It Began

Following the filing of the complaint with the clerk of the Federal District Court on that cold, blustery Monday morning in early March, copies were also sent to the agencies and people against whom the charges were being made. By the end of the week Simarski and Stack, the law firm representing the Department of Social Services, had a copy. The sixty-three numbered clauses of the document made five allegations, each supported by a set of factual recitations.

It was alleged, first, that the defendants had or should have had *knowledge* of the abuse to which Joshua was being subjected, given that "In 1982 or 1983 Chris DeShaney . . . reported to (them) . . . the fact of the ongoing child abuse." Further, "On or about November 30, 1983, Dr. T.L. Bowers . . . reported to the . . . defendants his diagnosis of child abuse . . . ," and, in addition, Joshua had been rushed to hospital emergency rooms on numerous occasions during the year in which the Social Service Department was presumably responsible for oversight. Hence, the defendants ". . . knew or by the exercise of even slight care reasonably should have known of the . . . strong likelihood and great danger of child abuse being committed upon" him.

Second, the department owed a *duty* of care to Joshua throughout the fourteen months that they oversaw his case. They had ". . . the duty, responsibility and authority under applicable law to supervise, monitor, oversee and promote (his) care, welfare, safety and wellbeing [*sic*] . . ."

But, they *breached* that duty because they ". . . permitted Joshua to be taken out of protective placement and returned to the custody of Randy. . . ." They ". . . actively concealed and withheld from Melody DeShaney all knowledge and information concerning . . . the danger to Joshua of ongoing, continuing child abuse." Insofar as Melody paid monthly child support, the defendants knew her address and telephone number and could have contacted her at any time. Had they done so she ". . . would promptly have sought and obtained a formal legal change of the custody of Joshua back to herself."

As a result of the breach of duty Joshua suffered grievous *harm.* On March 8, 1984, he was rushed to the hospital ". . . where he was seen to be profoundly injured, having suffered multiple abrasions, lacerations, edemas, ecchymosis, skull fractures, brain damage and diverse other physical, mental and emotional injury."

The defendants were not like casual neighbors, the complaint argued, having no duty to act even with knowledge of the torment being endured by the boy next door. The Winnebago County Department of Social Services had assumed responsibility for his well-being; they had assumed a *duty,* but had *breached* that duty, and as a result Joshua suffered grievous harm.

The complaint drew two conclusions from this recitation. First, the defendants' breach of duty violated Joshua's rights under the Fourteenth Amendment to the Constitution of the United States by depriving him of life and liberty without due process of law, and second it denied him his constitutional right to the equal protection of the law. And given the severe harm caused by the defendants' breach of duty the complaint asked for 50 million dollars in compensatory damages and 50 million dollars in punitive damages to be assessed against the defendants should Joshua and Melody prevail at trial.

The rationale set forth for the damage amount asserted that, "The actions, omissions, recklessness, misconduct, (and) indifference . . . of the Defendants . . . are so extreme, bizarre, unjustifiable . . . and utterly unacceptable in a civilized society as to warrant and indeed demand—the imposition of punitive and exemplary damages, both to punish these Defendants for their misconduct in this case and to deter these Defendants and others similarly situated from repeating or continuing in similar misconduct in the future as to other persons and other minor children entrusted to their care."[1]

A jury trial was demanded.

Others Similarly Situated

Sullivan and First understood from the outset that the outcome of the case carried implications far beyond the parties involved. Eventually a number of children's rights organizations would be drawn into the court battle on Joshua's side, while a dozen state governments and the solicitor general of the United States, representing the federal government, came to the defense of Winnebago County. They understood that an outcome in favor of Joshua would have much to do with how business was done regarding children in distress, given the countless other children who stood in Joshua's shadow. Their deterrence argument in support of the damage award suggested that the pattern of action and inaction that yielded Joshua's twilight state was unique neither to him nor to Winnebago County.

The wider implications of their case for Wisconsin and beyond were evident even as they crafted the arguments to be made on behalf of Joshua.

In Milwaukee, Barbara S., a twenty-year-old woman, was charged with causing the death of her fifteen-month-old son Paul, who died of starvation as a result of having been fed only two or three times a week. A visit from social services two weeks before the infant's death yielded the conclusion that a relative's report of abuse was unfounded.

In Medford, Wisconsin, Dean H., a twenty-one-year old man admitted to placing his seven-month-old son in a clothes dryer and turning the machine on. He also admitted to breaking the infant's leg and throwing him on the floor. The child had been in foster care but the parents were deemed fit to regain custody after receiving counseling.

In Friendship, Wisconsin, Donald 0., a twenty-five-year-old, was found guilty of child abuse following the death of his two-year-old daughter, Luann, from an internal rupture. The hospital examination revealed that the child had bruises on her neck, back, and abdomen. A caseworker had been in the home the week the child suffered the fatal injuries.[2]

Sullivan and First did not see themselves as arguing that mere mistake yielded liability. They understood that omniscience could no more be demanded of caseworkers than of lawyers. Rather, it was a question of gross negligence: negligence that shocked the conscience. Their concern was not the fallibility common to humans, but was directed instead at taken for granted patterns of institutional neglect, beyond punishment and exempt from restitution for the harm done to those least able to fend for themselves.

Half a continent away from Wisconsin, a Mayor's Task Force in New York found disturbing deficiencies in the city's child protective system that indicated, "If New York City's child protective system was working the way it should, death and long term injury would be avoided for many children."[3] About the same time the report was being compiled and published, a supervisor in the Brooklyn office of the Special Services for Children unit sought repeatedly to alert his superiors to the existence of negligence in the handling of child abuse cases.[4] Unable to persuade them to take his complaints seriously, he leaked information about specific cases to the press. In 1982 he was demoted, fined a month's salary, and transferred to another unit. In 1984, a report by the inspector general of the Human Resources Administration substantiated negligence in seventeen of twenty-two cases about which the alarm had been sounded. Nine children had died in the seventeen cases. Interviewed about the report, the director of the city's "umbrella child welfare agency" justified the demotion and fine on the grounds that the worker had released confidential information, and in any event, ". . . he could have contacted other superiors."[5] The unreasonable was commonplace.

Occasionally the nightmare case yielded public outcry and a gesture at reform. The Philadelphia Human Services Department lost its license temporarily in 1983, but was found later, following its renewal, to be responsible for the death of children because of ". . . lack of adequate resources, poor casework practices, faulty supervision and administration, and an administration . . . unable to resolve and understand (the) shortcomings."

In Chicago, south of Oshkosh, Jonathan Campbell's short, tortured life ebbed out as Sullivan and First were drafting Joshua's complaint. Jonathan died on his first birthday, shortly after a home visit by his caseworker. The autopsy revealed that his ears had been nearly torn off and that he had more than two dozen bruises on his body, many of long duration. As public outrage swelled, the caseworker was indicted on criminal misconduct charges for failing to report signs of child abuse.

Neither Sullivan nor First believed that the criminal justice system alone was the place to seek justice for Joshua or for all the others who stood in his shadow. Criminal charges had been lodged against Randy, but that did not reform the process that allowed Joshua to be abused in the first place. More importantly, reliance on the criminal process yielded a circumstance in which the state reacted only momentarily to public outcry over the outrageous case that happened to find its way into the newspapers. In Chicago, even as law enforcement responded to public outrage over Jonathan Campbell's fate, the caseload for childcare workers remained nearly twice the state average.

Periodic public concern and spasmodic official response to tragedy had not translated into structural reform anyplace in the nation. In Wisconsin, the child abandoned to the whims and impulses of the abuser as a consequence of the negligence, indifference, or incompetence of public agents charged with protecting his interests had no recourse under state law to substantial money damages as punishment, deterrence, and incentive to systematic, structural reform. *DeShaney* would seek to change that for Wisconsin and for the nation.[6]

Three weeks after Sullivan and First filed the complaint, Mark Mingo filed a general denial. Mingo, six years out of Marquette Law School, would be the lead attorney for the defendants as the case moved up through the legal system. Insurance defense was one of his practice areas. If Joshua prevailed, a damage claim of some substantial dollar amount would ultimately reach into the coffers of the insurance companies. It would fall to him to contest each and every element of Joshua's claim, and he was joined in battle by Wayne Yankala, also out of Marquette Law School.

Uncertain Destination

A good trial lawyer attempts to present a compelling and comprehensible story to the jury, and Donald Sullivan was a good trial lawyer. The development of Joshua's story required extensive pretrial preparation. As in any case the injured parties knew only part of the story. Melody had only bits and pieces of what had transpired between January 22, 1983 and March 8, 1984, and Joshua was incapable of rendering an account of what was done to him. Hence, the details of the story had to be uncovered by the taking of depositions, the questioning of the major and minor players under oath.

There was also an extensive paper trail: minutes of meetings, copies of forms, files of client records that indicated what responsibilities had been assumed by Social Services and what responses had been made to Joshua's increasingly dire situation. These materials would be solicited via a court order in the process aptly called "discovery." Sullivan's experience told him that defendants are not always readily forthcoming with potentially damaging material. As the case moved along he came to feel that there was increasing difficulty in obtaining key documents from the other side.

The depositions and the discovery material were essential to the job of shaping the story he would put before the jury. The details of the story had to prove the basic elements of the complaint: Social Services knew what was happening, they had a duty to intervene, they breached that duty by not intervening, and Joshua was severely harmed by that breach.

The task facing Mark Mingo and Wayne Yankala was to develop a plausible counternarrative for the jury. They would take depositions from the same participants and make use of the same documents, but would ask the jury to draw a different set of inferences from them with regard to the key elements of the complaint: knowledge, duty, and breach.

At the same time that the case was proceeding on the trial track it was also proceeding on the *dismissal track.* While the trial track involved the organization of a case to be presented to a jury of twelve laypersons, the dismissal track required the formulation by Mingo and Yankala of a substantial written legal argument for submission to presiding judge John Reynolds, asking him to dismiss the case. Their motion to dismiss and the legal arguments offered in support of that motion would contend, as such motions do, that even if the plaintiffs' factual allegations were true, even if everything Sullivan and First claimed had happened actually did happen that, as a matter of law, there was no basis for making a claim against the defendants.

As they moved ahead on the trial track, framing a counternarrative for presentation to a jury, contending that Joshua's factual allegations were not true, Mingo and Yankala were also proceeding on the dismissal track, marshaling a legal argument in support of the proposition that there was no basis for a constitutional claim even if they were true.

The Trial Track

Early in June of 1985, three months after the filing of the complaint and Mark Mingo's answer, the attorneys for both sides met with Judge John Reynolds for a status conference. Given the heavy federal court calendar, when could they expect to go to trial? They were looking at six months before the case could be heard. The attorneys knew that such delays are never welcome to clients and never completely understood by them. John Reynolds had other cases in various stages of argument. Don Sullivan and Curry First and Mark Mingo and Wayne Yankala had other cases to which they had to attend even as this case drew the bulk of their attention and energy. For Melody, Ann Kemmeter, and Cheryl Stelse, there was only one case. The surgeon may have many operations scheduled, but for the patient going under the knife the only life they have is at risk. Their clients, already anxious and afraid, would have to wait six more months.

The final pretrial conference was scheduled for January 17, 1986, and a trial anticipated to run seven days was scheduled to begin in February. Just as the student is never unhappy when the examination is rescheduled for a later date, the attorney may not be unhappy when a case is scheduled for a date far ahead. Six months would give Don Sullivan and Curry

First more opportunity to uncover the grim details about the bad thing that had happened in a small city on the edge of Lake Winnebago, and would give Mark Mingo and Wayne Yankala time to do what they could to take the edge off of those details.

In the meantime the taking of depositions began. On August 28 and over a span of several days, Don Sullivan deposed Ann Kemmeter. Years later when asked his impression of her, he indicated believing that the average social worker dealing on the front line with child abuse lasted only a few years. Daily confrontation with the limitless human capacity for evil proved too draining. It appeared from the record that Kemmeter had been in the child-abuse charnel house well beyond the normal span.[7]

The deposition went to the essentials of the case the plaintiffs would have to make at trial. Did she know or should she reasonably have known of the existence of abuse? Sullivan asked her about visiting Joshua and finding cigarette burns on his face. She parried, indicating that it "was purely a suspicion of mine that they may have been cigarette bums." Sullivan asked her to describe what she suspected might be cigarette burns. The marks "were noticeable on the bottom of his jaw towards the front, going towards the front of his chin."

Sullivan's questioning zeroed in on whether she suspected abuse: "I take it that you're telling us that you were not comfortable with the explanations that the adults were giving you for these various bumps and lacerations and so on?" She indicated being concerned "more that because of the numerous occasions I would be there when I would note lumps and bruises—not bruises, correction, it was lumps, lacerations, or the family had shared with me that the child had been at the emergency room. So I began to be concerned as to what was really happening in this family."

Sullivan then asked directly, "Were you concerned that these were the physical indicia of child abuse?" The answer parried the question. "I was concerned whether it was child abuse or whether this was simply a child that was accident prone."

Sullivan pressed the matter. Was she sufficiently concerned about child abuse that she asked to have someone team with her in making the visits?

Again, the answer avoided direct acknowledgment of the suspicion of abuse. "I was concerned enough that I requested that another worker join me on the case."

Sullivan posed the query directly. "My question is, at that point, were you suspicious that this was a child abuse case?"

Finally, the answer was direct: "Yes."

Later the coworker who had joined in the visits confirmed the reason for a teammate. She was asked did Kemmeter ". . . indicate to you that she was suspicious of child abuse" and answered "yes."[8]

Kemmeter was probed with regard to the duty triggered by evidence of child abuse. She indicated that, ". . . if there was evidence that this child had suffered severe injuries or was not safe in their home, we would request temporary physical custody of the child for placement outside the home till the matter could be heard in juvenile court."

But that had not been done in Joshua's case.

The deposition testimony of Melody DeShaney and her mother, Myrna Bridgewater, allowed Sullivan to probe the breach of duty claimed in the complaint and elicit testimony they would offer on the stand were the matter to go to trial. Under questioning Melody indicated that Kemmeter told her of Joshua's numerous emergency room visits, and that "She said that she knew one day she was going to get a phone call and that Joshua was going to be dead." Her mother spoke of hearing the same words. "She said there was a file of child abuse on Joshua, and I will never forget when she got done she says, 'I just knew the phone would ring some day and Joshua would be dead.' And she never did nothing to help him. She didn't even call us or nothing."

Person by person Sullivan fleshed out the story. His questioning was sharpened and focused by documents obtained through discovery, but his belief that Mingo was slow and reluctant in making documents available led to a bitter exchange as he sought to question Kemmeter regarding whether she had written in a report that Joshua had cigarette bums on his face. Mingo interjected, "If he wants to ask you that question take time to go get your report." But Sullivan would have none of it. "We've had enough stalling and bullshit today. We'll finish up for today." Mingo was incensed. "We're not going to have any more comments like that on the record. I don't want that type of language used in front of my client, and I don't like the implication, and I don't want it to happen again." But Sullivan refused to back down. "I don't like the implication either, Mark." But Mingo persisted, "Then don't make it. That's totally uncalled for." Then Sullivan put an end to it. "We agree to disagree."[9]

Sullivan and First believed that the testimony and documents to be offered at trial left no doubt that the Winnebago County Department of Social Services had dealt with Joshua in a manner that met the legal definition of gross negligence. They were prepared to argue that Social Service's duty to act on Joshua's behalf lay not merely in the fact that Thomas Hoare had called Ann Kemmeter on a cold January day in 1983, but also in Wisconsin law itself. Social Service involvement in Joshua's case preempted the field, precluding other agencies from attempting to act on his behalf. They offered no help themselves and their mere presence prevented others from attempting to offer help. Neither courts nor the police had the power to act based on firsthand knowledge of Joshua's circumstance, and they were not provided with information by Social Services enabling them to do so.

Sullivan and First were prepared to argue that there was absolutely no question but that the department had sufficient knowledge of Joshua's predicament. They actively managed a case file on him for more than a year. There had been more than twenty caseworker contacts with Joshua and his family at home, plus numerous contacts with doctors, the police, hospital social workers, and others over the yearlong period that the sad drama unfolded. There had also been a number of supervisory conferences at which Joshua's case had been one of the matters to be reviewed.

The case to be presented at trial looked very strong. The anticipated testimony, documents, and arguments to be made at summation pointed to the strong possibility that a jury would find in favor of Joshua and Melody.

Photographs and testimony from the numerous doctors who had ministered to Joshua would make a jury aware of the extent of his injuries. Ecchymosis and hematomas sounded serious and would be explained by the doctors, but photographs of the swellings, tears, lacerations, and bruises would say more to them than words could. Generally the victim can speak most directly and painfully about the injuries suffered in an assault, but this was not possible in Joshua's case, and that very fact would also be meaningful to the jury hearing his case.

A letter sent to Melody in late September by Lori Dickman, a social worker with the Social Service Department, also indicated what a jury would hear. Dickman had gone to see Joshua in the foster care facility where he had been placed following further surgery. The visit prompted her to write Melody indicating that his caretakers were concerned about his lack of progress. Indeed there had been regression in his ability to control his head and trunk. He was also having problems eating and digesting food. He had to be fed, but tried to avoid the spoon and had trouble keeping food down. When the physical therapist tried to exercise him he went glassy eyed, leading his caretaker to believe that he was in pain. The burden of taking care of him was too much; it took away from the time and attention that had to be given other children with severe needs. They were depressed over his lack of improvement despite the long hours devoted to his care and wanted him removed from their home by Thanksgiving.

The deposition process also allowed Mark Mingo and Wayne Yankala to begin building the case for the defense. Questions put to Thomas Hoare, the hospital social worker, were meant to establish that the decision to return Joshua to Randy following the first emergency room encounter in January of 1983 was justifiable. Hoare indicated that Joshua had been held in the hospital over the weekend pending the team meeting that was to decide whether he would be returned to Randy. He had been told by a nurse that whenever Randy came to see his son, ". . . Joshua would come running to him with his arms out wanting to jump into his arms and be hugged by him. . . ."

Mingo then moved in for the clincher. "Did that indicate anything in terms of whether Joshua was, in fact, a child abuse victim, with that abuse being perpetrated by Randy DeShaney?"

And the social worker considered the matter. "That's where the question comes in. Because of that behavior, I would have to question whether Randy was physically abusing his son."[10]

The testimony of Keith Nelson, the policeman who had investigated the possibility of abuse following Joshua's initial examination in the Theda Clark emergency room, corroborated Thomas Hoare's recollection. The evidence of abuse that he had gathered and that was considered by the Child Protection Team was inconclusive. Under questioning from Mingo, Nelson recounted the outcome of the team meeting. Everyone had agreed that ongoing supervision was needed, but no one had made the case for petitioning the court to take Joshua away from Randy.[11]

Mingo's questioning also sought to build an argument that the various doctors who examined Joshua in the months following his return to Randy did not explicitly communicate suspicion of abuse to the Social Service Department. He began by asking Robert Gehringer, the doctor whose examination of Joshua in the Theda Clark emergency room in January of 1983 had triggered the initial inference of abuse, as to whether he had had any subsequent involvement with the boy.

And, indeed, he had.

Joshua had been treated in an emergency room on March 14, 1983, by a Dr. DeMorest who then forwarded a report to Gehringer for addition to Joshua's record. Mingo's next question was straightforward. Did anything in that report indicate child abuse or possible child abuse? And the answer was straightforward. "Not in the record I have."

Mingo pressed the matter as to whether new suspicion of abuse had been communicated to the social workers, or indeed, whether there was any basis for new fear, but the doctor's responses suggested primarily increasing apprehension on his part as the incidents multiplied. At some point Joshua had been seen again in the emergency room for a laceration on his upper lip, sustained allegedly by a fall from a wagon, and had then been sent over to his office, leading him to notify Social Services, but Mingo moved to blunt the meaning of this statement. Was the new injury a sign of abuse or could it have been an accident? And Gehringer explained that the ". . . particular injury was probably by accidental means in that the history relating to it was appropriate and that falling on a wagon could certainly cause a laceration of that sort."

Mingo pressed the matter, seeking to shift the blame, if there was any, away from Social Services. "So you didn't indicate to the social service worker that you had any further suspicion of child abuse as of this time in that case . . . is that correct?" Gehringer conceded the point. "I don't remember stating it exactly like that. I'm sure that I told her that he had not . . . he missed his appointment and that this was his second injury and that I was concerned about the injuries."

But then Mingo pressed too far, ". . . I'm wondering did you make any statements indicating that you had new or further suspicions of child abuse. . . ." And the doctor shored up his response. "Yes, in that he's had two more injuries." Whereupon Mingo retreated to a review of the two occasions on which the doctor had seen Joshua. On either occasion had he concluded that there was child abuse? The doctor indicated he had not concluded definitively that there was child abuse, but instead said, "My concern was that a child who we had been worrying about child abuse because of injuries had two more injuries."

But, Mingo came at him again, asking. "If at any time subsequent to January 25th of 1983 you felt the child was abused once again, was there any action you could take to have the child once again placed in temporary physical custody?" And Gehringer conceded that he could have had Joshua committed to the hospital. "I'm sure . . . , if I felt that he was in immediate danger at that point. That was not my opinion."[12]

Mingo's objective was to raise questions about whether the Social Service Department had ever been told by the various doctors who treated Joshua that he was being abused. Gehringer's testimony suggested that he had tried to convey concern but never said explicitly, "This boy is being abused." The examination of a second physician regarding Joshua's trip to the Mercy Medical Center in Oshkosh in November of 1983, ten months after Social Services had assumed a role in Joshua's life, pursued a similar path.

This doctor, deposed in early September, about the same time as Doctor Gehringer, was asked specifically about his actions following his emergency room examination of Joshua: ". . . you're telling me that in November of 1983 you didn't pick up the telephone and attempt to reach the Department of Social Services with respect to Joshua DeShaney, correct?" And the response was unapologetic. "That's exactly what I'm saying. As a matter of fact, I didn't really fill out the report that went to the Department of Social Services. I specifically avoided filling out that report because it would have given me greater likelihood of being called to testify . . . if the nurse fills out the report, then they most likely would talk to her as opposed to me, and my physical findings as noted are documented."[13]

He sought to justify his reluctance to get involved in terms of the demands on his time as an emergency room doctor. "I see every patient that comes in and I don't have time to sit down and fill out a two or three page report hand written [*sic*] about a case of child abuse at the time. And I know that that report was filled out immediately after that patient left the department."

The questioning pressed toward his perception of his responsibilities and what he had done or not done. As he understood it, his only responsibility was to see that a report was sent to the "appropriate agency." He was asked, "Who is the appropriate agency?" As he understood it, the Social Service Department of Mercy Medical Center was the appropriate agency.

After further commentary, there was an interjection, "Can I stop you for just a second? When you use the term Department of Social Services . . . are you always referring to the Department of Social Services at Mercy Medical Center?" And when the doctor indicated that he was, there was a follow-up question. "Okay. And that's something different from the Winnebago Department of Social Services?" And the doctor indicated. "I really don't know."

Three weeks later Mark Mingo sought permission from the District Court to file and serve a third-party complaint. He asserted that the second physician ". . . testified at his deposition that . . . he diagnosed child abuse . . . yet he failed to so state in his emergency room report and he failed to report such diagnosis to the proper authorities." The third-party complaint also alleged that he had failed ". . . to follow internal hospital policy and procedures in notifying the defendants, Department of Social Services, and Ann Kemmeter of his diagnosis." Hence, although all of the defendants named by the plaintiff denied having done wrong, should a jury decide otherwise and find them liable for the harm done to Joshua and Melody, that physician should share in that liability and the financial consequences thereof.

The motion also asked the court to make the Oshkosh Police Department a third-party defendant. In the course of discovery Mingo had learned that the Department, in response to a call, had taken a statement from Joshua indicating possible abuse. "It was learned . . . that despite a statement on the bottom of (the report) indicating that same was forwarded to the Defendant, Winnebago County Department of Social Services, said report was never forwarded by the Oshkosh Police Department to the Department of Social Services." Hence, again, should a jury find the defendants liable, the Oshkosh Police Department ought to share in that liability.

Were the matter to go to trial, Melody DeShaney would be a key witness; indeed the impression she made on the jury might be decisive. She was a mother pleading that she had lost her only child through the negligence and indifference of the defendants. Money could not fill the void, but money would allow her to pursue the best medical care available for him. Punitive damages, in addition to the damages necessary to meet Joshua's medical needs, would serve to deter others from the same folly, as well as punish those responsible for robbing Joshua of his future.

It was crucial to the defense that Melody's character and motives be brought into question. How much had she been concerned about her son in the past? What was her real objective now? The deposition indicated the direction in which cross-examination would go at the anticipated trial. Wayne Yankala's questions went to the circumstances under which she had given up custody of Joshua in Cheyenne in 1980. At that point she had physical custody of her son but was to surrender him to her ex-husband and his new wife, Christine. She was asked whether she had been interested in meeting Christine "to get a better understanding about her." When she indicated that that was not ". . . really in my mind at the time," her interrogator painted a harsh picture. "So what you did, you took Joshua and dropped him off at your mother's and then just left?'

But her answer painted a different picture. She waited for her uncle to come over with the modified divorce decree. She had refused to sign the initial decree because it denied her visitation rights with Joshua. The modified decree afforded her the possibility of seeing him.

But how had she cared for Joshua when he was in her care? Wanton disregard was hinted at. "Did you ever give Joshua any sort of sedative such as alcohol to calm him down when you had him?" But there was a firm denial. And how concerned had she been about getting Joshua back? "After Joshua's custody was transferred to Randy in December of 1980 and up until March 8th of 1984 did you ever request that custody of Joshua be transferred back to you?"

She had not.

The questioning then moved to whether she had made any attempt to keep in touch with Joshua after he had been taken back to Wisconsin. She indicated having made attempts to contact Randy to find out how her son was but to no avail. She felt that "Randy was trying to stonewall (her) out of Joshua's life . . ." And that led to sparring about whether Randy was really inaccessible and whether she had voiced concern about being excluded from Joshua's life to her mother, who did have periodic contact with her ex son-in-law.

A jury would have to decide whether Melody was a mother in torment or a poseur seeking to profit from her son's tragedy. The question did not go directly to the issue of the Social Service Department's responsibilities. Melody could be a poseur and the Social Service Department might still have been negligent. Who she was did have something to do with the scope of the tragedy and might, therefore, have something to do with the magnitude of damages were she and Joshua to prevail.

The deposition put the horrific details of Joshua's torment before her again, as would an impending trial. Undoubtedly a jury would also hear about the counseling and therapy needed to help her cope with the emotional vortex brought on by the tragedy, and a jury would hear her assessment of her emotional circumstance. "Maybe it is a little bit of the healing process to be able to fight back. At least you're doing something."[14]

In the same week that Melody gave her deposition, another train began to move on a second track, raising the issue of whether there would be a trial at all.

The Motion to Dismiss: The Second Track

On October 21, Mark Mingo and Wayne Yankala filed a *Brief in Support of Motion to Dismiss for Failure to State a Claim upon which Relief Can Be Granted* with the District Court. The seventeen-page document advanced the proposition that even if the factual claims regarding Joshua's abuse were true there was no legal basis for going forward in federal court.[15]

Three arguments were made in support of this proposition, the first of which went to the claim that Joshua's constitutional rights had been violated. Curry First and Donald Sullivan had relied on section 1983 of the Federal Code in advancing the argument that Joshua and Melody had been deprived of their right to due process of law under the Fourteenth Amendment to the United States Constitution. Section 1983 gave citizens the right to seek justice in federal court when an agent of government, acting in an official capacity, or as the language of the statute phrased it, "under color of law," deprived them of a right conferred on them by the Constitution.

Mingo and Yankala cited *Jackson v. City of Joliet* and other cases in support of their contention that not every injury suffered by a citizen is a result of official negligence, incompetence, indifference, or malice necessarily infringed on a constitutionally guaranteed right. In *Jackson*, the estate of the driver and passenger in a car that veered off the road and crashed and burned brought suit in federal court arguing that the Joliet policeman who came on the scene and took charge caused the deaths of their loved ones by failing to call an ambulance and by directing traffic in such a way that other potential rescuers were prevented from reaching them. His conduct, they argued, was actionable under section 1983 as a deprivation of the lives of their loved ones life without due process of law.

A court held otherwise on the grounds that the Fourteenth Amendment protects citizens from being directly abused by the state but does not provide a constitutional guarantee of a minimum level of competence in the services the state provides. In other words, there was no constitutional right to competent police service. Presumably had the Joliet police officer maliciously run the car off the road and then impeded rescue efforts, there would have been a constitutional claim. Mere incompetence did not provide such a claim.

The motion to dismiss implored Judge Reynolds to apply the *Jackson* conclusion to the facts of *DeShaney*. Wisconsin could be held to account constitutionally for injuries its agents might directly inflict on children, but it could not be brought to account under the Constitution for harm caused by their mere negligence. This analysis yielded their conclusion. "While all will agree that the injuries to Joshua DeShaney are unfortunate, the fact remains that he had no Federal right to non-negligent child protective services . . . ," even assuming the truth of the charges made against the Department of Social Services.

They noted, however, that there was an exception to the proposition that harm occasioned by the negligence or indifference of the state's agents does not yield a constitutional claim. In a number of cases courts had concluded that where the state has a "special relationship" with an individual it may be liable for failure to meet a minimum standard of care. Where it has explicitly assumed responsibility for an individual it may be held to some a minimum standard. But this case was different, they argued. The facts of *DeShaney* could be easily distinguished from those of the cases in which courts had found a special relationship to exist between the state and the plaintiff.

In particular they sought to draw a distinction between what had happened to Joshua and what happened to the plaintiff in *Doe v. New York City Department of Social Services*, a case that seemed to support Joshua's claim. In *Doe*, the plaintiff had been placed in foster care and had been physically and sexually abused by her foster father. Her claim against the city was met with a motion to dismiss which was denied, allowing the case to move forward.

But, Mingo and Yankala argued, expanding on the difference between that case and *DeShaney*, that in *Doe* ". . . the alleged child abuse was perpetrated by a state-certified foster parent. The foster home and the foster parent were subject to direct regulation by the State and the State had actual custody of the child." By contrast, in *DeShaney*, ". . . the Winnebago County Department of Social Services did not have custody or control over either Joshua . . . or his father. . . ." Hence, the "special relationship" found in *Doe* was lacking in *DeShaney*, thereby defeating the plaintiffs' argument that there was sufficient state action as to yield a constitutional claim.

Rather, they contended, the circumstances of their case were closer to those of *Martinez v. California*, a case decided four years earlier by the United States Supreme Court. In *Martinez* a teenage girl had been murdered by a parolee with a history as a sex offender five months after his release from prison. The suit against the state brought by her survivors failed on the grounds that the girl's death was too distant a consequence of the parole board's action to hold it responsible under Federal Civil Rights Law. At the time it voted to release Martinez, the board could not reasonably have foreseen that he would commit a heinous act.

An analogy could be drawn between *Martinez* and *DeShaney*. Mingo and Yankala contended as they sought to persuade Judge Reynolds to dismiss the charges. "Similarly, in (this) case . . . the injuries to Joshua DeShaney are too remote a consequence of the defendants' actions to hold the defendants responsible under the . . . Civil Rights Statute. . . . the Department . . . did not have custody over Joshua . . . the injuries occurred at the hands of his natural father. The defendants had absolutely no control over Randy DeShaney, nor was he an agent of the state. . . . Plaintiffs' complaint fails to establish a sufficient causal nexus between the action of the . . . defendants and the plaintiffs' injuries and should be dismissed . . ."

The motion to dismiss also offered an indirect and somewhat convoluted argument that the defendants should be protected by the doctrine of "qualified immunity," which recognizes that government functionaries, policemen, foremen, social workers and the like are required constantly to make judgment calls. Under the doctrine of qualified immunity they should be shielded from liability when a call turns out to be wrong and even harmful, save if the call is outrageous, contrary to accepted policy, or violates the law. None of these circumstances obtained in this case, Mingo and Yankala argued.[16] John Reynolds would have to either grant the motion to dismiss the case or set a trial date and let it go forward. Based on his record both sides had reason to hope and cause to fear. He brought a varied and distinguished background to the moment. He had been the state's attorney general and had served as governor for one term, and now he was chief judge of this prestigious federal circuit. He brought a sense of calm and competence to his interaction with the often passionate, driven attorneys who appeared before him and would, had he chosen a different profession, have been cast often as a judge in Hollywood courtroom dramas, given his air of authority and Midwestern decency. Before his appointment to the federal bench, he had established the state's first women's commission, and had defended academic freedom at the state's public universities and colleges, and when he became a judge, he ordered Milwaukee's Board of Education to end racial segregation in the city's schools, overseeing a busing program to achieve that end.

Don Sullivan and Curry First would submit their answer to the motion to dismiss to him, and as autumn gave way to an early winter chill they set about working on it, point by point.

CHAPTER SEVEN

IN A DISTANT PLACE

By the fall of 1985, Winnebago County had been under the shadow of a lawsuit for more than a year. The outcome of the suit was still in doubt as events unfolded in Milwaukee courtrooms and law offices ninety miles to the south. Although the suit might have galvanized the state to action, it could not be said that sense of urgency was widespread in the county.

In July the county board voted against creating a new social work position for Social Services even though the entire salary would have been paid by the state's Child Welfare Fund. In August the state undertook a review of the department's procedures for handling child abuse and neglect cases, mandating that reports of abuse be investigated within twenty-four hours, whereas it had been taking Winnebago County seventy-two hours to initiate inquiry.

In September the Social Service Department was found in violation of not commencing investigations within the required time, and a renewed plea to the board resulted in approval for a new position for 1986 to be funded by the state. In November the Department drew up a set of guidelines for investigating child abuse cases establishing priorities: some reports would be looked into immediately, some within twenty-four hours, some within seventy-two hours, and others within five days or more. The reports designated to receive the urgent attention were to be those involving children showing bruises and welts and children reported to have been repeatedly hit, and the condition of the child was unknown.

Plaintiffs' Response

On November 20, Curry First filed an Answer to the motion to dismiss.[1] A substantial document, nearly twice as long as Mingo and Yankala's missive, it offered a response within the constraints of the format required for legal rebuttal, but passion pressed up against those constraints and, at the end, broke through in a detailed and systematic recitation of the horrors that had brought the parties to the courtroom in the first place.

Each point made in the motion to dismiss was addressed, beginning with the argument that Joshua had not been deprived of a right secured by the Constitution and hence could not bring a claim under section 1983, which requires that an officer or government agent, acting in an official capacity, have inflicted the injuries on the aggrieved party.

A number of cases were cited in support of the contention that courts interpreted the due process clause such as to include the kind of harm done to Joshua. *White v. Rockford,* decided three years earlier, had stated that "Although it would be impossible to catalogue and describe precisely each 'liberty' . . . protected by the Due Process clause, it can hardly be doubted that chief among them is the right to some degree of bodily integrity." If Joshua had lost nothing else, First argued relying on *White,* he had surely lost his right to bodily integrity.

First recognized that his opponents acknowledged the harm done to Joshua but had argued that Social Services did not have a "special relationship" with him such that they could be held responsible for allowing him to be harmed. He countered, arguing that although there were a number of federal cases close to home that supported Joshua's claim that a special relationship had existed, *Estate of Bailey v. County of York,* a case out of Pennsylvania decided a few months earlier, spoke most directly to his situation and supported his claim.

The grim facts of that case were similar to those of the case now being argued. In 1982 the York County Children and Youth Services agency received credible evidence that five-year-old Aleta Bailey was being abused. The child was taken from the custody of her mother and the mother's boyfriend, Larry Hake, and placed with the mother's aunt.

The next night Aleta was taken from the aunt and returned to the custody of the mother and the mother's boyfriend. A month later she was dead as a result of injuries inflicted on her by the mother and the boyfriend.

A trial court had dismissed the case based on arguments similar to those that Mingo and Yankala now offered in seeking the dismissal of Joshua's claim, ". . . Aleta was not in legal custody when killed and . . . neither her mother nor Rake were under state control or supervision, hence, York County was not responsible for what they did to Aleta." Mingo and Yankala had argued that Joshua was not in the custody of the Winnebago County Department of Social Services and the department did not have supervision or control over Randy, hence it was not responsible for what had happened to Joshua.

The Court of Appeals had rejected the defendant's argument in *Estate of Bailey* and First now asked John Reynolds to reject Mingo and Yankala's arguments on the same grounds. In *Estate of Bailey* the court concluded that ". . . where the state had expressly stated its desire to afford affirmative protection . . . ," and where ". . . the state knew of the victim's plight . . ." or was in a position to know, a special relationship could be said to exist. In Joshua's case, First argued, the department had involved itself deeply in Joshua's life and knew or should have known of the violence to which he was being subjected. If the defendant's motion was rejected in *Bailey*, it ought to be rejected here.

He was dismissive of Mingo's argument that the Social Service Department was free of liability if it had not itself directly inflicted injury on Joshua. He cited cases in which police officers had been found to have a Fourteenth Amendment duty to stop fellow officers from beating prisoners, and analogized to the Social Service Department doing nothing even though it knew of the beatings being inflicted on Joshua.

He also gave short shrift to their argument that qualified immunity shielded the defendants because they were merely public servants exercising discretion in discharging their responsibilities. The exercise of discretion could be so derelict as to fall outside the furthest boundaries of the reasonable.

The major submissions were now in. In early December Mingo would file an answer to First's brief, but the major arguments had already been made.[2]

Winter War

On January 21, 1986, virtually two years to the day after Randy and Marie had brought Joshua to the Theda Clark emergency room claiming he had been accidentally injured, Don Sullivan and Curry First submitted a pretrial report to John Reynolds, along with a set of proposed jury instructions, rules that he would give to the jury as to how they were to go about reaching a verdict. The pretrial report reviewed the negligent acts that formed the basis of the plaintiffs' case and the harm yielded by that negligence:

> Joshua is now retarded, wheelchair-bound, speaks poorly, and has limited use of his right hand and virtually none of his left.

> It will require approximately $60,000 per year, at present levels, for adequate care and therapy. . . .

Mingo and Yankala also submitted proposed jury instructions to Reynolds for his review. Reynolds understood that the proposed instructions submitted by each side were slanted to yield an advantage. Indeed, the proposed instructions submitted by Mingo would have made it extremely difficult for a jury to find against the Social Service Department. Negligence or carelessness would not have been enough to ". . . constitute violation of a constitutional right . . ." The jury would have to decide that there had been "gross negligence . . . a deliberate indifference to the rights of others and a gross departure from ordinary care." But even that would not have been enough. Even if they found that Kemmeter and Stelse acted with reckless disregard and deliberate indifference to Joshua's rights, they would still not be liable if the evidence suggested that they ". . . neither knew nor should have known that reckless disregard and deliberate indifference to Joshua's rights violated federal laws . . ."[3] In other words, their proposed instructions would have required a jury to find not only that the defendants had done wrong but that they knew at the time that what they were doing violated the law.

John Reynolds would sort the matter out, reviewing the proposals submitted by the contending parties and coming up with a set of jury instructions that he felt were clear, fair to each side, and true to the law.

Two days after submission of the pretrial report and proposed jury instructions, the parties set February 21 as the date for the final pretrial conference and March 3 as the date for the trial to start. But then matters began to change.

On January 29 Reynolds canceled the March trial date and rescheduled the start of trial for Tuesday, May 27 at 9:30 a.m., the final pretrial conference to take place on Friday, May 9. But in early May, Mingo sent a letter to John Reynolds. He wanted the trial date postponed and on May 7 Reynolds rescheduled the trial for September 22, and then a short while later rescheduled it again for October 27.

But they never got to October.

Decision and Order

On June 20 John Reynolds handed down his decision and order on the motion to dismiss Joshua's claim.[4] Years later he would say that it had been a difficult decision, but he had felt comfortable with it. When asked about the broad range of factors that played a role in where he came out, he indicated having taken an aptitude test earlier in his life that showed him to have an affinity for social work. Also the experiences of a close relative who was a social worker made him aware of the decisions they had to make daily under crisis circumstances. He wondered if they should have to toil in the shadow of a lawsuit where events went awry. On the other hand, the facts of the case were horrendous. He felt for Joshua.

His decision and order were concise. The order of business was set forth directly. "Presently before the Court is the motion by the defendants . . . to dismiss the complaint for failure to state a claim upon which relief can be granted . . ."

A recitation of the facts was followed by legal analysis.

His initial observations gave no hint as to the direction in which he might move. He cited well-settled law to the effect that, ". . . when a municipality puts a particular individual in a position of danger from private persons it creates . . . a special relationship with such an individual, from which relationship a duty to provide . . . protective services may arise."

The tenor of that statement seemed to bode well for Joshua's cause.

"Knowledge by a state official that his action or inaction while under a duty to act subjects a particular person to known dangers may amount to gross negligence and subject the official to liability. . . ."

His next statements offered no hint of where he would end up. The courts had not settled on a "bright line test" whereby a special relationship might be said to exist, but a number of cases provided guidance. "Examples of actions by officials which create . . . a special relationship include leaving minor children stranded in an automobile after arresting the guardian . . . deliberately exposing mental patients or prison inmates to known risk of assault . . . deliberately denying a prisoner needed medical treatment . . . and merely being present when a fellow officer begins to beat a person in custody. . . ."

Then ambiguity disappeared. "This case is not sufficiently similar to such cases as to support a finding that a special relationship existed between Joshua DeShaney and the public defendants." Three reasons were given for reaching this conclusion. Referring to the final March 8 beating he indicated, "Neither Joshua nor Randy were in state custody . . . at the time or immediately prior to the beating. None of the public defendants were present when the beating took place. Nor can the Court say . . . that the public defendants deliberately exposed Joshua to known danger."

He then moved to expressly reject the decision of *Estate of Bailey* in which the Third Circuit Court of Appeals had found a special relationship between a social service department and an abused child on facts similar to those now presented. The Third Circuit was wrong, he asserted. *Estate of Bailey* had been wrongly decided.

This had to be the case, he argued, otherwise every assumption of public responsibility by government would carry the possibility of constitutional liability. "Every social welfare program would . . . become a charter of constitutionally sanctioned social and economic rights." The implications of the Pennsylvania case were not supportable and hence could not serve as guidance as to how to resolve the issues presented by the Joshua's case.

Throughout his analysis, for reasons that are not clear, Reynolds focused only on the final March 8 beating rather than the yearlong involvement of the Social Service Department with Randy and Joshua. The narrow focus and a literal conception of "custody" facilitated concluding that a special relationship had not existed. "The fact that the Theda Clark . . . Center held Joshua under a protective custody order for three days some thirteen months prior to the March 1984 beating indicates no more than that efforts were made at that time to protect a child in the legal custody of one of his natural parents from possible child abuse." Such temporary custody did not give rise to a special relationship.

His conclusion followed from his analysis. "The Court finds . . . that the public defendants are entitled to judgment as a matter of law. . . ."[5]

It made no difference if every assertion in the complaint was true. It was of no consequence if all that was alleged to have occurred had indeed occurred; the law, Judge Reynolds concluded, offered Joshua no shelter.

There would be no trial after all.

In an interview years later about the decision, he offered comments suggestive of those of Captain Vere following allowing the execution of the saintly midshipman, Billy Budd, in Herman Melville's classic book. "Our vowed responsibility is this: that however pitiless the law may operate, we nevertheless adhere to it and administer it." There was also an echo of Plato's recitation in *Apology*, "The judge's oath requires him to judge according to the law, not according to his pleasure."

Sullivan and First had a decision to make. They could go forward and appeal Judge Reynolds's decision to the Seventh Circuit Court of Appeals in Chicago, or they could fold their hand. Even if the Seventh Circuit reversed, that did not mean there would be a trial anytime soon. The other side would almost certainly seek to take the case to the United States Supreme Court.

It was also understood at some level that if *DeShaney* moved to the Circuit Court level and then on to the United States Supreme Court, the dispute would become as much about the purposes of the law as about the proper inferences to draw from technical legal arguments. At its heart the case had always been about values. If the Constitution did not protect Joshua and other children similarly placed it would be because a panel of judges said that it did not, not because the language of the Constitution dictated that conclusion. The judges who would now rule on the case could not bend the language of the Constitution to any purpose that suited them, but ambiguities in the language did leave room to make choices about which values and interests receive constitutional protection and which do not.

Throughout much of the country's history the rights of African Americans were not protected by the Constitution. And then they were. The language of the Constitution did not change. The interpretation the courts brought to that language changed. A choice was made within the limits of the language of the Fourteenth Amendment in *Plessy,* giving the ancient evil of racial discrimination the shelter of the Constitution, and a choice was made within the limits of the same language a half century later in *Brown,* denying racial discrimination the continued imprimatur of constitutional legitimacy. Both decisions helped make America. *Plessy* gave enormous impetus to legal segregation; *Brown* contributed enormously to the national climate within which the civil rights movement developed.

DeShaney also carried the potential to make a difference. Were the Circuit Court and then ultimately the Supreme Court to rule that the Constitution afforded Joshua protection when government knew of the violence being done to him but remained indifferent, serious attempts at institutional reform might replace momentary gestures at reform in response to public outrage generated by the particularly horrific case occasionally coming to public attention. In the end the case was about the meaning of the law and a Constitution for what?

A month after John Reynolds's ruling came down Don Sullivan filed a *Notice of Appeal* with the District Court, informing it that the plaintiffs, Joshua and Melody "hereby appeal to the United States Court of Appeals for the Seventh Circuit from the *Decision and Order* of this Court dated June 20, 1986."

There was one more piece of business however. The American legal system, like most Western legal systems, requires the losing party in civil litigation to pay a portion of the costs borne by the winning party. A commentator on this policy explained its multiple purposes, "A plaintiff's decision to sue imposes an obvious cost on the defendant and on the taxpayers who foot the bill for public legal institutions. . . . it (also) affects litigants in other cases by crowding the courts, by delaying the resolution of other disputes in the system . . ."

A *Bill of Costs* signed by the attorney for the Winnebago County Department of Social Services was submitted to the clerk of the District Court. Joshua DeShaney, "a minor, by his *Guardian ad Litem*, Curry First, and Melody DeShaney" were to reimburse the defendants just over eight thousand and six hundred dollars for expenses incurred in their successful effort to defeat the claim that they had been negligent in seeing to his care.[6]

In the Land of Oz

In the ancient world all roads led to Rome. In the modern world of federal litigation all roads lead to a Circuit Court of Appeals. In 1891 Congress divided the nation into eleven districts and created a circuit court within each to hear cases on appeal from judgments and decisions at the district court level. The circuit courts stood between the district courts and the United States Supreme Court. The Seventh Circuit included Illinois, Wisconsin, and Indiana. Within those states all cases on appeal arising from the districts courts went before the Seventh Circuit Court of Appeals housed in a grand tower in downtown Chicago overlooking Lake Michigan.

The court was in its second grand structure. Its initial home, a Beaux Arts edifice topped with a dome and decorated inside with oak, mahogany, and bronze, was bombed in 1920 by radicals associated with the Industrial Workers of the World, doubting that justice could be found, even in the halls. The court and the building survived the bombing, but by the 1960s the building was no longer adequate to the needs of an ever-busier circuit. It was replaced by the steel-and-glass tower proximate to Lake Michigan that housed the office of Richard A. Posner, the judge who would preside over the proceedings involving *DeShaney v. Winnebago County Department of Social Services.*

Within the legal profession a circuit court of appeals judge has nearly reached the top, a seat on one of these courts being one step below and often a stepping-stone to the United States Supreme Court. As Eisenhower- and Kennedy-era appointees to the Supreme Court began to retire, the names of two circuit court justices were floated by the Reagan administration as possible nominees: Robert Bork, from the District of Columbia Circuit Court and Richard Posner, from the Seventh Circuit Court of Appeals.

A seat on a circuit court of appeals also required presidential nomination and ratification by the Senate. Although probity and a distinguished career in the profession were, presumably, the major considerations in the nomination and ratification process, political ideology had increasingly become important. Richard Nixon had promised the electorate in his 1968 campaign that he would "reform" the Warren Court by nominating "strict constructionists" to the bench, justices less likely to find civil rights and reform of the criminal justice system in the language of the Constitution. Elected as a more explicitly conservative ideologue than Nixon, Ronald Reagan promised to complete the transformation of the Supreme Court.

In an astute assessment of how American law is made, Reagan's Attorney General, Edwin Meese, felt that the conservative judicial revolution would not be complete until courts in the federal system below the Supreme Court were transformed by the nomination and selection of conservatives. In 1981, the first year of the Reagan presidency, Richard Posner was appointed to the Court of Appeals.

Posner had begun his journey to conservative prominence from an unlikely place. Twenty years before his nomination to the Seventh Circuit bench he clerked for Supreme Court Justice William Brennan, an icon of liberal jurisprudence. Brennan was still on the bench. In his *DeShaney* dissent two years later he would comment negatively on the position taken by his former clerk.

Following a stint in Washington after clerking for Brennan, Posner took a position at Stanford Law School. There, according to his later commentary, the apparent breakdown of the social order attending protests against the Vietnam War abroad and various grievances at home began to move him toward a place far different from that occupied by Brennan and some of the other distinguished legal figures for whom he had labored. He would, in time, be cited by some as "America's greatest living judge . . ." and as "an icy rationalist."[7]

His 1973 book, *Economic Analysis of Law* described the place he had arrived at in his thinking and made him a nationally and internationally known legal scholar. The book also gave new prominence to the "law and economics" mode of legal analysis. This approach rested on the premise that the principles of economics, understood to mean free market capitalism and cost benefit analysis, should be used in assessing whether existing or proposed laws made sense or did not make sense. As one commentator phrased it, the approach rested on the premise that ". . . law should be designed to ensure that assets and opportunities are in the hands of those who can and would pay the most to have them. . . ."

Posner brought elements of his economic mode of analysis to the bench. He was skeptical of the notion that judges were impartial and disdained the more conventional modes of legal analysis. As one commentator put it, he was of the view, ". . . that judges base their opinions on 'guesses' and personal ideology, while hiding behind a veil of precedent . . ." By contrast, the economic framework, whatever criticisms were leveled at it, provided a "principled" basis on which to examine the issues petitioners brought before the court.

Always a prolific writer as a law professor, Posner continued to be prolific as a judge, rapidly turning out decisions on the cases before him. A commentator quoted him to the effect that a judge, makes ". . . a large number of decisions in rapid succession, with little feedback as to their soundness or consequences. People who are uncomfortable in such a role . . . and perhaps they are the most introspective, sensitive, and scrupulous people—do not become judges, do not stay judges, or are unhappy judges." Perhaps the law and economic framework provided him with a calculus for quickly resolving the varied issues presented by the cases the court heard.

1986 had seen changes in the composition of the Supreme Court. Warren Burger had retired and been replaced by William Rehnquist as chief justice and a former University of Chicago Law School faculty colleague, Antonin Scalia, had been appointed to high court. In the fall of that year the Reagan administration promised further changes in the Supreme Court and Posner's name was floated by people who claimed to be in the know. But whatever was happening in Washington, as a new year dawned, he was still a member of the Seventh Circuit Court of Appeals and was still scheduled to hear the appeal in a case out of Wisconsin involving a social service agency and a battered boy.

Snow had fallen overnight in Chicago but the morning of January 13 was crisp and clear. Court convened a little later than scheduled. The three-judge panel presided over by Posner had received briefs and supporting material from each side. The briefs familiarized them with the arguments made at the District Court level and the repertoire of cases cited in support of those arguments. Their clerks might have done additional research and supplied them with concise statements of the main issues and a summary of the arguments pro and con. Ostensibly, Don Sullivan and Mark Mingo would offer an oral argument and amplify the points made in their written submissions. Their major challenge however would be to withstand the inevitable inquisition from those judges hostile to their position.

As with any attorney going into oral argument Sullivan had prepared a list of major and minor points that he wanted to make, but as an experienced trial attorney he also knew that there was no telling how many he would get to make. Oral argument was a supremely high-stakes battle of wits in which the physical setting and the rules of engagement converged to make the contest unequal. The judges sit above and look down on the attorney. The rituals of decorum dictate that the attorney maintain deference and respect in word and manner while the judge may exercise any degree of abuse that disdain, malice, or simple disagreement with the lawyer's arguments commend short of physical assault. In the end the judge will make the decision, hence the attorney dare not stray from deference lest the client pay the price.

Don Sullivan would say later that the assault from Posner came early and was relentless. He was prepared for questions but felt that he was being approached as a not particularly promising student in Judge Posner's classroom being lectured on why his claim lacked the saving grace of even a small degree of merit.

In his various writings Posner had drawn an analogy between judges and spectators at a play. He indicated that watching the drama unfold as the lawyers vie against each other was one of the pleasures inherent in the judge's role. Sullivan perceived Posner to be a playwright in the *DeShaney* hearing insofar as his incessant commentary shaped the direction in which the drama went, turning oral argument into a monologue and Sullivan into a bit player.

The numerous articles Posner had authored, the many books published and the steady stream of judicial holdings indicated that he wrote very quickly. His office in the courthouse looked out over Lake Michigan but he worked with his back to the window letting little distract him.[8] His *DeShaney* decision was published on February 12, less than a month after oral argument.

It began with a recitation of the facts and stated that those facts had yielded a suit by Joshua and his mother under section 1983 of the Federal Code against the Winnebago County Department of Social Services and various other named parties, alleging that, acting under color of law, they had deprived Joshua of his right to life, liberty, and property under the due process clause of the Fourteenth Amendment.

He then parses Joshua's claim, examining it in two parts. First, it was being argued that the Social Service Department was liable for failing to protect Joshua from Randy's violence but, he asserted, it was settled law in the Seventh Circuit that ". . . the state's failure to protect people from private violence . . . not attributable to the conduct of its employees is not a deprivation of constitutionally protected property or liberty."

It followed therefore, he offered, that in order to pursue their claim, Joshua's attorneys would have to argue that the Social Service Department was complicit in the harm done to Joshua. And if that was their argument the details establishing their complicity had to be spelled out. But plainly, neither Ann Kemmeter nor anyone else in the Social Service Department had assaulted Joshua, nor could their involvement in the case be said to have encouraged Randy or any other assailant to greater ferocity. Presumably, Joshua would have been beaten whether Ann Kemmeter made visits or not. The involvement of the Social Service Department in his case could not be said to have brought more harm to him than he would have suffered in any event. Hence, the department contributed little to the quantum of injury done him and bore no liability for any portion of the harm he suffered. "That the state's inaction may have brought about a trivial increase in the probability that Joshua would be severely injured by his father does not enable a conclusion that the state deprived Joshua of his right to bodily integrity."

He then turned to *Estate of Bailey*, the case out of the Third Circuit, relied on by Curry First in his District Court response to Mark Mingo. "We reject the proposition . . . that once the state is aware of the danger that a particular child may be abused, a special relationship arises between it and the child and places on the state a constitutional duty to protect the child from the abuse."

Economic considerations were also a factor in reaching this conclusion. "The concept of special relationship, when extended as far as the Third Circuit extended it . . . makes it more costly for a state to provide protective services to an individual in need, since by doing so it may be buying itself a lawsuit should its efforts fail." In addition, the courts were not competent, he opined, to determine whether an agency had acted with a minimum degree of competence in attending to the welfare of children.

His conclusion followed from his analysis: the proposition that a state had an obligation to intervene on becoming aware that a child whom it serves is being abused ". . . is not grounded in constitutional text or principle."[9]

Curry First had entertained little hope from the outset that Posner would reverse Reynolds's decision. Nothing in his holdings in his years on the bench and nothing in his broader writing or philosophical view suggested that he would. Nevertheless, this holding was crucial. If, as anticipated, he ruled against them, their quest to take the case before the United States Supreme Court would be in the form of an appeal from what Posner wrote.

In the nature of things, the attorney rising to face the court, poised to make oral argument, has to believe that there is chance of prevailing, that the situation is not hopeless. The small quantum of hope that Don Sullivan might have had vanished quickly under the hostile barrage directed at him by Posner. He commented years later when asked about *DeShaney* that he believed Posner had made up his mind beforehand, citing the short turnaround time for the written opinion. Oral argument was a mere ritual, a predicate to Posner's foreordained conclusion. It was a variation on *Death in the Afternoon.* In the bull ring the sweeping moves of the cape, the matador's graceful pivots as the bull charges by are all ritual drama. The bull has no chance.

The next step was to prepare a petition for submission to the United States Supreme Court requesting that they hear the case. They would, in formal language, seek a writ of certiorari. The Supreme Court did not have to take their case, indeed, it denied most petitions. But, if they decided to hear the case, Posner's decision would be the terrain over which the battle would be fought. The briefs submitted by the opposing sides would show subtle and complex analysis of the Supreme Court's own rulings on the reach and purpose of the due process clause. It could be expected that a number of interest groups would petition the Supreme Court to be allowed to submit briefs, child advocacy groups on one side, state and local governments on the other.

Judge Posner's position rested on an interpretation of the historical purposes of the Fourteenth Amendment, suggesting that it was meant to deter government from harming people but did not impose any obligation on government to offer help, save under very limited circumstances. The debate at the Supreme Court level would allow for extended examination of the circumstances yielding a Fourteenth Amendment in the years immediately after the Civil War and an exploration of the intent of the people who framed it. Did they truly intend that the language have the limited reading Posner gave it?

Judge Posner's holding also rested on policy considerations yielded by law and economics analysis. Presumably, a decision in favor of the Joshuas of the world would expose the state to excessive financial risks from damage suits. The legal discourse attending a battle before the Supreme Court held the possibility of exploring the underlying value issues presented by the case and by the type of prudential concern Posner articulated. At one level his conclusion was wrong even within the law and economics framework, as Wisconsin would have to pay tens of thousands of dollars a year for Joshua's care. Diligence by the state's agents would have prevented the beatings that necessitated the care and the attending enormous economic costs.

At another level the law and economics analysis applied to the facts of the case yielded a strange conclusion. Had Joshua died, there would have been no economic burden on the state at all, save for the possible lawsuit brought by Melody. Within a law and economics framework the state would benefit more where the abuser kills the child, rather than where the child survives but is impaired. It would cost less to keep murderers in prison or execute them than care for such children for the rest of their lives. The analytic approach adopted by Posner implicitly yielded the question of whether a sane or civilized society should base law and policy on a framework in which it is better for the state if an abused child dies than if that child lives.

The movement of the case to the United States Supreme Court promised an exploration of the purposes of the Constitution. Nine justices would determine what the document meant for Joshua and for all who shared his dark place. Whatever doubts and fears Don Sullivan and Curry First had as they prepared to petition for the Supreme Court to take their case, Melody voiced faith in the law. "This is America, and you have to believe that what is right will happen in the end."

CHAPTER EIGHT

THE SUPREME COURT DECIDES

Two-year-old Laura Lynn Lazarovich was rushed to the Pittsfield Berkshire Medical Center on a cold February day in 1986. An abused child, she had sustained her third skull fracture and showed evidence of brain damage. She was paralyzed on one side and blind in one eye. Eight months earlier her parents had been indicted on assault charges for beating her, leading the New Jersey Division of Youth and Family Services to petition Family Court to have her placed in foster care. On May 15, 1985 her parents failed to show up in court to face the assault charges. Four days later a Family Court judge signed an order returning her to her parents. Eight months later she was rushed to Pittsfield Berkshire Medical Center. Neither Youth and Family Services nor Family Court could explain the sequence of events.

In 1987 only a fraction of the thousands of aggrieved parties seeking permission to appear before the United States Supreme Court were successful, hence, it was by no means certain that Don Sullivan and Curry First's petition for a writ of certiorari would be granted. Among the factors that came into play in terms of the court's decision to grant or reject a petition is the existence of an important constitutional question and a difference among the Circuit Courts of Appeal as to how that question ought to be answered. *DeShaney* presented both.

The Seventh Circuit Court of Appeals, speaking through Richard Posner, said that the Constitution imposed no duty on public agents to protect citizens from private violence. In *Estate of Bailey* the Third Circuit said that it did. The grim facts of *Bailey* were, as recounted, similar to those of *DeShaney*. On January 3, 1982, two adult relatives of four-year-old Aleta Bailey noticed bruises on her body. A week later they saw more bruises, prompting calls to a child hotline and to the police. The next day an employee of the York County Child and Youth Services Bureau took Aleta to the local hospital. The evidence of abuse was clear and the recommendation was unequivocal. Larry Hake, the mother's boyfriend, should be denied access to the child, and if Aleta's mother, Jo-Ellen, was unwilling or unable to shield her daughter from Hake, Aleta should be taken from her. A Child Protective Services worker informed Jo-Ellen that she had twenty-four hours to get Hake out of her house and that he was to have no further contact with the little girl. The following day Aleta was returned to Jo-Ellen's care. A month later she was dead of injuries inflicted by Jo-Ellen and Larry Hake.

Aleta's father, Cameron Bailey, brought suit against Child Protective Services Bureau and York County, making three claims: Child Protective Services had made no effort to determine whether Larry Hake had been expelled, nor had it taken steps to move Aleta to a safe environment and, further, the county had been negligent in its oversight of the Child Protective Services. The court dismissed all three claims.

On appeal the case was heard by a three-judge panel, the county's attorneys offering the type of argument later made by Mark Mingo in his submissions to John Reynolds and Richard Posner: Aleta was the victim of private violence. She had been beaten to death by her mother and the mother's boyfriend. Had she been in the county's custody, the county would have been responsible for her fate, but that not being the case, the county was not liable for what had happened.

Two of the three justices would have none of it. If ". . . the state puts a man in a position of danger from private persons then fails to protect him, it will not be heard to say that its role was merely passive." They were sensitive to the fact that agencies have to make difficult judgment calls that might turn out to be wrong, but allowed that ". . . an error of judgment, an unforeseeable tragic event, a good faith but misinformed professional decision or (even) . . . negligence" would not bring liability. A jury would have to find that an agency showed "reckless disregard" or "callous indifference" to a child's welfare before finding that agency liable for the child's injuries.[2]

The Third Circuit decision in *Estate of Bailey* and the Seventh Circuit opinion *DeShaney v. Winnebago County* were in conflict. Given that the Constitution is a charter of national rights, a citizen is supposed to have the same rights in Maine as in Nevada, in New York as in New Mexico.

When Circuit Courts of Appeal are in conflict on a constitutional question the Supreme Court may take up the matter to say once and for all what the Constitution means.

On July 14, 1987, Don Sullivan and Curry First filed their petition. They urged the Supreme Court to consider the outcome in *Estate of Bailey* and drew the court's attention to what was at stake, ". . . one can expect that there are presently alive in this country children who are being physically abused who will benefit directly from a Court encouraged increase in vigilance . . ."

The split in the circuits boded well for the Supreme Court granting their petition, but it almost did not happen, the roadblock being yielded by sympathy for their position rather than opposition to it. Ordinarily the flood of petitions coming into the Supreme Court are read by law clerks rather than the justices themselves, and clerking for Justice Thurgood Marshall was a bright, young attorney, two years out of law school, named Elena Kagan, two decades later herself appointed to the Supreme Court.

In September of 1987, she drafted a three-page memo to Justice Marshall. The facts of the *DeShaney* case were "horrific" she noted, and some of the circuit courts had found a state duty to intervene on the kinds of facts *DeShaney* presented. Posner's position that the Constitution is a charter of "negative rights" with the state having no duty to intervene even though knowing of a child's torment was an outlier in terms of the direction of most lower courts before whom the issue had come. But, she feared, a majority of this Supreme Court might affirm Posner's position, thus converting his minority view into the law of the land. Perhaps it was too great a risk to take; perhaps Justice Marshall, because he supported the arguments Sullivan and First were making, ought to refrain from signing on as one of the four justices necessary for a petition to be granted and for the petitioners to have their opportunity to argue before the full Supreme Court.

And indeed, on the first go-round the petition failed, only Justices William Brennan and Byron White voting to hear the case, leaving Sullivan and First two votes short. Refusing to let the matter rest and animated by the existence of the split in the circuits, Justice White importuned Harry Blackmun and Thurgood Marshall to reconsider, and eventually they came on board, Kagan's fears regarding the human cost of a loss notwithstanding.[3]

The Supreme Court's language was brief. The case would be heard. What had begun in a small town in Wisconsin would end in a courtroom in Washington. The next day the *New York Times* brought the story to national attention. A feature article alluded to Richard Posner's assertion that ". . . the Constitution imposes no duty to protect children from their parents." Quoting Don Sullivan and Curry First, the story also succinctly stated Joshua's claim, ". . . the deliberate refusal of child protection officials to protect [a] child already under their auspices and . . . known to them to be in extreme danger . . ." violates the due process clause of the Fourteenth Amendment.[4]

On March 21, 1988, Don Sullivan received a terse letter from the office of the clerk of the Supreme Court specifying details as to the court's strict procedures and time requirements. All that remained was to be informed of the date Sullivan and Mingo would appear before the court in oral argument, gladiators in the arena, more than one life at stake.

> *Thelma Steward and her mother were arrested in the Bronx, New York, charged with breaking the arm of Thelma's three year old son, Wayne. Three months earlier Thelma had been arrested for breaking Wayne's leg. The boy was placed in the Custody of Thelma's mother. Mother and daughter lived together.*[5]

On The Eve of Battle

Early Saturday morning, the day after Easter, two weeks after the Supreme Court agreed to hear the *DeShaney* case, dozens of Oshkosh children gathered in South Park for the annual Easter egg hunt. Bundled against the lingering chill still in the air, they were a carnival of sparkling eyes and excited voices. Parents huddled along the sidelines, clapping and cheering as the children, some hardly more than toddlers, scattered for the hunt. Bags of candy, stickers, and balloons awaited the young scavengers, and later the Easter bunny would entertain them. Parents took photos, capturing eight-year-olds tumbling in the grass, a four-year-old in awe of the Easter bunny, a six-year-old clutching an Easter egg, a treasure beyond measure.[6]

Four years earlier Joshua had been rushed to Marcy Medical Center from a home not far from the South Park, suspended between life and death. Hours later he had been wheeled from the operating room, not dead, but far from being alive. His life since then provided no memories of splashing in the pool at Amity Park on warm summer days, or of sliding down Morris Hill Christmas morning on a borrowed sled before rushing home to open presents, and there would be no memory of hunting for Easter eggs in South Park on a clear day in April, a month after his ninth birthday.

As children frolicked in South Park, dreaming of summer fun to come, a thousand miles away Don Sullivan's thoughts turned to the coming showdown over who was responsible for the terrible thing that had happened in Wisconsin four years earlier. The rules of the Supreme Court were explicit and very detailed. He and Curry First had sixty days to submit their brief to the court. Mark Mingo had thirty days to submit a reply brief. Sometime after that he and Mingo would appear before the Supreme Court for oral argument. And sometime after that the court would hand down a decision.

He needed time to prepare. Every day was precious. But in the end time was what he did not have. Two crises arose. The first was manageable. The second threatened to end the case in disaster.

On April 21 Sullivan wrote a letter to Joseph Spaniol, clerk of the Supreme Court. A major illness had struck down a member of his family. The nearest hospital able to offer treatment was in Boulder, a hundred miles from Cheyenne. For the last month he and his wife had made the trip back and forth three or four times a week, and it appeared they would be doing so for another four weeks, perhaps longer. He asked for an extension of time in order to ". . . complete the briefing . . . in a manner appropriate to my obligations both to my client and to the Court." Four days later Spaniol replied, granting him a two-week extension. He had until June 4.

On May 11 Mark Mingo sent a letter to Spaniol. He seemed worried about a possible advantage the other side might have gotten. He did not object to the extension of time granted Sullivan but argued that as a practical matter he and his team could not begin working on their brief until they received the brief Sullivan and First submitted on behalf of Joshua and Melody. It appeared, as matters stood, that the other side would have the original sixty days plus the extension while his side would be confined to the initial thirty days to formulate a reply to their opponents. He asked for forty-five days to submit his answer to Sullivan and First. On May 17, Sandy Nelson, assistant clerk of the court, telephoned Mingo. They were not prepared to address his request now. He could raise the matter again, after Sullivan and First had filed their brief.

The next day, May 18, Sullivan sent a letter to Mingo. A dispute had arisen regarding what would finally be submitted to the Supreme Court. This dispute reflected the fact that the resources available to the contending sides were not equal. Mark Mingo could rely on the resources of the state while Sullivan increasingly had to reach into his own pocket to keep the battle going. As a case works its way up through the court system a voluminous record of depositions, documents, records and transcripts of court proceedings develops. Given the situation, Mingo had less need to be parsimonious about what portion of the record would be printed up and submitted to the Supreme Court than did Sullivan. Normally the attorneys for each side attempt to reach a consensus on what portion of the material that has developed in a case will be reproduced and submitted to the court in a so-called joint appendix.

A communication from Mingo a few days earlier had prompted Sullivan to call Sandy Nelson at the Supreme Court with a complaint. Mingo's recitation of what he wanted in the joint appendix seemed excessive. Nelson agreed with him. The letter of May 18 to Mingo was blunt. "To make a long story short, your designation is vastly beyond what the Court either needs or wants." He invited Mingo to phone if he had any questions. Several days later Nelson conducted a conference call with the two antagonists. The sides agreed on what supporting documents would be submitted in the joint appendix and on an extension of time for both.[7]

Matters were back on track. In late August Don Sullivan received a letter from Spaniol. Oral argument was scheduled for Wednesday, November 2.

Years later Sullivan described his preparation. "I had one previous case before the Supreme Court but this was the first in which I would do oral argument. I read every case, even cases remotely connected to the issues. It was a matter of matching the facts to the law. I read significant cases until I understood them. I tried to figure out the lines of argument and after reading enough cases the lines of argument began to suggest themselves. I rehearsed. Friends and colleagues here played The Court. What were the tough questions? How could I answer quickly, sharply, to the point?"[8]

And then it appeared it might not happen.

On Wednesday, October 24, two weeks before oral argument, Curry First received a call from Sullivan. Melody had fired him. While he was still trying to absorb the news, First learned that Melody's complaints also embraced him.

Melody laid out her grievances in a letter to Thomas Williams, the Wisconsin judge responsible for seeing that Sullivan and First represented Joshua effectively and fairly. The letter recited an array of complaints against Sullivan, ". . . he does not return phone calls . . . I had to go to a shopping mall to fire him, as he was running a political campaign . . . Mr. Sullivan had promised me that during the two weeks prior to oral argument he would do no more campaigning and devote all his time and energy to reviewing my son's case, which clearly he has not." And as for First, upon learning of Sullivan's firing he had, she alleged, sent ". . . a self-serving letter to all parties . . . without immediately contacting me to find out what my reasons were for such an action." But the final allegation was the most stinging. "I feel Mr. First is more concerned with financial gain than with my son's interests."[9]

Copies of the letter had been sent to Joseph Spaniol, Supreme Court clerk, and to William Rehnquist, chief justice of the Supreme Court.

First was in his Milwaukee office when the call came from Judge Williams. The accusations of misconduct had to be addressed immediately. Williams wanted a conference call between his office in Oshkosh, First in Milwaukee, Sullivan in Cheyenne, and Melody wherever she might be. His professional reputation and the fate of the case on the line, First asked Judge Williams if he might drive up to Oshkosh and be on the phone from his office during the conference call. He wanted the judge to see him as he talked with Don and Melody, to understand what he had brought to the case over the preceding four years, and to understand how much, for Joshua's sake, he did not want to see it die this miserable death. Williams granted his request.

The conference call was made from the judge's chambers with Judge Williams, First, and a court reporter present. The multiple exchanges were tense, but eventually they began to feel dry land under their feet, and toward the end of the drama First made a plea to Melody. Years later he sought to recall the exact words, ". . . for Joshua's sake will you now promise and commit that you will do nothing between now and the end of oral argument. We need you to promise that if you need to do something you will go to Judge Williams in Oshkosh, but do not go to the Supreme Court, and if you are going to do that we need to talk some more for Joshua's sake." And when she said "yes," he sought reassurance: ". . . will you say 'yes' to Judge Williams?" A word from Melody and the crisis was over.

He acknowledged, reflecting on the matter after the passage of years, that he did not know what would have happened had she not gone along.[10]

Don Sullivan also reflected on the matter several years later. "Melody was under enormous emotional pressure. She had become a bit of a public figure. There was a *New York Times* Sunday magazine article in which she was a featured figure. There were TV programs in which she was featured. For the first time in her life she was a minor celebrity. She started to need an enormous amount of handholding. Some of it was justifiable, some of it got in the way of preparing for the Court."[11]

The ship was back on course, but the roughest seas lay ahead.

Visions in Conflict: Rehnquist and Blackmun

There is no way of knowing whether any of the place names in *DeShaney* resonated with William Rehnquist, chief justice of the United States. They would have been echoes from his Wisconsin childhood. As a child he had lived on North Prospect Avenue in Milwaukee, and his father had worked at the Johnson Box Company across town. The Rehnquist family had deep roots in small town Wisconsin, as did the DeShaney family. His mother had been born in Berlin, a small town in Green Lake County, not too distant from Neenah and Oshkosh. Talent and ambition had taken him from the modest cities and small towns of his native state. Following service in World War II he entered Stanford University. In six years he earned a Bachelor of Arts degree, two master's degrees, and a degree from Stanford Law School.

While talent brought him from his Wisconsin roots, ideology brought him to the Supreme Court. An ardent conservative, supporter of Barry Goldwater and Richard Nixon, he had taken a post in the Justice Department following Nixon's 1968 election to the presidency. Three years later Nixon nominated him to the Supreme Court in an effort to give the court a more conservative cast. In the ensuing years his performance on the bench did not defeat conservative expectations. In 1973 he had been one of two dissenters in the *Roe v. Wade* case protecting a woman's right to abortion from state interference. Five years later he dissented from the *Bakke* conclusion that race might properly be used by colleges and universities as one factor among many in deciding whom to admit. He also dissented from the *Johnson v. Santa Clara County* assertion that an employer might make gender a plus factor in evaluating candidates for a position for which no woman had ever been hired.

Following Warren Burger's retirement in 1986 Ronald Reagan nominated him to be chief justice. The nomination revived a controversy from his initial confirmation hearing years earlier. In 1953, fresh out of law school, he was a law clerk for Justice Robert Jackson when *Brown v. Board of Education* came before the court. *Brown* challenged a half century of state-mandated racial segregation in the public school systems of the South and asked the court to reverse *Plessy v. Ferguson*, the case on which legal segregation rested. A memo was found among Jackson's papers in which his young clerk argued that *Plessy* was still good law, advancing the view that the Constitutional rights of a minority are whatever the majority chooses to say they are, "To argue that the majority may not deprive the minority of its constitutional rights, the answer must be that while this is true in theory, in the long run it is the majority who will determine what the constitutional rights of the minority are." At his initial confirmation hearing and his hearing to be elevated to chief justice, Rehnquist denied having defended racial segregation, claiming instead that he had merely responded to a Jackson request for a memo exploring all sides of the issue. Not everyone believed him, and Elsie Douglas, longtime secretary to the deceased Jackson, accused him of smearing a "great man," but no one was able to prove his story was a lie.[12]

The other Midwesterner on the Supreme Court, Harry Blackmun, brought a different sensibility to the law. Rehnquist had met conservative expectations, but Blackmun had not. Nixon had nominated him to the court in 1970, and he was easily confirmed. There was little in his Minnesota background and long career in the law following graduation from Harvard Law School that suggested an affinity for the grievances of minorities, women, or the weak and dispossessed. Within three years of his appointment, however, he began to speak in a distinctive judicial voice. He wrote the majority decision in *Roe v. Wade*, arguing that a "right to privacy" could be inferred from the language of the Constitution even though the word *privacy* does not appear in the document, and that this privacy right allowed a woman choice with regard to the termination of a pregnancy. His concern with privacy as constitutional right was also reflected in a case that came before the court two years before *DeShaney*, challenging a Georgia law criminalizing sexual relations between consenting adults of the same gender, essentially a law criminalizing homosexual conduct. He dissented from the majority decision upholding the law, asserting that: "This case is about . . . the right most valued by civilized men, namely the right to be let alone."

And in the end he never lost sight of the fact the law was about life and not merely a set of abstract concepts. He was described by one of his former law clerks as sensitive to the fact that ". . . legal cases arise from the unseen anguish of real people." Another clerk described him as attempting to ". . . weave silken threads of sympathy across the gap between what is law and what is just." He was said by some whom he had mentored to be "a voice for the outsider" who could ". . . connect with . . . ordinary people and take an interest in their problems." He was ". . . determined that the 'modest pleas' of the downtrodden . . . not go unheard."

Had he been asked what ends the law has, what purposes the Constitution serves he would have given a very different answer than Rehnquist. Their differences went to more than arcane judicial interpretations of the document, each had written decisions that changed American society.

Their clashing visions of the Constitution would shape the coming final battle over *DeShaney*.[13]

DeShaney would ask Rehnquist and Blackmun and the other members of the court to decide whether there need be opposition between what is "constitutional" and what is "just." They were guardians of the Constitution and understood that their task was to discern the relationship between the document's language and the grievances citizens brought before them. Although the word *privacy* was not found in the Constitution, a majority of the court had concluded that a fair and honest reading of the document suggested that it afforded citizens a "right to privacy" from state intrusion into such matters as decisions about reproduction. There were no words in the Constitution stating that a state must protect a child from abusive parents, but Sullivan would seek to persuade a majority of the court that a fair and honest reading of the document's text should yield a decision saying that the Constitution offered Joshua shelter, even if Wisconsin chose to look the other way.

May It Please the Court

Don Sullivan rose early Wednesday morning, the day of oral argument, having not slept well on the eve of the final battle. He had come to Washington within days of resolving the crisis with Melody and spent time in grueling mock oral argument sessions, attorneys from child advocacy groups playing members of the Supreme Court. Now, as he dressed, he went over the arguments he would make and the possible exchanges with various justices. He allowed himself guarded optimism. The justices were not likely to throw an argument at him that had not been anticipated.

Still, it might be an uphill fight, not because of the Constitution, but because of the composition of the Supreme Court. Over the course of a decade or so the court had changed. Beginning in 1954, under the leadership of Earl Warren, the court had taken the lead in extending the reach of the Constitution to African Americans and those who had been left out. *Brown v. Board of Education* struck a blow at racial segregation. A series of decisions after *Brown* opened up voting rights and struck at racial discrimination in the workplace and public accommodations. The Warren court even afforded the criminally accused greater constitutional protection.

Warren Burger replaced Earl Warren as Chief Justice in 1969, and despite the hopes of critics who felt that the Warren court had been too liberal, continued to offer an expansive reading of the Constitution as reflected in its 1973 *Roe v. Wade* abortion rights decision. The Reagan administration taking office in 1981 sought to change the direction of the Supreme Court by nominating more conservative justices. Two or three justices were unlikely to be in Sullivan's corner, and two or three who might be persuaded by his representations, and that left two or three who might go either way. If he had bet on the matter, Sullivan allowed years later, it would have been five to four, perhaps even six to three in his favor.

He met up with Curry First and they drove to the court building, arriving early as instructed. A cold sun glinted off the steps leading up to the front entrance; already knots of tourists were clustered about, waiting for the doors to open. They went to a side entrance and were met by a clerk who ushered them into an office. There they were instructed in the protocol of the court and told what would happen when their turn came; then they were shown around the building. The calm and graciousness of the clerks had a soothing effect, easing growing tension. Sullivan could hear the echo of debates past in the quiet corridors and stately chambers. He looked forward to joining in a conversation that would shape the nation.

Just after ten o'clock the nine justices entered the courtroom and took their seats, the chief justice in the center, the others on either side in order to seniority, the newest justices sitting at each end. Court clerks bustled about and there was some minor business, then the chief justice summoned the combatants to the lists, "We will now hear *DeShaney v. Winnebego County Department of Social Services.*" Don Sullivan rose and advanced to the lectern. He had thirty minutes to make his case. He paused, cleared his throat, then began.

"Mr. Chief Justice, and may it please the Court."[14]

He moved first to head off any hint that he was a utopian dreamer. He was not there to argue that Wisconsin had to do ". . . all good things to all people . . . prevent all harm or all sadness," nor was he arguing that the State had a ". . . constitutional duty to protect all children in all cases . . . ," but when Wisconsin took steps to protect Joshua and learned that he was in danger it had a duty to act.

And then Rehnquist challenged him. This was the first confrontation. Was there any language in the Constitution that gave him a basis for making such a claim? It was the opening minutes of round one. Years later he described what he thought and felt as the battle began. "I stood up and uttered a few sentences of what I hoped to say then a voice that sounded like God or a higher power spoke: Mr. Chief Justice Rehnquist."

As Rehnquist bore in on him his reply was uncertain. "Take the situation where the child is locked behind the door with his protector and the protector becomes the predator and a proceeding is brought at the extreme end of the child protection spectrum to terminate the parental rights . . . the Court has already said the Constitution governs that relationship . . . any of us has a constitutionally protected right to . . . bodily protection."

But the Chief Justice pressed his challenge. The Constitution shielded a citizen from state violence but not from violence at the hands of private parties, was that not the case? Sullivan's response was brushed away as Rehnquist adopted the tone of an impatient professor instructing a slow student. "Well, why don't we start with the language of the Fourteenth Amendment which says that a state shall not . . . deprive any citizen of life, liberty or property without due process of law." The document said nothing about a wife attacked by her husband or a child attacked by a parent having a constitutional claim. Sullivan seemed to be in a corner. He advanced an example that could be taken as confirming Rehnquist's point. "I agree with that, Mr. Chief Justice . . . if you were to hold otherwise, then the police department would have an obligation to prevent the mugging and a whole host of things that are simply unworkable and are not found in the Constitution . . ." And along the way he offered that, ". . . what I'm saying to you is that . . . this is a question that had not been addressed to my knowledge by the Court . . . If you have the parent and the child in an intimate relationship and the Constitution lies . . . in that setting, and if the rights of the parent with all his natural powers . . . are recognized, why should the rights of the child be less recognized?"

Then Sandra Day O'Connor joined in. The first woman to sit on the Supreme Court was something of an enigma to those who looked to the Constitution as a source of shelter from the swirling tides of bigotry, oppression, and neglect. She had been raised in a southwest that still carried echoes of the frontier. A child of the depression years of the 1930s, she had seen her ranch-owner father struggle to survive in the face of falling agricultural prices, uncertain markets, and the vagaries of nature in a dustbowl era. She was no stranger to the limits prejudice imposes on talent. She had entered Stanford University at sixteen, graduated at nineteen, and entered Stanford Law School, one of five women in that year's class. Rehnquist was one of her classmates and like Rehnquist she was on the board of the *Stanford Law Review*; she also finished among the top students in her class. But unlike her male peers, including Rehnquist, she had difficulty finding a job upon graduation. Rehnquist had been offered a Supreme Court clerkship, while she had been offered a job as a legal secretary by a Los Angeles firm, and eventually wound up with the San Mateo County attorney's office, working on civil cases. It was an era when few women entered the legal profession. She had done very well academically but no Supreme Court clerkship awaited her as it did Rehnquist. Avenues opened to white male law school graduates were closed to her.

A changing world and great ability brought her to the Supreme Court, but it was not clear that she brought the realities of her own life to her decisions in cases involving the fortunes of the weak and the needy. She had been, at best, an inconsistent vote in support of choice in the abortion cases the court had considered and was an unreliable vote on civil rights matters.[15]

Now she confronted Don Sullivan and her opening salvo removed any doubt as to her stance. It was more a statement of alarm rather than a question. "If your theory were accepted it seems to me it would have a real deterrent effect on state child abuse programs . . . Why would a state want to undertake a child abuse program at all if they faced liability if they guessed wrong . . . I think you're asking the Court to take a step that is . . . quite unwarranted and quite dangerous."

The starkness of the comment, its abstract, uninvolved quality brought Sullivan back into the fight. This was not a philosophical discussion, or a college cafeteria bull session. There really were broken bodies out in the world beyond this courtroom, and what this court said and did would have a lot to do with whether there would be more broken bodies. He brought the exchange back to Joshua and what had happened in Wisconsin and what was happening to other Joshuas, and whether the law need be a stranger to their torment by moving to allay O'Connor's alarm and turn the court's gaze to the grim facts that had brought them to this place at this time.

He pointed out that merely guessing wrong would not expose an agency to legal action. There had to be gross negligence, knowledge that a child was in danger and deliberate indifference to the child's fate, and both of these, he argued, were found in *DeShaney*, ". . . I lost track of how many different doctors' reports of abuse there were and how many different nurse abuse reports there were . . . and how many direct observations on separate occasions by the caseworker. But I suggest to you that after two years . . . of this, when the caseworker goes to the home and sees cigarette burns on the face of the child, I suggest that's knowledge."

And as the encounter unfolded, William Brennan joined in, also moving to keep the focus on the horrific facts. "Mr. Sullivan, let me put it this way. The child was severely injured." Sullivan agreed and Brennan continued, "and the state placed him in a position of extreme danger, did it not?" Sullivan took the ball and ran with it. "Eventually they did, yes sir . . . this caseworker . . . the evidence before the Court demonstrates that she told witnesses, and I think I'm accurately quoting . . . 'I always knew the phone would ring someday and Joshua would be dead.' "

Then Brennan put an exclamation point on it. That there would now be a claim seeking to make the state accountable for assuming a duty of care, then ignoring Joshua's torment ". . . doesn't shock me as much as it seems to shock my brethren."

Pushing forward through an incoming barrage of questions seeking to knock him off his feet, Sullivan returned to the facts, linking the legal abstractions with which some members of the court were playing to a horrific reality, implicitly asking, "what are you going to do about it?" The Department of Social Service case file recorded the tragedy as it unfolded. ". . . In January of 1983 they had a doctor report . . . a case of child abuse . . . Three days later they send the child back to the abusive home . . ." He sought to bolster his argument by citing a number of cases in which the Supreme Court itself had held the state to account for harm done to a citizen.

Rehnquist was not persuaded, but his verbal thrust was wide of the mark, doing little damage at all. "I don't see how you can turn that around and say from these limitations on the state we also derive a duty on the state." But Sullivan stood his ground and came back strongly. The state had assumed a duty of care, knew Joshua was in danger and did nothing about it.

Then John Paul Stevens joined in. He seemed skeptical, but one could not always tell from his questions where he would come down in the end. The question was quite specific and potentially very difficult relative to Joshua's claim. If a constitutional violation had occurred, when did it occur? Had the Constitution been offended when Joshua was returned to Randy's care by the Child Protection Committee? Sullivan allowed that it had not. Had it been offended when Kemmeter made her first visit to the home? Again, Sullivan allowed that it had not. However difficult the line of questioning, it allowed Sullivan to return attention again and again to the horrific facts. Certainly as the number of reports from doctors and nurses and the police accumulated, and as the number of occasions on which Joshua was seen with injuries multiplied, failure to act crossed a line from mere negligence to the kind of extreme and gross negligence that constituted a deprivation of constitutional rights.

And then Antonin Scalia interjected. He sought to place Sullivan in a box, offering that he did not see what the problem was. Joshua was already in Randy's household and all the state had failed to do was remove him from that household. Was he claiming that a social worker has a constitutional duty to remove a child from a home if she suspects abuse? He moved to lock the box with Sullivan inside. What if a caseworker visited an elderly person, saw that the person was without food, and failed to provide it. Would there be a constitutional violation? In effect, was Sullivan really arguing that the state should prevent all harm, all sadness? But Sullivan prevented the lid from slamming shut, restating his basic position—the state was complicit in the dire circumstances besetting Joshua, in other words, the caseworker was not just somebody who happened to drop by but was implicated in Joshua being in that home in the first place.

And as the round neared an end Sullivan asked the court for permission to reserve two minutes of his time for rebuttal should that be necessary.

Taking Sullivan's place at the lectern, Mark Mingo repeated the argument he had made previously as the case moved up to the high court—Joshua's father had beaten him into oblivion and the state had nothing to do with it. True, they might have had custody of Joshua for a few days, but they could not be faulted for handing him back to Randy.

And then an extraordinary exchange commenced between Mingo and Antonin Scalia, the Supreme Court's most conservative justice. He was an exponent of a school of constitutional interpretation called "originalism," the idea that the language of the Constitution, as applied to contemporary issues, should be given the meaning it had in the late eighteenth century when the document was drafted or, in other words, modern judges should adhere to the "Framers' understanding" of the language when addressing the conflicts before them.

He had come to the court with a reputation for pugnacity and his tenure on the bench suggested that the reputation was well earned. His manner was pressing, insistent, impatient with those less able to quickly grasp what he viewed as the subtle twists of legal reasoning that yielded the one true answer.[16] Yet, he was indulgent with those fortunate enough to argue the position he regarded as correct, and thus he now proceeded to indulge Mingo by leading off with a comment and a question. "So what you're saying is that what makes a difference is whether you're just returning him to that status he was in before you took over temporary custody. Is that the difference?"

Mingo agreed and added that the key question was whether restoring Joshua to Randy's custody ". . . can fairly be said to have increased the risk of harm to that child."

Scalia then cleared away the brush from the dismaying path along which they were traveling, "Increased it from what? From what it was before the state took custody or from what it was when the state had custody?"

Mingo helped him clear the brush away. "From what it was before the state interjected and took custody."

Scalia's skepticism became sanctimony in Justice Kennedy's contribution, and along the way Joshua became "it": "well you were just returning it to the person who had the legal right to custody."

And Mingo's reply, supported by Justice Rehnquist, affirmed the sanctimony: "The parents certainly have a constitutional right which might be observed by the social worker."

They had reached their rhetorical destination. Some of the justices of the Supreme Court and the attorney for the Winnebago Department of Social Services were in agreement. If the state took a child from abusive parents and then returned the child to those parents, how could anyone say the state's action made the child worse off? *It* was being abused before and *it* was being abused again. Why should the state be held to constitutional account?

And then Mingo resumed his discourse, the interjection of his supporters increasingly yielding questions that were to trail from the case: what is the relationship between law and justice? A Constitution, for what? He came back to the hospital team meeting that initiated public involvement in Joshua's case. "Every one of the professionals . . . concurred . . . They all concurred that there was no evidence to substantiate a claim of child abuse." And nothing that happened subsequently implicated the state in Joshua's tragic fate. The only duty the Department of Social Services had under state law was to investigate reports of abuse. There had been only one such report, and the social worker had been followed up on.

Rehnquist moving to help Mingo bolster his case, joined in. ". . . Your point really is that she was not under a constitutional duty to do certain things that your opponent says she was under a duty to do."

And Mingo politely acknowledged, "Yes, Your Honor, you're quite right . . ."

They were nearing the end but there was still time for the bizarre. Justice Byron White, otherwise a minimal participant in the proceedings, put a question to Mingo: ". . . under your theory I take it, if two policeman see a rape and watch it just for their own amusement, no violation of the Constitution." Mingo allowed that "We would concede that there is no constitutional violation in that particular case." To which White replied, "You're not . . . You're arguing it as well as conceding it." Whereupon there was laughter in the courtroom.

Whatever had happened in Wisconsin was an abstraction, an occasion for quips and a good laugh. And after a few interjections by Rehnquist, Mingo's time was up.

Sullivan and Mingo were through but there was one more attorney to be heard from—Donald Ayers, deputy attorney general in the Attorney General's Office, represented the Reagan administration. In the month following the Supreme Court's decision to hear the case, a number of parties had sought permission to file "Friend of the Court" briefs in support of one side or the other. Various child advocacy groups filed briefs in support of Joshua's claim while New York, Connecticut, Maryland, Oregon, Pennsylvania, and Wisconsin joined in submitting a single brief in opposition. The federal government's fear of this claim also drew the Reagan administration into the fray and now the administration's attorney stood before the court.[17]

He seemed to be concerned about the possibility of federal courts becoming an arena for suits against failing child protection agencies. Child abuse might be a problem, but it was someone else's problem, ". . . it is clear . . . that the area of child protection is not one that is crying out for constitutional oversight . . ." He raised the specter of child protection being abandoned by the states if Sullivan and First prevailed. Then he was through.

An hour or so after Sullivan had stepped to the lectern, Chief Justice Rehnquist intoned, "The case is submitted." And it was over.

> *Time stopped for Michael Anthony Baker in the winter of 1988. Less than a year old, he was found dead in a Bronx, New York apartment. His two-year-old sister was barely alive. Their mother had turned on the heater and left the children alone while she spent the night with a boyfriend. The temperature in the apartment had risen to 110 degrees. Investigation revealed that Family Court had ordered a city agency to monitor the family on a monthly basis. Two social workers had been assigned to the case, but the family had not been seen for nearly a year.*[18]

The nine justices would now deliberate, and for the attorneys and the parties they represented there would be weeks or months of waiting. If the decision went in favor of Joshua the case would go to trial in federal court in Milwaukee. That was all that was being asked for. A jury would decide whether gross negligence on the part of the Department of Social Services had deprived Joshua of a meaningful life. The Department of Social Services had contended that the evidence of abuse was never sufficient to sustain an effort on their part to remove Joshua from Randy's custody. Ann Kemmeter had denied ever saying that she expected to receive a call telling her that Joshua was dead. If the five justices found in Joshua's favor they would have an opportunity to make these arguments before a jury.

For Kemmeter and the other named parties, the period of deliberation meant more time in purgatory, not knowing whether their lives would go on much as before or take a new and harrowing turn marked by courtroom appearances and testimony and long nights of "what if."

On December 8, seven weeks after oral argument, Sandra Day O'Connor sent a note to William Rehnquist. She was willing to join in his draft opinion rejecting Joshua's claim. The next day Byron White followed suit. Normally cases heard at oral argument are discussed and debated in a weekly conference. A majority had emerged against Joshua, and Rehnquist had assigned himself the task of writing the draft opinion. The court's history showed that majorities were not always stable, dissenters in closely divided cases often nurtured the hope of bringing a vote or two over to their side as draft opinions were circulated.

On December 23, John Paul Stevens sent a memo to Rehnquist suggesting changes in his draft opinion. The language was too rough, the tone too brusque. Was it necessary to accuse the justices sympathetic to Joshua's claim of bending and distorting the law? It seemed a ". . . harsh slap at those who may disagree with our resolution of the novel issue this case presents."[19]

The next day Rehnquist responded. He would be happy to tone down the language. On December 15, Antonin Scalia indicated he would sign on to Rehnquist's draft. The majority was complete. That same day,

> *The police found Jessica Cortez dead in an apartment in the Bushwick section of Brooklyn, her neck broken. Nicholas, her nine-year-old brother, was found in a closet, beaten and malnourished. According to the police Jessica had been beaten and sexually abused for months by a mother with a documented history of abuse and neglect. Jessica's relatives charged that child welfare officials had ignored danger signals.*
>
> *The year before, New York City had responded to criticism about heavy caseloads in its Special Services for Children Unit by shifting cases to other units. By 1988, according to public officials, the average case load in Special Services had fallen to a target figure of twenty. They did not reveal that the average load in units to which cases had been shifted had risen to over fifty. Hundreds of cases sitting in boxes went unattended for months. Among them was Jessica Cortez's.*[20]

The End Game

In late January Thurgood Marshall sent a memo to William Brennan indicating that he would be happy to sign on to his dissenting opinion. More than any of the other justices, Marshall brought a lifetime of experience to the Supreme Court that allowed him to weigh the abstract language of legal argument against the brutal and absurd realities yielded by claims that whole categories of people did not enjoy the constitutional protections afforded others. His long journey to the high bench had taken him through courtrooms in which he argued that the right to counsel applied even to poor black defendants, and that black students had a right to attend state university professional schools that their tax monies helped fund, and, in the group of cases argued as *Brown v. Board of Education*, that state-sponsored school segregation offended the Constitution and did damage to black students.[21] Perhaps, as much as any of the justices in dissent, he could appreciate the baroque conclusion yielded by the reasoning of the majority: Randy, in prison for assaulting Joshua, enjoyed the protection of the Constitution because he was "in custody" and not able to protect himself from private violence, whereas Joshua, in an institution because of assaults by a private party, did not enjoy the protection of the Constitution because he was not "in custody" when beaten and had been, presumably, able to fend for himself.

Shortly after Marshall joined Brennan in dissent, Harry Blackmun did the same, although he also set about writing his own dissenting opinion.

Compassion Exiled: The Decision

February had been unusually mild, but a cold wind blew across the Great Plains toward Cheyenne on the night of the twenty-second, leaving a slight morning frost on the trees along Main Street. More than three months had passed since oral argument, but Don Sullivan did not know whether the passage of time bode well or ill. In the meantime life went on. It was past noon and he was down the street from his office in the stately halls of the Wyoming Legislature when the call came telling him that a decision had been reached.

An hour earlier the court had handed down a split decision. Rehnquist's thirteen-page majority opinion conceded that the facts of the case were ". . . undeniably tragic . . ." but did not support Joshua's claim. The opinion tracked Richard Posner's reasoning. The Fourteenth Amendment prohibits states from denying citizens life, liberty, or property without due process of law. Joshua's injuries were inflicted by his father, Randy, not the state. The state had no constitutional obligation to come to his aid, even with knowledge of his distress. And at the end of the opinion Rehnquist cautioned Judges against letting unseemly emotion interfere with the sober application of the law. "Judges and lawyers, like other human beings, are moved by natural sympathy in a case like this to find a way for Joshua and his mother to receive adequate compensation for the grievous harm inflicted on them. But before yielding to that impulse, it is well to remember once again that the harm was inflicted not by the State of Wisconsin, but by Joshua's father."[22]

Silken Threads of Sympathy

William Brennan's dissent carried the weight of the opposition argument. In his thirty-third year on the court, Brennan was by now a lion in winter. An affable New Jersey Judge, nominated by Eisenhower, he came to the Supreme Court with no discernable judicial philosophy or point of view on the great matters of the day. But in the twilight of his tenure he had become, in the view of Antonin Scalia, his colleague and philosophical opposite, one of the "most influential" justices of the twentieth century.

Two years before sitting down to write his dissent in *DeShaney* he had given a speech in which he said that "We do not yet have justice, equal and practical, for the poor, for members of minority groups, for the criminally accused, for the displaced persons of the technological revolution, for alienated youth, for the urban masses. . . . Ugly inequities continue to mar the face of our nation. We are surely nearer the beginning than the end of the struggle."[23]

He saw the Constitution as a living document whose language was to be interpreted in such a way as to move the nation forward in the struggle to erode unjust inequities. It offered hope rather than foreclosing possibilities. In an interview with the journalist Nat Hentoff he commented on his view of the Constitution by quoting from William Butler Yeats's play *Cathleen ni Houlihan*. " 'Did you see an old woman going down the path?' " asks Bridget, " 'I did not" replies Patrick, who came into the house just after the old woman left. 'But I saw a young girl and she had the walk of a queen.' " Some might see the document as old, but it was still young and full of promise. Its brightest possibilities lay ahead.

Now in the minority in a Supreme Court increasingly inclined to read the Constitution as a document hostile to change and indifferent to the problems of the weak and the marginal, he crafted a dissent offering a point-by-point refutation of the position taken by the *DeShaney* majority. He went back to their central argument: Joshua had not been harmed by the inaction of the Department of Social Services because the beatings had been inflicted by his father. But, Brennan offered in rejoinder, "I would begin from the opposite direction. I would focus . . . on the action . . . Wisconsin has taken with respect to Joshua and children like him . . ." And he offered a reason why: ". . . a State's prior actions may be decisive in analyzing the constitutional significance of its inaction."

He then spelled out the implications of this framework for assessing Joshua's claim. Wisconsin had established a child protective system that channeled reports of child abuse to local departments for evaluation and action. Under that system doctors, neighbors, the police, and an ex-spouse forwarded information to Social Service regarding suspected abuse of Joshua. Without doubt all of these parties thought that the signs and portents that aroused their fears were being looked into. Through its system the state relieved ". . . ordinary citizens and governmental bodies . . . of any sense of obligation to do anything more than report their suspicions of child abuse. . . ." If Social Services ignored these warnings, ". . . no one will step in to fill the gap." The consequence in this case, he argued, was that the system ". . . effectively confined Joshua DeShaney within the walls of Randy DeShaney's violent home . . ."

It ". . . simply belies reality," he concluded, "to contend that the State 'stood by and did nothing' "; it had "actively intervened in Joshua's life . . . ," thereby shutting out other potential sources of rescue. It could not now contend that the disastrous consequences of its handling of the case were beyond the reach of the courts because its agents had not themselves assaulted Joshua. And in support of his conclusion he drew a direct analogy between the facts of *DeShaney* and those of the prison and hospital confinement cases in which the court had found that the state could be called to account constitutionally for the consequences of its failure to tend to the welfare of those in its charge.

Blackmun's dissent was shorter and a more somber and stark commentary on the outcome of the case. He spoke directly to Rehnquist's canard about sentimentality. "Today the Court purports to be the dispassionate oracle of the law, unmoved by 'natural sympathy.' But in this pretense the Court itself retreats into a sterile formalism which prevents it from recognizing either the facts of the case before it or the legal norms that should apply to those facts."

He compared the majority to the pre-Civil War jurists who had found words in the law to justify slavery: "like the . . . judges who denied relief to fugitive slaves . . . the Court today claims that its decision, however harsh, is compelled by existing legal doctrine." But, he argued, Supreme Court justices are not prisoners of the law: ". . . the question presented by this case is an open one . . . our Fourteenth Amendment precedents may be read more broadly or narrowly depending on how one chooses to read them. Faced with the choice, I would adopt a 'sympathetic' reading, one which comports with the dictates of fundamental justice and recognizes that compassion need not be exiled from the province of judging."

He concluded with a lament for what was, and for what would never be.

"Poor Joshua! . . . It is a sad commentary upon American life, and constitutional principles—so full of late of patriotic fervor and proud proclamations about 'liberty and justice' for all, that this child, Joshua DeShaney, now is assigned to live out the remainder of his life profoundly retarded."[24]

In his sorrow Blackmun echoed in tone John Marshall Harlan's dissent in *Plessy v. Ferguson* nearly a century earlier. Louisiana had mandated that blacks and whites on public carriers ride in separate cars. Homer Plessy challenged the constitutionality of the Louisiana law, thereby challenging the constitutionality of "separate but equal" itself. Could a state make racial distinctions in law without offending the Constitution? Eight justices of the Supreme Court said "yes," while John Marshal Harlan said "no." Few had doubts as to the grim realities attending racial segregation, but the majority had found reason to conclude that state-mandated racial discrimination was beyond the reach of constitutional reform. Harlan understood that a sad choice had been made that would in the end cost lives and stain the court. Blackmun's dissent bespoke the same mourning for the lives that would be lost by a decision that would cast a shadow over the court.

According to *Los Angeles Times* writer David Savage, other justices had "mocked" Blackmun for his "Poor Joshua" cry from the heart in the courtroom and in his dissent. Following Blackmun's death in 1994, Linda Greenhouse of the *New York Times*, who covered the Supreme Court for decades, had the opportunity to go through his papers. "Poor Joshua" was, she wrote, ". . . such an unusual expression of judicial sentiment that I had wondered where it came from." Who had decided to leave it in his written commentary? She was gratified to find that it was Blackmun himself rather than one of his clerks. There in the file, in tiny handwriting on lined paper, was his dissent ". . . almost precisely as it was later published."[25]

The Unspeakable Terror

The decision was immediately controversial. Syndicated columnist Nat Hentoff shuddered in print, referring to Rehnquist's observation that Joshua was no worse off than if the state had ignored him in the first place as "eerie reasoning." But nationally known columnist, Ellen Goodman, felt herself ". . . in rare agreement with the conservative court." She feared that if ". . . this case had gone the other way in our lawsuit happy world, any firefighter, police officer, ambulance driver or social worker might (be) sued by a citizen claiming protection . . ." Had the case gone forward ". . . it would have tipped the scales further in the direction of 'rescuing' children from their parents." She opined, and asked, "Do we want that?" She empathized with those in the frontline. "I do not envy the caseworkers we have assigned the task of determining how violent a family is, how vulnerable a child is. When there is trouble in a home these risk-assessors face dilemmas the rest of us can only ponder."[26]

But nationally syndicated columnist, Mona Charen argued that ". . . reverence for the family must stop at the whip's end . . ." She dismissed the fear of endless lawsuits as groundless and misplaced: ". . . if the social welfare agencies, fearing to be dragged into court, become too aggressive about removing children from their parents, the mistake is temporary and remediable. On the other hand, when social welfare agencies are too timid, too reluctant to interfere . . . the results are Joshua DeShaney's—permanently and irremediably."[27]

Debbie Ratterman, writing in *Off Our Backs: A Women's Newsjournal*, offered a striking and prescient critique of the majority decision. "None of the justices mentioned the fact that the lack of state enforcement of child abuse laws encourages abusers to continue beating children. Ineffective or indifferent agency protection may make the abuser confident that he will escape detection or punishment."[28]

Austin American columnist, Jim Fain, spoke directly to Rehnquist. "The chief justice of the United States says it's too bad about Joshua DeShaney, but it's not his problem . . . any judge is bound by the law as he understands it, but I'd be more comfortable if I thought he wept when he wrote the opinion."[29]

Constitutional scholar and law professor, Cass Sunstein, in a piece called "Constitutional Politics and the Conservative Court," written a few years after the decision came down, placed it in the context of the trajectory of an increasingly conservative body. "With increasingly firm insistence, the majority on the Court claims that the Constitution creates only 'negative' rights, not 'positive' ones, that is, only rights against state power, not rights to state assistance to prevent private acts of violence or to guarantee even minimal living conditions. . . ." Yet, he was still taken aback by this ruling. "But it is still surprising to read the Court's ruling in *DeShaney* that the Constitution had no bearing on a social welfare agency's refusal to protect a two-year-old child from severe beatings. . . . after the service had received repeated warnings . . . of imminent danger."

And years later Harvard professor Laurence Tribe recalled sitting in his office in the spring of 1989, a bright sunlit day, discussing the case with his research assistant, ". . . a lanky kid in jeans and a leather jacket . . ." Both he and the young Barack Obama were horrified by the facts of the case and less than persuaded by the majority decision; ". . . the Supreme Court found no violation because, in the reasoning of . . . Justice William Rehnquist, the state's agents had been guilty of nothing more than 'inaction,' Barack and I both agreed that the distinction between 'action' and 'inaction' was not significant enough to justify so brutal a result."[30]

And Tribe in a talk before the City Bar Association of New York a few months later enlarged on defects in the decision: "The majority's question in *DeShaney* was simply, 'Did the state of Wisconsin beat up that child?' and not, 'Did the law of Wisconsin, taken in its entirety, warp the legal landscape so that it in effect deflected the assistance otherwise available to Joshua DeShaney?' " The Court had asked the wrong question, Tribe asserted, and therefore got the wrong answer. Had it asked the right question it could not have plausibly concluded that the State had nothing to do with Joshua's torment.

Even supporters of the majority decision expressed pain. Writing several years later, columnist James Kilpatrick harkened back to *DeShaney* as he commented on a more recent abuse case: "There's a difference between law and justice. Justice is what we deserve: law is what we get. Contrary to popular impression, the high court's function is not to dispense justice, but to interpret law. As a matter of constitutional law, Rehnquist was clearly right. As a matter of justice, poor Joshua! . . ."

But the holding probably brought satisfaction to the author of a letter to the *New York Times* and those sharing his point of view questioning why the Supreme Court had taken the case in the first place. He blamed the litigation on Melody who, he offered, ". . . By her own admission . . . abandoned custody of her son to her husband, Randy. She must have known of his violent tendencies. After all, she lived with him. Ann Kemmeter, the social worker, did not . . . [Melody] did not seek visitation rights and made only halfhearted attempts to find her son. In her suit, she is seeking to blame the Wisconsin Department of Social Services for her own failure as a parent. You can't simply abandon your children and expect the Government to take care of them for you. . . ." She was, in his view, in it for the money.

News of the decision spread rapidly in Oshkosh. By late afternoon the local papers were describing Winnebago County officials as being "relieved." Had Joshua won it would have cost the county more money to protect itself, according to a county executive. The *Northwestern* applauded the decision in its editorial and took a swipe at Blackmun: " 'Poor Joshua,' indeed—to quote dissenting Justice Harry Blackmun . . . but a plight so worthy of pity does not mean that society itself has wronged him." The editorial contended that a decision going the other way placed caseworkers in the crosshairs of a lawsuit for every wrong decision and ". . . would have been harmful to the class of youngster needing their help, the other Poor Joshuas of this world."[31]

County Social Service director, Mark Quam, looked at the human dimension of the tragedy, if you are a case worker: ". . . you ask yourself a million times, what if I had done this, what if I had done that?" His words bespoke existential anguish. "I don't know how you can touch anything bad and not feel a sense of responsibility." But, on the other hand, "How much power do we have to stop bad things from happening?" He feared that the pendulum had swung too far in favor of the rights of parents. "Hopefully, out of this soul searching and tragedy we'll find middle ground."

And for no one had the lost possibilities of yesterday been more haunting than Anne Kemmeter. The *Post-Crescent* spoke with passion of the meaning of the five-year ordeal to her. "Joshua DeShaney has gotten a raw deal in life. So, too, has Anne Kemmeter. The difference is that 9-year-old Joshua, who lost half his brain . . . will be forced to spend the rest of his life in an institution. Kemmeter was—and is—one of the best caseworkers in the Winnebego County Social Services Department, and much of her life and career remain ahead of her. Her reputation has been sullied because of one-sided, unchallenged statements made in the course of a precedent-setting lawsuit involving Joshua, but she will carry on."

Reporters sought her out soon after the decision had come down and she spoke of the toll the case had taken on her. She had been depressed and had ". . . almost became a recluse and didn't want to talk to anybody or see anybody." She had thought about the case "every day since the action was filed. It never left me."

But the favorable decision went a long way toward lifting the cloud hanging over her head. "I feel I can lift my shoulders a little higher, like a thousand pounds has been lifted off . . . but it's going to be gradual . . . I'm more comfortable reporting to work each day and doing the best I can without tremendous anxiety and fear. . . . I can go on without fear."

She had suffered Joshua's pain. "I went through the grieving of Joshua's surgery . . . any abused child hurts . . . there are a lot of emotions at stake. . . . Joshua will always have a . . . special place in my heart." But, in the end she felt vindicated. "Throughout the entire litigation you only had the plaintiff's version of the story . . . no one has heard our version of the story . . . I wish we could have done more . . . but, on the other hand, we're not the ones who physically abused the child."

Some of her colleagues felt the decision offered the opportunity to look again at the law. John Mueller, a local Children's Services director, worried that the law leaned too heavily in favor of parents. "I'm all for parental rights; I'm all for trying to see that these kids remain in the home. But I guess my gut would tell me we have a tendency to be a little bit more involved with the parent than the kid."

But other observers saw a silver lining in the decision for social workers. Tom Birch, counsel for the National Child Abuse Coalition, felt that it "should have a positive effect on child protective services throughout the country." He and others were reported as believing that the "ruling alleviates social workers' fears of being sued . . . a ruling against the workers could have affected their judgment in reporting cases."[32]

And as for Melody, the fight for Joshua had sustained her, according to her therapist. But, "when this is all over," she asked, "what happens to Melody?"[33] And now, it was all over.

Curry First saw the negative implications of the case for those similarly situated. He represented the survivors of a woman who died while following instructions on treating herself for ventilation given by a fire department dispatcher. He was arguing essentially the same legal points advanced in *DeShaney.*

Whatever silver lining some saw in the ruling, Don Sullivan begged to differ. At first he spoke from the head: "this is bad for the people and bad for the country in terms of cutting back on the constitutional rights of people."

Then he spoke from the heart. "I've got a picture in my head of what an enraged big person looks like to a little kid. And that big person may be swinging a fist, a belt or the tip of a cigarette. I feel the unspeakable terror of that little kid, of all these little kids. And today my heart is breaking for these little kids. We owe our children better than this."[34]

On March 5, 1989, days after the decision came down, a letter arrived at the Supreme Court addressed, "Dear Justice Blackmun." It was from Sandra Taylor living in Vancouver, British Columbia, and read as follows: "As a teacher for 26 years of grade 1 children, and caring deeply for them, I was shocked to read about Joshua DeShaney in a March *Time* article. I applaud your statements. The picture of this beautiful child holding his cat, breaks my heart, when I realize what his condition must be now. I am enclosing a cheque for $25.00 in the hope that it can be used to help him in whichever way you wish. You have my greatest admiration and best wishes."

CHAPTER NINE

THE CRYING GAME

There is a cycle in terms of the attention the public gives to child abuse, a kind of grim dance that plays itself out over and over. A horrific incident occurs and is reported in the newspapers and on television. A child barely out of infancy has been found battered, starved, and sexually abused. Neighbors had called the police on several occasions. The family was known to Social Services. Caseworkers had visited the home. And yet there on the evening news is the snapshot of an infant, bright-eyed, happy, unknowing of good or evil, now battered beyond recognition, or dead in the city morgue.

The public is outraged. Angry public officials decry the situation and demand an explanation. Social Service professionals cite enormous caseloads, heavy backlogs, and the law's ambiguity about when a child may be removed from the home. Public officials promise reforms—caseloads will be reduced, spending will be increased, communication between agencies responsible for child welfare will be improved, negligent caseworkers will be removed. But within a week or so public attention shifts elsewhere, drawing the attention and promises of the political community with it. A few reforms are implemented, but before long the situation is much as it was prior to the horror that provoked the outrage. It remains so until the next broken body is found, a year, or two years, or three years later. Then the dance starts again.

This macabre waltz played out in events that unfolded in Wisconsin in the summer of 2002, not far from the venues that witnessed Joshua's torment. Late in November of that year Christian Cisneros, two years old, was buried in an unmarked grave outside of Hobart, a small town twenty miles east of Neenah, where Joshua's road to oblivion had begun. Few events offer testimony to the legacy of the *DeShaney* decision with as much eloquence and anguish as the short, unhappy life of Christian Cisneros. Few speak as powerfully of the need to revisit that decision.

This Is What Happened

November 5, 2001

The Brown County Department of Social Services receives its first report about Christian Cisneros, a little boy barely out of infancy. The doctor treating him noticed bruises on his body and patches of hair missing from his head, explained away by his stepfather, Israel Figueroa, as the result of an accidental spill of cleaning fluid. The Brown County Department also learns that Christian had been treated for a broken shoulder several months earlier caused, according to his stepfather, by a fall from a high chair. Christian's mother, Kimberly, is questioned and warned that further evidence of injury to the boy might result in action by the Department.

February 7, 2002

Christian is brought to St. Mary's hospital in Green Bay, Wisconsin, with an elbow injury, leading hospital personnel to report possible child abuse. Under questioning Israel admits to having yanked and pulled on his stepson. Four days later Christian and his three-week-old sister are placed in foster care.

March 29

Christian is returned to his mother and stepfather who, in the light of their troubled history as parents, are required to undergo counseling. Christian is enrolled in the Cuddle Care daycare center in Neenah, four blocks from the Theda Clark emergency room to which Joshua had been rushed eighteen years earlier.

July 19

A social worker meets with Christian's parents following a report that bruises have been seen on his back. The caseworker does not see abrasions on his back, but there is a bruise on his side due, Kimberly claims, to a fall from a shopping cart. There is also a bruise on his temple, attributed to a car accident.

Despite the caseworker's conclusions and protestations of innocence by Israel and Kimberly, Cuddle Care staff become increasingly concerned about Christian's welfare. When he shows up with scratches on his shoulders and under an eye they are told that he fell out of a car. When he shows up with a black eye, Kimberly claims that he ran into a table. Eventually, concern about a severe bruise on Christian's leg prompts Cuddle Care to make a report of possible child abuse to Social Services. They do not receive a return phone call, but continued worry prompts a second call.

October 30

A public health nurse visits the Figueroa home. Kimberly attributes the scratch on Christian's nose to rough play.

November 6

A caseworker sees Christian, but notes no injuries.

November 8

The Department of Health and Human Services receives another report of possible abuse. There was blood inside Christian's right eye and there were scratches on his nose and back.

November 11

Another report is received. Christian has an arm injury, a cracked lip, and a bruise under his right eye.

The multiple reports prompt another home visit. Suspicious marks are seen on Christian, caused, the adults claimed, by rough play at home and at the day care. The caseworker concludes that the marks are not consistent with abuse and are not uncommon for a child of Christian's age. It is noted that Christian seems to be an active boy, not afraid of his mother or stepfather. The situation is deemed to not warrant ". . . major concern."

November 26

Cuddle Care makes a third report of suspected abuse but does not receive a return call.

November 29

Christian is rushed to Appleton Medical Center with major head injuries, and from there is sped to Wisconsin Children's Hospital in Milwaukee.

November 30

Christian dies without ever regaining consciousness. The Milwaukee County Medical Examiner concludes that blows to the head and a blow to the stomach severing his spine caused death. The autopsy shows previous breaks to both shoulders, the right elbow, and the right collarbone.

Shortly after Christian's burial, reporter Dan Wilson chronicled the story from beginning to end in the *Post-Crescent* newspaper. A daycare worker told him how the staff learned of Christian's death. "His mother came and said something to the people in our office that he had stopped breathing . . . I went out to my car on my break and I just sat there and cried."[1]

Christian's story played out in the same towns as Joshua's story eighteen years earlier and set in motion the same minuet. There was public outrage and there were demands for reform. The childcare professionals offered explanations in the language that is part of the ritual. "Suspicion is not enough . . . Credible evidence that probable cause exists . . . You can't always be right . . . It is not a good idea to rush in when you don't have all the facts . . . It is pretty serious to take a child away from their parent . . . They are under a lot of pressure and I can sympathize with that. . . ." Joshua's tragedy years earlier prompted the same language; "Kids are injured all the time, but to take them out of the home you have to show abuse."

And as part of the minuet attending Christian's tragedy, an outraged political community promised reform. There was yet another report with the same recommendations that earlier reports had recommended in the wake of earlier tragedies: ". . . better coordination with police, better training of social workers and better communication with doctors." Similar good intentions trailed eighteen years earlier in the wake of Joshua's tragedy. "I think this should be an opportunity to look at what the laws are for this kind of a situation, and what we can do about it."[2]

And then all is forgotten—the horror, the promises—until the next occasion for the crying game.

The Legacy of *DeShaney*

In the years after it was handed down, *DeShaney* became the rock on which many cases foundered. Bruce Powell's suit on behalf of his deceased son, Bruce James Powell Jr., returned to his ex-wife despite clear signs of abuse, was dismissed by a court relying on *DeShaney*,[3] as was a claim by the Simpson brothers, abused by their mother and her various boyfriends while state social workers repeatedly investigated, but did nothing.[4] *DeShaney* also denied recourse to children placed in foster care. Keena White died from blows to the head, allegedly inflicted by foster parents in the home where she had been placed by the state of South Carolina. The Court of Appeals cited *DeShaney* in turning back the suit filed on her behalf. South Carolina had no duty to protect her from abuse in the foster home in which they had placed her because she was not actually in state custody.[5] Across the country in Missouri, Larry and Gary Bass, eight years old, were scalded to death by abusive parents a few weeks after the Department of Family Services failed to investigate despite receiving multiple reports of the boys' being abused. Citing *DeShaney,* the Eighth Circuit Court held that Missouri was not responsible for the welfare of the boys because they were never in its custody and, in any event, the state's failure left them in no worse circumstance than they were in already. The facts were horrendous, they allowed, but *DeShaney* admonished judges to restrict themselves to administering the stern dictates of the law rather than be swayed by unseemly emotion.[6]

Children in danger from lethal parents were the most immediate victims of *DeShaney,* but its impact went beyond childcare. Other victims were swept under in its wake, including battered women, the handicapped, and schoolchildren. If the state had no duty to protect children, neither did it have a duty to protect others whom it knew to be exposed to lethal threat.

The legacy began to take shape quickly.

On the night of March 10, 1989, eighteen days after *DeShaney* was handed down, Carole Pinder's ex-boyfriend, Don Pittman, broke into her home, punched and kicked her, and threatened her children. A neighbor restrained him until the police arrived, but Pittman continued to threaten her in the presence of the children, screaming that he "wasn't going to jail for nothing this time; this time it would be for murder." The police placed him under arrest and took him outside to the patrol car. One of the officers then returned to the house and spoke to Pinder, who told him that Pittman had threatened her before and that he had just finished serving a sentence for attempted arson following an unsuccessful effort to set her home on fire. She was concerned for the safety of her children. She could remain at home with them rather than return to work.

The officer assured her that Pittman would remain in custody until morning and would then be brought before a county commissioner. Relying on that assurance Pinder returned to work. At the police station the officer lodged two minor charges against Pittman and then brought Pittman before a county commissioner that evening, despite what he had told Pinder, and because the charges were minor Pittman was released on his own recognizance. He promptly returned to Carole Pinder's home and set it afire. Her three children died in the blaze.

Pinder brought suit against the Cambridge, Maryland Police Department on behalf of herself and her deceased children, stating that she had relied on the officer's promise to keep Pittman in custody overnight, otherwise she would have remained at home. That promise yielded a duty on his part, she argued, to protect her children from Pittman's threatened violence. His failure to honor that promise cost her children their lives. She urged the court to find that gross negligence on the part of those sworn to uphold the law had led to the death of her children, depriving them of their lives in violation of their rights under the Fourteenth Amendment to the United State Constitution.

The United States District Court for Maryland agreed with her, as did a three-judge panel of the Fourth Circuit Court of Appeals, whereupon the Police Department then asked the entire 4th Circuit to hear their appeal. Relying on *DeShaney*, the full court reversed the earlier decisions, asserting that the Police Department had no duty under the Constitution to protect Pinder or her children.[7]

DeShaney also soon came to defeat the claims of battered women.

Jena Balisteri had suffered beatings at the hands of her ex-husband and had been subjected to ongoing threats, harassment, and vandalism. She repeatedly and unsuccessfully sought police help, imploring them to enforce the terms of a restraining order. Eventually she brought suit against the local police department, claiming that they showed indifference and hostility to women plaintiffs in domestic violence cases. *DeShaney* was "controlling" in the matter, the court that dismissed her case stating that there is ". . . in general, no constitutional duty of state officials to protect members of the public at large from crime."[8]

DeShaney also defeated Flor Maria Soto's claim against the police for failure to protect, the final scene in the tragedy beginning on Wednesday, April 17, 1991, when her husband, Angel Rodriguez, assaulted her badly. When he passed out drunk she gathered up their two children and fled to her mother's house. Soto had a nine-year history of beatings and abuse at Angel's hands but had not gone to the police because she feared his wrath. Now, accompanied by her mother and at her urging, she went with her children down to the police station to lodge a complaint. She told them of the latest assault and showed them her bruises. She also informed them that Angel had threatened to kill her and her family if she went to the police.

Angel was known to the officers to whom the complaint was made, having done odd jobs around the station and repaired automobiles. As the complaint was being taken they referred to him as "Rafi." Flor Maria later claimed that after she left the station an officer told Angel about the complaint even though he knew Angel had threatened lethal violence. Four days after Flor Maria's trip to the station Angel took the children and went to the beach. When Flor Maria showed up to bring them home, one of the youngsters warned her off, whereupon Angel shot and killed both children, then turned the gun on himself.

Relying on *DeShaney*, the district court dismissed Flor Maria's claim on behalf of her children because ". . . a State's failure to protect an individual against private violence simply does not constitute a violation of the Due Process clause."[9]

DeShaney also denied parents recourse for any harm befalling their children while in school. Again, there are many cases, but a few will suffice.

In 2007–08, nine-year-old Jane Doe was taken from her elementary school six times by Tommy Keyes, despite the fact that his name did not appear on a form identifying the adults who could pick her up. On each occasion she was sexually assaulted. Her guardian brought suit unsuccessfully on her behalf, but the Fifth Circuit Court of Appeals turned the plaintiffs away, offering in 2012 that "The question we have addressed is simply whether the failure to check Keye's and take Jane amounted to a constitutional violation."

DeShaney persuaded them that it did not.[10]

But the school failure went back to the beginning. Three years after *DeShaney* was handed down, suit was brought on behalf of two female students who had been sexually and verbally abused by male classmates over a period of weeks. The plaintiffs alleged that the students' teacher and her superior knew of the abuse but took no action to stop it.

The complaint also argued that compulsory attendance laws and the school's authority over students during the school day yielded an obligation to provide a safe environment, but the court rejected D.R.'s claim. The school's authority over D.R. during the school day did not create the kind of custodial relationship necessary to claim an exception to the *DeShaney* rule that public authorities have no constitutional duty to prevent harm within their bailiwick, even with knowledge that harm is occurring.[11]

In short, given *DeShaney*, the state has a greater constitutional obligation to protect a convict in prison from harm by other convicts than a school has to protect a student from other students.

A year after the *D.R.* decision, Roberson, a high school student, was stabbed to death in his classroom by three other students. In the subsequent lawsuit his mother also argued that compulsory attendance laws created a "special relationship" between the school and the child, but the court disagreed, citing *DeShaney* for the proposition that schools do not have a constitutional duty to create a safe environment for students.[12]

One year after the *D.R.* decision and a thousand miles away, Ted Niziol, also a high school student, brought a 22-caliber handgun to school. Shortly after 9:00 a.m., classmates informed a teacher that Niziol had a firearm, and the teacher immediately told the school principal. Sometime between 9:30 a.m. and 11:00 a.m. a school counselor was also informed of the situation; the counselor in turn told another school officer. Just after 1:00 p.m., one of Niziol's classmates was questioned, but he denied any knowledge of the gun. An hour later Niziol met his sister and other students. The local newspaper recounted what happened next. "As he pulled his Toyota 4-Runner out of the parking lot . . . minutes after school let out, he passed the gun to Steven Moschella, sitting behind him in the backseat. Moschella took the gun out of the soft leather case and brandished it in both hands. Not knowing the gun was loaded . . . Moschella pulled the trigger. A bullet sliced through the driver's seat 'at the heart level,' Pasco school officials said. Teddy . . . opened the door of the Toyota and fell to the ground. Within seconds, the school resource officer was giving the boy CPR, but he never found a pulse. Teddy was pronounced dead soon after at North Bay Medical Center. . . ."

Niziol's parents brought suit against the school board and various named parties, alleging that no effort was made to even question their son despite knowledge of his reckless action. Again, a court relied on *DeShaney* in finding that inaction by the state did not yield liability, no matter what was known or could have been done.[13]

Nor was there liability under the reasoning of *DeShaney* for another school, aware of the bullying to which a special needs student was being subjected, when that student locked himself in a bathroom and committed suicide.[14]

But despite *DeShaney*, cases continued to be brought in the lower courts by plaintiffs who refused to stop believing that the law must offer the hope of justice to the injured.

On August 5, 2013, Rockne Newell opened fire during the monthly Ross Township supervisors meeting, wounding several and killing three, including James LaGuardia.

Frances LaGuardia later brought suit against the supervisors and various officials, including the county sheriff, citing a tortured history involving Newell and local government. He had brandished firearms and made lethal threats when efforts were made to confront him regarding numerous, serious violations involving a panoply of laws and codes regarding the upkeep of his property. They knew or should have known of his lethal propensities and should have taken steps to shield the innocent from his wrath at the town meeting. Constrained by *DeShaney* and its progeny the District Court in 2016 disagreed, asserting that ". . . as explained by the Supreme Court in *DeShaney,* the Due Process Clause of the 14th Amendment was intended to protect people from the State, not to ensure the State protected them from each other."[15]

DeShaney also helped defeat James Pal Reat's claim on behalf of his deceased relative, Ran, even as the court conceded that "The facts of this case are tragic." Menaced by thugs who threw a bottle and broke the rear windshield of his car as he was driving with friends, Ran Pal fled across the Denver line into an adjacent community and called 911 seeking police protection, only to be told that he needed to return to the spot where the attack occurred in order to receive aid. Despite pleas citing injuries and being in a state of shock, and injuries to his passengers, Pal was told he had to return to the location of the incident, and finally he did so, only to find no police on the scene. Nor it turned out later, had the 911 dispatcher sent them. And inevitably the marauders soon returned, firing shots as a terrified Pal and his passengers cowered in the car, and Pal was killed.

But, according the Tenth Circuit Court of Appeals in August of 2016, there was no liability under a theory of "state created danger" as that doctrine evolved from *DeShaney*. The 911 operator " . . was not present at the scene of the attack . . . He . . . merely informed the victims, however incompetently, that to get help from the police, they would have to return to Denver." And another case went unheard.[16]

DeShaney also left social workers in a strange, unhappy limbo, the National Association of Social Workers observing in a brief filed before the Supreme Court in 2014 that its continued silence on the case failed ". . . to provide guidance to those charged with the difficult task of protecting child welfare . . ." and that, indeed, it created "a perverse incentive structure for case workers to err on the side of permitting abuse to continue. . . ."[17]

Also, unforeseen at the time, *DeShaney* provided a simple, straightforward, compelling argument for advocates of private gun ownership. If the government has no obligation to protect citizens, citizens must see to their own protection. David Murley captured the essence of this argument in his law review article, referring to *DeShaney* as being ". . . unwittingly . . . the most important Second Amendment case ever decided by the Supreme Court." Insofar as the court made it clear that government has no constitutional obligation to protect citizens from violence, it follows that the Second Amendment has to be read as giving citizens a private right of gun ownership.[18]

Broadly similar sentiments are expressed on blogs such as *Guns Save Lives*, "The Supreme Court has . . . ruled that police officers at all levels of government have no duty to protect the citizens of this country. . . . We are on our own for protection."[19]

Whatever the meaning of *DeShaney* in terms of gun ownership, the essential legacy of the decision falls most heavily on the weak and helpless, those who cannot arm themselves, those who must rely on the state for protection. Data published by the Department of Health and Human Services in 2010 indicated that annually child protection caseworkers received more than 3,000,000 notifications of suspected abuse involving almost 6,000,000 children. Between 2008 and 2011 there were 750,000 substantiated cases of child abuse in the country. Approximately 1,500 children died annually as a result of abuse, most five years of age or younger, with one or both parents being the likely perpetrators.[20]

Both the gross numbers and particular stories bespoke tragedy and the need to pay attention. In a searing series of articles in the *Denver Post*, David Olinger reported that in 41 percent of the state's child abuse deaths over the preceding decade, officials had warning of the impending disaster. Hospitals had sent children home with fractured skulls; police had failed to investigate domestic violence; caseworkers had seen injuries and not followed up. And in the end it came down to the individual death: nine-year-old Michelle Moore ". . . slumped over her clarinet, beside the music she was practicing when she died . . . ," shot by a father who had killed her mother and six-year-old brother, Charlie, before turning the gun on himself.[21]

Olinger chronicled one kind of tragedy, but the nightmare imagination can conjure others—the call made to the police at the sound of an intruder, but there is no response, the frantic call made for an ambulance as a loved one lies gasping, but it does not show up; the call made to the fire department as the flames spread, but they do not come; the call made to a child abuse hot line, but there is no answer. And of all these possible nightmares only the call made to a child hot line, with there being no answer actually routinely occurs. Nearly 42,000 calls to Pennsylvania's child abuse hotline went unanswered over an extended period of time. There were long wait times on the phone, and there was a shortage of caseworkers, and there were questions of adequacy of funding, even as even as the state auditor lamented that ". . . any single of those calls could have lead to a life or death situation for a child."[22]

And beyond the children, dead at an early age, there was the pain of the survivors, not captured in any statistic. There was Brenda Hudak visiting her granddaughter's grave regularly. The calls she and others had made to the county's child abuse line had failed to bring action. Amanda Gallegos, nineteen months old, died from being repeatedly struck or squeezed. An autopsy revealed broken ribs that had healed and been broken again. "Toward the end, all she did was cry a lot," her grandmother said. "I could always see the fear in her eyes." The marker was simple: Amanda was born. She lived a short time. She died.[23]

As he pondered the *DeShaney* decision years after having argued on Joshua's behalf before the Supreme Court, Don Sullivan, as recounted, compared himself to Albion Tourgee, the attorney who argued and lost *Plessy v. Ferguson.* That decision gave racial segregation the stamp of constitutional approval. For half a century it was the rock on which efforts to end open, unashamed, legally enforced racial segregation foundered. On May 17, 1954, a long, tenacious, uphill battle, led by Thurgood Marshall, culminated with the *Brown v. Board of Education* decision overturning *Plessy.* If Don Sullivan saw himself as Albion Tourgee, the attorneys arguing *DeShaney* by another name will be stepping into the shoes of Thurgood Marshall and Robert Carter and Jack Greenberg and Spottswood Robinson, fighting an uphill battle on behalf of those cast outside the protection of the Constitution by a cruel prior decision.

Somewhere in America a tragedy is in the wings. On a quiet street, in an ordinary-looking house, in a small town a child is being beaten. In a cramped apartment, in a crowded high rise, in a big city a child is pleading that she will "be good" as the next blow comes down. In a small Midwest town, still gray with the soot of the mills that shut down years ago, home to a dwindling population making ends meet with part-time jobs at fast-food joints, a child is on life support in the emergency room, the victim of suspected abuse. One of these children will die, or wind up brain damaged, or crippled for life, and a lawsuit will be yielded against the agencies that failed to protect. The lawyer taking the case will be well aware of *DeShaney* and its legacy but will press ahead in any event, driven by a sense that justice not sought will never be obtained.

But the imagination need not conjure up horrors trailing in the wake of *DeShaney.* They are a constant reality. On January 8, 2014, a cold, grim day in New York City, four-year-old Myls Dobson died following repeated beatings at the hands of his father's girlfriend. Two years earlier Child Services had removed Myls from his mother's custody and placed him with his father, a figure with a criminal history. During the weeks preceding the final, lethal assault caseworkers visited the residence several times, apparently unaware that Myls's father was behind bars on new charges and that the boy was therefore wholly in the hands of the girlfriend.[24]

A year and a half later, on September 26, 2016, six-year old Zymire Perkins was rushed to the hospital by his mother, but it was too late. He was already dead. The postmortem examination revealed a skeletal, malnourished body, carpeted with bruises. There were also ribs that had been broken and fused back together. Further inquiry revealed that Zymire had not been a stranger to public agencies. In July of 2015 an anonymous caller reported that Zymire had been struck at least twenty times at a picnic by Rysheim Smith, his mother's boyfriend, for "not listening" and was threatened with more punishment when they returned home. In August of 2015 Zymire told investigators that Smith had held him nude in a cold shower to punish him, Smith not denying the accusation. In February of 2016 his mother told teachers concerned about bruises on Zymire and a missing tooth that appeared to have been knocked out that he was "clumsy and fell a lot." And in May of 2016 he had complained of pains in his legs at school and told at least one of the child protection agencies contacted of being beaten with a belt by his mother. In addition, a neighbor had contacted an agency regarding the little boy nearby who seemed constantly to be in such bad shape. And, indeed, the household had been investigated several times with no permanent alternative placement being put in place despite the lack of electricity in the apartment, the mold, and the vermin.

And following Zymire's death the crying game played itself out. The commissioner for Children's Services appeared before the City Council in tears. The mayor accepted blame and spoke of "Procedures . . . not followed, common sense . . . not exercised. . . ." And the protestations of remorse were genuine, as they had been for Elisa Izquierdo in 1995 and Nixzmary Brown in 2006 under similar circumstances, and as they would be for future Zymires unless something changes.[25]

The call for the Supreme Court to return to *DeShaney* has been a constant since the decision was handed down. On July 1, 2001, nationally syndicated columnist James Kilpatrick recounted a story out of Martin County, North Carolina. Over a period of weeks, ten-year-old Alex Stevenson was harassed and assaulted on school grounds and in classrooms by classmates. Pleas to school officials did not bring effective intervention. The grim story ended with a final, vicious assault and with Alex, suffering from contusions, lacerations, and ". . . a temporary eye dysfunction" transferring to a private school.[26]

The Fourth Circuit Court dismissed a suit brought by Alex's father in language echoing *DeShaney:* ". . . although school officers may have been . . . ineffective in not heeding the warnings . . . they had not themselves inflicted the injuries on Alex. Kilpatrick drew an analogy to *DeShaney*: "Poor Joshua in Wisconsin! Poor Alex in North Carolina! The high court ought to take a fresh look at this one." And a decade and a half later another case involving a school prompted the *South Carolina Law Review* in September of 2016 to print a piece arguing that "It's Time for the Fourth Circuit to Rethink *DeShaney*."[27]

And others made a similar plea, *New York Times* columnist Linda Greenhouse writing in 2010 that ". . . two decades later, the *DeShaney* decision remains the subject of contention . . . the Supreme Court is regularly asked to revisit . . . and regularly declines . . . to do so."[28]

But at some point it will.

CHAPTER TEN

REARGUING *DESHANEY*

> *On December 9, 2009, Eugene, Oregon Police received a 911 call regarding a person in distress. Rushing to the home of the address given by the caller they found fifteen-year-old Jeanette Maples in a bathtub covered with bruises. Despite strenuous attempts to revive her, Jeanette died. According to the medical examiner she weighed barely 50 pounds at the time of her death. Her mother and step-father were charged but investigation also revealed, according to the* Oregonian *newspaper, that "For three years people in Jeanette's life tried to get child welfare authorities involved, to no avail. Her step-grandmother, a concerned parent of a friend, and educators all called the state Department of Human Services because she was bruised, constantly hungry and said she had been beaten at home . . . at the funeral, grieving friends, their parents, teachers and family members said they trusted that . . . [the professionals] would rescue Jeanette, but they never did."*[1]

Manifestly, *DeShaney* was wrongly decided, not only in moral terms, but as a matter of law, and an unholy mess has trailed in its wake as lower courts have struggled to adjust its abstract, formalistic categories to the complex realities of everyday life. As was observed in a 2012 *Notre Dame Law Review* article, "In the twenty-three years since the decision, *DeShaney* has foreclosed . . . claims in many child abuse cases . . . And child abuse deaths continue to rise in the America. Abused children continue to die daily under watchful state agency care. The public is always suitably outraged, and yet these agencies . . . are not liable when they fail. Because of *DeShaney* this system is unlikely to change."[2]

The outrage among law professors was immediate and palpable: ". . . Chief Justice Rehnquist's opinion for the majority in *DeShaney* is an abomination," wrote Aviam Sofier in the *George Washington Law Review*. "It is illogical and extremely mechanistic: it also abuses history, fails to consider practical impact, and demonstrates moral insensitivity. Not only that, it is wrong."[3] And, Peter Edelman in the *Manhattan Lawyer* contended that ". . . it might be a much more appropriate statement of where we stand as a society if our constitutional doctrine were to say that what happened here is unacceptable and will not be tolerated."[4]

Constrained by *DeShaney*, courts recognize only a few exceptions to the proposition that the state has no constitutional obligation to see to the well-being of citizens in distress. A state is liable when it places a person "in custody," and then fails to provide some minimal level of care. In a variation on this category, it is also liable where it has a "special relationship" as, for example, between a school and a student, but as was observed in a 2013 *St. John's Law Review* piece on school cases where *DeShaney* came into play, ". . . the current analysis used by courts in determining whether a special relationship exists is impractical, opaque, and overly subjective."[5]

The state is also liable where through negligence or recklessness its actions place an individual in an even worse position. This is called "state-created danger," but some courts find state-created danger only where the state's actions "shock the conscience," an inane standard, without clear meaning, subjecting similar facts to vastly different readings from one jurisdiction to the next, depending on the elasticity of a court's conscience. In *Montgomery v. City of Ames*, in which the plaintiff unsuccessfully sought police protection from a predator violating a court order, not even ". . . gross negligence . . ." on the part of the police was sufficient to shock the court's conscience.[6]

Rearguing *DeShaney*: The Long View

On October 5, 1953, Earl Warren was sworn in as chief justice of the United States. Considered a moderate Republican by President Eisenhower, he had in 1948 been the party's nominee for vice president on a ticket headed by Thomas Dewey. There was little in his background to suggest an affinity for radical causes or movements. In the early months of World War II he had, as California attorney general, supported the relocation of Japanese citizens to internment camps, and after the war, as governor of a state rapidly growing in population, pursued infrastructure development and expansion of the public university system. He had little judicial experience prior to being named chief justice by Eisenhower, but a long career hewing close to Republican orthodoxy promised an unexceptional approach to the issues likely to come before the court.

In the autumn of 1956 Eisenhower put forward the name of another seemingly safe pick for the Supreme Court, William Brennan, the son of Irish immigrants who, through talent and hard work, had risen in the world. Following a stint with a respected firm after finishing Harvard Law School, he had worked his way up through the jungle of New Jersey politics, becoming along the way a Superior Court judge and a member of the New Jersey Supreme Court. Unlike Warren, he had extensive judicial experience, but there was little to suggest that he held extreme views on the issues of the day.

A decade later Brennan and Warren were being denounced in some quarters as avatars of radicalism, and celebrated in others as jurists seeking to give meaning to the language of the Constitution. They had led the court in formulating a series of decisions that revolutionized constitutional jurisprudence and dramatically impacted on American society. The language of the Constitution did not change, but the way in which that language was interpreted did. In effect, for Brennan and Warren, and the Kennedy and Johnson appointees who joined them, the aspirations for equity implicit in the language of the document provided markers by which to examine the *actual* inequities in the social system, the hydra-headed manifestations of racism, the myriad inequities of the criminal justice system, the taken for granted abuses by the powerful.[7] By 1968 there were billboards in the land calling for the impeachment of Earl Warren as a dangerous radical, and the composition of the Supreme Court had become an issue in the presidential contest that year between Richard Nixon and Hubert Humphrey.

The election of Nixon set in motion a judicial counterrevolution. Having run against the Warren court, Nixon set about changing the Supreme Court ideologically, the selection of William Rehnquist being part of that strategy. By the time *DeShaney v. Winnebago County Department of Social Services* came before the court, the judicial roulette associated with Supreme Court nominations had created a knife-edge situation. The court was beginning to tilt, but Brennan, an aging warrior, was still there, as were Thurgood Marshall and Harry Blackmun, a Nixon appointee, whose constitutional jurisprudence had moved him away from the conservative camp.

In a letter to Harry Blackmun, written by Warren Burger in 1969, before either was on the Supreme Court, Burger lamented the court's direction under Earl Warren and opined that newly elected President Richard

Nixon would be able to straighten the place out only ". . . if he gets four appointments."[8] And in short order Nixon got four appointments—Burger, Blackmun, Rehnquist, and Powell—but the court did not abruptly change course, given that serving might itself have been a learning experience that influenced the judicial views of some of his appointees. The Burger Court was not the Warren Court, nor was it the court that foes of the Warren court envisioned.

And in the years following *DeShaney*, the court continued to balance on a knife's edge, its tilt depending on judicial retirements or deaths in relation to the political dynamic yielding replacements. Was a George H. W. Bush making the nomination, or a Bill Clinton, a George W. Bush, or a Barack Obama? But whatever the court's tilt may be over any stretch of terms, a case raising *DeShaney* issues will inevitably be argued before it again, and the outcome will be uncertain. The history of the court is replete with instances of justices whose jurisprudence was other than anticipated by the presidents who nominated them, Earl Warren and William Brennan, for example; or whose jurisprudence on a given issue evolved over time, Oliver Wendell Holmes on race, for example; or who were driven by the facts of a particular case to depart from their usual judicial stance, John Roberts in *Foster v. Chatman,* for example;[9] or who brought particular sensibilities to the reading of the Constitution, Harry Blackmun, for example. Hence, whatever the perceived tilt of the court this year or that, there can be no confidence either way as to how *DeShaney* reargued would be decided. Whatever the cast of the court, the charge for the attorneys calling for reversal remains the same.

The Supreme Court will return to *DeShaney* with a chance to reverse it when four justices agree to take a case with similar facts and the same issue. At that point briefs will be filed, the case will be scheduled for oral argument before the nine justices, and the attorneys for each side will begin preparing for the most important day of their professional lives by combing through the relevant law and cases, formulating complex arguments, and rehearsing their presentation again and again before colleagues.

And then the day will come. The attorney representing Jessica or Richard or Lucy will go first, standing before the nine justices, prepared to argue that the state betrayed a battered child by failing to act even with knowledge of the child's torment, and that a lower court, bound by *DeShaney v. Winnebago Count Department of Social Services,* had not allowed a lawsuit filed on the child's behalf to go forward. What will that attorney contend and what arguments will have been advanced in the briefs?

The voluminous and passionate criticisms of *DeShaney* fall into several categories, the attorney's seeking its reversal beginning, perhaps, with an argument regarding the reach of the Constitution.

The Constitution Is More Than a Charter of "Negative Rights"

The chief justice opened his rejection of Joshua's claim with an expression of sympathy. The facts of the case were "undeniably tragic," he opined, but a fair and impartial reading of the Constitution mandated rejection of his claim. The language of the Fourteenth Amendment prohibits states from depriving its citizens of life, liberty, or property without due process of law, but does not require them to aid citizens in distress. Savage harm had been done to Joshua by a private citizen, not the state, hence he had no claim. His articulation was not new or idiosyncratic but represented the direction in which a more conservative court had been moving.

This was the majority's key claim; according to Justice Brennan in dissent, all else flowed from it. "(By) leading off with a discussion (and rejection) of the idea that the Constitution imposes on the States an affirmative duty to take basic care of their citizens, the court foreshadows—perhaps even preordains—its conclusion. . . ."

And Rehnquist was correct with regard to much of the document. Mississippi, for example, cannot block an eligible person from voting, but has no duty to assist that person in getting to the polls even with knowledge that they otherwise will not be able to vote. His error, and that of the majority, lay in stretching this limited proposition into a blanket assertion regarding the entire document, overlooking, for example, the positive right in the Sixth Amendment mandate that in ". . . all criminal prosecutions the accused shall . . . have the assistance of counsel for his defense." And if the accused cannot afford counsel, the state must provide counsel for him, this obligation not being limited by any notion that it does not have to do so unless it caused the accused to be indigent, or only if the accused is in custody. The obligation exists apart from anything the state did or did not do.[10]

In support of his contention that the Constitution is only a charter of negative rights, Justice Rehnquist cited the intention of those who drafted the law under which Joshua sought redress, but, as many critics pointed out, "The historical record is not as unambiguous . . ." as the chief justice suggested.[11]

The Fourteenth Amendment broadly and the language under which Joshua's suit was brought specifically were yielded by the seismic violence that swept the South in the decade after the Civil War, as the defeated rebels sought to reimpose domination over the newly free black population. Whippings, arson, and murder targeting blacks and their supporters drove an escalating anarchy, spurring a response from a Congress still strongly impacted by the personal consequences of the war—brothers, fathers, sons, cousins, and friends having died, and now part of what they had won on the battlefield with their lives was being wrenched away by the defeated rebels after the guns had fallen silent.

In 1866 the nation's first civil rights act was passed, and in 1867 parts of that act were incorporated into a proposed Fourteenth Amendment. Neither piece of legislation was a Platonic exercise in how to create "the good society." Both were meant to address immediate problems, including official negligence in the face of private violence being directed at black citizens and their sympathizers in the South.

In addition, a series of so-called Klan Acts were proposed, leading to extended debate in Congress and a vote on April 20, 1871, ratifying a statute containing the language under which Joshua brought his suit a little over a century later. And when challenged during the debate to justify reach of this new law, its supporters pointed to ". . . evidence of Klan terrorism that had elicited no response from the local sheriff."

In other words, officials should be held to account for what they did not do as well as for what they did. The clear intent of Congress ". . . was not to place limitations on the government's ability to act, but rather to expand states' obligation to offer protection to their citizens."[12] The law ". . . was aimed at least as much at the abdication of law enforcement responsibilities by Southern officials as it was at the Klan's outrages."[13]

The operative language under which Joshua sought redress prohibited officials "acting under color of law" from denying a citizen life, liberty, or property. They might do this directly or they might "cause" a citizen to suffer the loss of rights, the term *cause* embracing inaction, negligence, or indifference.

The essential thrust of the argument here would be to refute the claim that the Constitution is wholly a charter of negative rights, thereby negating any claim on behalf of a plaintiff in Joshua's circumstance. Clearly, the Congress that drafted and passed the law under which Joshua sought redress and under which successors would likely seek redress was meant to address official inaction as well as official action. "Justice Rehnquist sought to ignore and rewrite the intent of the Fourteenth Amendment," one critic argued, "and Joshua DeShaney was granted no recourse from the failure of the state to protect his life."[14]

A *DeShaney* reargument might also draw on the extensive criticism of Rehnquist's decision, arguing that, for purposes of the law, age is a factor.

Children Are Different

"*DeShaney*'s libertarian logic suggesting that private persons can usually take care of themselves, so the government isn't responsible when they get hurt doesn't make sense when applied to minors," observed one critic.[15] Another pointed out that, "Children at risk because of parental behavior are treated differently under the law from other citizens in need of protection."[16] And it is also the case, observed a third, that "Children are in a protected class. As such they are inherently in a 'special relationship' with the state," with the state having a heightened duty to see to their welfare.[17] And three years before *DeShaney*, Rehnquist, in his majority opinion in *Schall v. Martin*, agreed with this. Fourteen-year-old Gregory Martin claimed that the New York law permitting the detention of juveniles for days prior to a determination of whether there was sufficient evidence of wrongdoing as to charge them with having committed an offense violated their rights under the due process clause of the Fourteenth Amendment. The lower court agreed with him, New York appealed, and the case came before the United States Supreme Court.

In upholding the law, Rehnquist invoked the doctrine of *parens patriae* granting the state the power to protect persons unable to protect themselves: the mentally impaired, those who are legally incompetent to conduct their own affairs, children. "Children, by definition are not assumed to have the capacity to take care of themselves" he wrote; "They are assumed to be subject to the control of their parents, and if parental control falters, the State must play its part as *parens patriae*."[10]

If the state "must," under the doctrine of *parens patrie*, exercise the authority to hold a child in detention solely in order to shield him or her from a destructive environment, it would be perverse to suggest that having released that child into such an environment and knowing that the environment is destructive it no longer has a duty see to the child's welfare.

Joshua's situation was an analog. The state first became involved with him when he was brought into the Theda Clark Medical Center. There was evidence of abuse and the state, pursuant to state law and its authority under *parens patrie*, declined to release him to Randy, his father, even though on the evidence they had at that point Randy had a constitutional right to reclaim his child. Joshua is then released but the state retains oversight for his welfare, discerns evidence of abuse, but does not act. Under Rehnquist's *Schall* reasoning the state had a duty when Joshua was brought into the emergency room, and there is no principled way of concluding that the duty ceased once Joshua was carried from the hospital, given their continued involvement in his case and ongoing knowledge of his problematic situation.[19]

Other challenges to *DeShaney* also derive from the unique place children occupy for purposes of the law, Akhil Amer and Daniel Widawsky in the *Harvard Law Review* arguing that the Thirteenth Amendment abolishing slavery should be looked to for redress, having been pointed in that direction by Justice Blackmun's passionate dissent in which he ". . . compared the majority . . . to the antebellum judges who denied relief to . . ." blacks fleeing bondage. "Like an antebellum slave, an abused child is subject to near total domination and degradation by another person, and is treated more as a possession than a person. Unless the state acts to protect an abused child, the child's status bears an eerie resemblance to that of the pre-Civil War American slave . . . . Even if he could not be sold, Joshua was treated not as a person, but as chattel, as a thing, as—quite literally—a punching bag." The Thirteenth Amendment, they contended, spoke to the misdeeds of private individuals which, in the case of child abuse, was often the father, the mother, the abusive boyfriend.[20]

Davenport[21] and Douthett[22] argued, in yet another approach, that the next Joshua has a claim under a theory of "entitlement," resting on the notion that the state vests a child with a type of "property" when it confers a benefit and cannot then divest the child of that benefit without due process of law—or, in other words, child abuse and child neglect laws should be seen as vesting a child with a type of property claim to life and liberty free of gratuitous violence or deliberate deprivation. If the state's negligence then robs the child of life and liberty, those speaking on the child's behalf could look to the language of the Fourteenth Amendment for redress: "No State shall . . . deprive any person of life, liberty, or property, without due process of law . . ."

The Razor's Edge

But beyond the question of how the Constitution should be understood with regard to positive and negative rights, and what leverage the special status of children under the law provides in arguing for a reversal of *DeShaney*, the attorneys representing another Joshua will have to address the "razor's edge" issue.

In an interview in his chambers years after he had written the first decision in *DeShaney* denying Joshua's claim, Federal District Court Judge John Reynolds enlarged on some of the matters that concerned him. Social workers would be in a tough spot, he opined. Often it was not clear whether abuse was occurring. If his decision had gone Joshua's way, a social worker might be liable for guessing wrong and letting a child stay in an abusive home too long, but could also be in trouble if a child was pulled out of a home on flimsy evidence.

His views mirrored those offered by social work professionals. Rudolph Alexander, writing in the journal *Social Work*, argued that child abuse cases often pose a set of cruel choices for workers in the field. A diligent attempt to document a parent's abuse by, for example, questioning neighbors, could result in a libel suit; but, on the other hand, ". . . they can face criminal and civil liability for failure to take action . . ."[23] The Winnebago County Department of Social Services presented itself as confronted with this dilemma in the months leading up to the final assault on Joshua.

When the case reached the United States Supreme Court, a hostile Sandra Day O'Connor challenged Don Sullivan with the razor's edge argument. Victory for his side would, in her view, create ". . . a quite dangerous" situation. Many who supported the decision after it was handed down also alluded to the razor's edge danger. The local Oshkosh newspaper put it succinctly: "On a practical plane, the decision means that social workers . . . will not be subject to second guessing . . . That is a tremendous burden lifted from them. . . . the *DeShaney* case had the prospect of making any wrong, or even any questionable decision, a matter of suit."

But these sincere reservations mask what is otherwise an intolerable situation; "Up to 40 percent of abused children die under the care of a child welfare agency," according to a 2012 *Notre Dame Law Review* article.[24] Indeed, the present circumstance creates an incentive for agencies ". . . to avoid taking children into custody, for by doing so they give rise to liability that they would never have merely monitoring children in their own abusive homes."[25]

Without doubt the razor's edge argument will be raised again when a *DeShaney* case comes before the courts. The contention has a kind of surface plausibility but, ultimately, presupposes that the law itself cannot dull the razor's edge. The argument that the law can fix this problem is straightforward and uncomplicated.

In a perfect world the social worker would not be presented with the cruel choices outlined by Alexander and lamented by John Reynolds, Richard Posner, and Sandra Day O'Connor. In a perfect world there would be no such thing as a false report of child abuse; nor would social workers draw mistaken inferences of abuse where none had occurred. But in an imperfect world malicious neighbors or spiteful relatives will make false reports, and there will be mistaken inferences of abuse where an accident or other innocent explanation accounts for a child's injuries.

Ambiguity characterizes the real world of child abuse, and in that world the social worker may make one of two types of errors. There may be failure to act when a serious problem of abuse actually does exist. This can be called a *type-one error*. On the other hand, action may mistakenly be taken against a parent who has not been guilty of abuse. This can be called a *type-two error*. A decision to act may be a mistake. A decision not to act may also be a mistake.

The razor's edge dilemma may be resolved, however, by looking at the cost of a type-one error against the cost of a type-two error. If the social worker makes a mistake and leaves the child in an abusive home, the price paid by the child is loss of life or limb, or the eternal twilight of a Joshua DeShaney. If the social worker makes the mistake of intervening where intervention was not necessary, the cost to the parent is mental anguish, possible loss of reputation, and loss of time resolving the matter. These are serious costs, to be sure, but less serious than death, brain damage, or permanent disability. The innocent parent or guardian harmed by an incorrect decision has a chance to be made whole. The battered child—Joshua, Jessica Corteze, Michael Baker—does not.

Resolution of the "choice of error problem" should be a straightforward matter for the law and the courts. Without a doubt, the social work profession should sustain a preference for keeping families intact, but in a world of ambiguity, where danger looms, doubt should be resolved in favor of the child. It follows that the law ought to protect the social worker from liability in the same way that it now protects those who make good faith, but mistaken, reports of child abuse.

The proper response to choice of error was recognized by a social worker interviewed in the wake of the *DeShaney* decision. "We're really talking about a very vulnerable, weak, defenseless population. I think we always have to err a little more on the side of people who can't protect themselves." In other words, in a world in which there are no guarantees, the only rational thing to do is make the mistake that carries the least cost.

Issues of law, policy, and justice are inextricably intertwined. In the end, the law is not an end in itself but is intended to promote larger social objectives. These objectives may affront common notions of decency and justice, like the laws that protected slavery and Jim Crow, or they may advance ends that most people would agree are humane and just, like laws to protect children from abuse. People make the law. The law is not an external force visited on society like the weather or the rotation of the earth.

In that sense, most of the dangers cited by the Rehnquist majority had the decision gone Joshua's way—proliferation of lawsuits against social workers or other public servants, hesitation by states to offer social services for fear of being sued—are easily averted. The same kinds of arguments could have been made in the 1960s against reporting statutes: Won't there be malicious reports? Won't mistaken reports lead to a flood of defamation suits? This has not happened in the decades since reporting of suspected child abuse became a legal mandate. The problem was anticipated and easily dealt with. Those who report in good faith are protected from liability. In the same sense, immunity should shield a social worker from liability where scrupulous examination of the evidence suggests that the threat faced by the child in the home was not sufficient to justify removal.

Resolution of the razor's edge problem rests with lawmakers. The principle is straightforward: a public officer should be immune from suit where removal of the child from the home is based on a good faith interpretation of the evidence, even though later, more thorough investigation reveals that interpretation to have been incorrect. Surely objections will be heard to this kind of proposal: won't there be a rash of unjustified removals? To this there are two answers: the same kind of objection could have been made to laws mandating that teachers, emergency room doctors, and the like report suspected abuse, and, in any event, public agencies and the public would learn to live with the law. A working sense of what kind of evidence constituted justification for removal would evolve just as a working sense of what constitutes evidence sufficient to justify reporting has evolved over the decades.

Eaton and Wells argued that the *DeShaney* decision created a perverse incentive to resolve ambiguities in ways most likely to harm children in danger. Both before and after *DeShaney*, removal of a child could bring on a lawsuit by the parent, subject to the defense that the caseworker had made a reasonable professional judgment as to the danger the child faced. *DeShaney*, they argued ". . . tells the social worker that it is safer from a standpoint of personal liability to leave an endangered child in the home than to attempt to remove him." In other words, *DeShaney* created a preference for making the mistake most likely to harm the child while at the same time, according to a 2012 critique based on close observation, creating a regime in which agencies are overburdened but immune from suit for the unfortunate consequences.[26]

But in the end, if the law opted to err on the side of removal, lives would be saved. Surely errors would be made. That is inherent in the human circumstance, but just as surely there would be fewer photographs in the newspapers of the Joshuas and Christians and Jessicas, caught in a happy moment of respite before fist and boot broke them into pieces.

And What Would Victory Look Like?

It is the day after the United States Supreme Court in a split decision has reversed *DeShaney v. Winnebago County*, fervently argued opinions having been offered on each side. The dissenting justices, relying on Friend of the Court briefs submitted before by state and local governments and various professional associations, predict that reversal will lead to widespread dislocations and breakdown in the delivery of services to the public. They foresee numerous lawsuits filed against the police, child and family care agencies, schools, and public hospitals for judgment calls made by their employees that turn out to be wrong. They envision public agencies being wary of expanding services and many consciously pulling back in order to avoid being sued, and others exercising a degree of caution in the delivery of services tantamount to curtailment. They predict that less will be offered in the way of child and family services, and that there will be fewer patrols by the police. They anticipate that there will be a proliferation of paperwork as agencies seek to establish strict adherence to specific procedures in order to protect themselves in the event of a lawsuit. And the real losers, they contend, will be the people these agencies were created to serve—children, families in distress, the poor, the elderly, the infirm.

A year or two pass and an investigative reporter or a group of academics undertake a study of the consequences of the *DeShaney* reversal and publish their findings in a series of articles. In all likelihood there will be four conclusions.

First, there will indeed have been lawsuits brought against public agencies—police departments, school districts, child protection services—

for harm inflicted on aggrieved parties by private individuals—husbands, fathers, boyfriends—alleging that agency dereliction allowed the private party to inflict harm, the kind of suit that would surely have failed before a *DeShaney* reversal.

Second, the public agencies will have defended, sometimes successfully, sometimes unsuccessfully by (1) disputing the facts—calls were returned, home visits were made, the medical record was not conclusive, or (2) by arguing that even if the accuser's factual claims are accurate, agency performance did not constitute "negligence" or "recklessness" as defined in law.

Third, in response to the *DeShaney* reversal many agencies will (1) have reviewed and improved procedures and (2) successfully sought and received enhanced funding from governments, realizing that it is more fiscally responsible to invest in service delivery than pay damages from lawsuits.

Fourth, social workers, schoolteachers, police officers, and others impacted by the institutional response to a *DeShaney* reversal sense less of a gap between the realities of their work lives in terms of rules and resources and the desire to serve that drew them into their professions in the first place.

Indeed, it will be clear that the original *DeShaney* decision was, ultimately, harmful to social work as a profession. In the real world there are heavy case loads, there is underfunding, there are opaque and conflicting bureaucratic rules, and one of the consequences of *DeShaney* was that states and cities continued to have no incentive to address any of these problems. Wisconsin capped damages for the type of suit brought on Joshua's behalf at fifty thousand dollars, and no state or city has an incentive to increase the limits of its own liability, to increase its exposure to potentially extraordinarily substantial damages. Nor is there any sustained incentive to address heavy caseload issues or issues of bureaucratic inefficiency, each crisis, each Joshua-like tragedy instead being addressed by "the crying game," expressions of sympathy for the injured by public officials before the television cameras and unreliable promises to do better.

As students of the situation have noted, *DeShaney,* in eliminating potentially heavy state liability, eroded the state's incentive to allocate child welfare resources more frugally and more efficiently. And the villains in each tragic case played out in nightly television news stories and chronicled in newspapers headlines are the caseworkers, accused of being indifferent to the signs of child abuse, careless in monitoring the welfare of young charges.

The *DeShaney* decision did no favors for the social work profession.

A reversal of *DeShaney* would provide an incentive for states and cities to address funding and staffing issues more seriously and to engage in the often difficult business of identifying and eliminating bureaucratic inefficiencies. Rather, the decision allowed agencies to remain overburdened and underfunded, the blame for the inevitable tragedies being shifted wholly to the caseworkers, rather than allocated in terms of a more precise calculus of blame. Social work as a profession would benefit from a reversal insofar as it would provide an incentive, potentially, for state legislatures and city councils to address the issues attending child care with sustained attention, greater seriousness, and more money.

The *DeShaney* Community

The daily occurrence of child abuse without adequate response yields the sense in many quarters that something is terribly wrong with a system of law that cannot find a way to offer redress to the most helpless of victims. And it is this lingering sense of justice deferred, of basic human decency deflected, that has yielded what might be termed a nascent *DeShaney* community.

The *DeShaney* community, implicit rather than self-consciously organized, is made up of the law professors who have probed the inadequacies of the Rehnquist decision and offered alternative formulations that would honor the rights of parents, respect the ambiguous realities encountered by social workers, yet protect the most vulnerable in the society from lives defined by needless suffering.

The nascent *DeShaney* community also includes social workers who have studied the decision and written about it, and who every day confront the ambiguities of a home in which Joey or Jane or Jasmine, indeed, might have fallen from his tricycle as Dad says or might have been struck by a father unable to deal with the challenges and frustrations of parenthood.

The nascent *DeShaney* community has in its ranks reporters who have seen humankind at its best and at its worse, but who are bothered, nevertheless, by a Supreme Court decision that seems so at odds with basic human decency.

The nascent *DeShaney* community is made up of laypeople who have read about the case, who are not schooled in the intricacies of legal argument, who neither know nor care how "substantive due process" differs from "procedural due process," but who know in their hearts that something is terribly wrong when the law is said to free the state of any obligation to restrain the clenched fist from battering a child's face.

The nascent community also includes scholars such as Lynne Curry whose book on the *DeShaney* case articulated some of the tension between what happened and what a sense of fairness suggests should have happened.[27]

All these people form an implicit *DeShaney* community, looking in their different ways for change. And as with any community, strength comes from sharing knowledge, from interacting, from speaking to one another in ways that both inform and promote the possibility of effecting change.

The *DeShaney* website allows the nascent *DeShaney* community to be an actual community, open to all to post, share information, offer comments, have positions of every character commented on and evaluated. The premise is that the understanding of the issues presented by the case is promoted by exposure to the research and views of others, and that ultimately the strongest arguments for change, offered in every forum, from local legislatures to the Supreme Court, are yielded by drawing on the accumulated information, insights, arguments, reservations, propositions, and formulations of the community.

Some will simply want to keep abreast of the latest postings, others will want to contribute, some will engage in discussion and debate, others will want to draw on the site as they write articles, research briefs, or prepare for oral argument. Engagement in the community will take many forms as members address *DeShaney v. Winnebago County*.[28]

Conclusion

In the end the Supreme Court decision was an unsatisfactory outcome for the law and ultimately for all of the parties to the case, even the apparent winners.

That the law suffered damage is without question. Within two years after the decision was handed down more than thirty articles appeared in law journals. In the ensuing decade articles and commentary continued to appear, many reflecting a sense of outrage at a judicial stance that isolated the law from a reasonable and humane response to horrifying facts.

Neither did the outcome vindicate the Winnebago County Department of Social Services or any of the named parties. The Supreme Court decision said, in effect, that Don Sullivan could not go to trial because Joshua did not have the kind of claim that could be pursued under the Constitution, not that the underlying facts were not true. Responding to reporters' questions after the decision was handed down, Anne Kemmeter, while expressing relief that the case was over, lamented not having an opportunity to tell her side of the story. Neither the state nor the Department of Social Services wished to face the possibility of heavy monetary damages should they lose at trial, but in avoiding that danger they also lost the opportunity to respond systematically to the plaintiff's factual allegations. Hence, in one sense they won, but in another sense, they did not win.

The outcome was immensely unsatisfactory for Melody. Had the matter gone to trial and the Department of Social Services prevailed, there would have been the bittersweet satisfaction of knowing that Joshua had not been the victim of gross negligence or reckless indifference. Had she prevailed at trial there would have been satisfaction yielded by a sense of justice being done.

The Supreme Court decision left questions unanswered. In effect, the decision cast those questions into an eternal limbo. What had happened? Was anyone responsible? Were there profound questions of moral responsibility that could be closed only by a jury passing on the credibility of the competing stories about what had happened?

The *DeShaney* story is about a tragic event in Wisconsin and about countless other tragic cases. The continuing vitality of *DeShaney* derives from a persistent sense that the majority decision was both legally incorrect and profoundly at odds with the meaning and intention of the Constitution. *DeShaney* therefore is also about the purposes of the law. The majority and the dissenters did not differ in terms of legal sophistication or powers of analysis, they differed primarily in their conception of what "the law" is about. Why does it exist? Neither lawyers nor other professionals ponder why their profession exists, but occasionally the question is thrust on them so forcefully that no matter which way they turn they have to finally confront it. The passionate reaction to *DeShaney* and the ongoing vitality of the case can be explained by the questions it poses about the meaning and purposes of the law. What is the law about? A Constitution—for what?

The dissenters in *DeShaney* likened the posture of the majority to that of pre-Civil War judges who claimed that the law mandated support for the claims of slaveholders. The majority regarded that as a canard, proof that the dissenters were driven by sentiment rather than faithful adherence to the law's stern dictates.

In truth the Constitution is a flexible document. Its words are not subject to any old meaning a judge chooses to give them, but neither are they a linguistic straitjacket. Given the limited but real margin for choice in terms of the meaning the words may be accorded, the decision in any given case is both a legal conclusion and a social choice. The social choice made by the *DeShaney* majority struck many as horrific, a prescription for a Dickensian world, presented as the only "correct" answer to be drawn from a sober and responsible reading of the Fourteenth Amendment.

Constitutional scholars speak of an "indeterminate Constitution." The document lends itself to choices within limits. In his *DeShaney* dissent, Justice Harry Blackmun pointed out that "(T)he question presented by this case is an open one, and our Fourteenth Amendment precedents may be read more broadly or narrowly depending upon how one chooses to read them . . . Faced with the choice, I would adopt a 'sympathetic' reading, one which comports with the dictates of fundamental justice and recognizes that compassion need not be exiled from the province of judging."

Ultimately *DeShaney* is about different visions of the social order and the uses to which the law is put. The Constitution is not a mandate to "do good," but it is a document under which much good has been done. At its best, it is about the quest for justice. When *DeShaney* is reargued it can be an instrument for achieving justice.

On April 6, 1994, a sunny day in Washington, DC, President Bill Clinton summoned reporters to the White House. Justice Harry Blackmun was retiring. With Blackmun standing beside him, Clinton offered a heartfelt valedictory that went to the core of what he saw as Blackmun's contribution to the Supreme Court and to American society. "Those of us who have studied the law can at times be lost in its abstractions. The habits, the procedures, the language of the law can separate lawyers from the people who look to the bar for justice." But the man standing beside him was an exception. "Justice Blackmun's identification was firmly and decisively with the ordinary people of this country, with their concerns, and his humanity was given voice not only in majority opinions but in dissents." And then the president quoted from one of those dissents. "What is required of us is moral ambition. Poor Joshua. It is a sad commentary upon American life and constitutional principles that Joshua and his mother are denied by this Court the opportunity to have their rights protected."

On November 18, 2015, funeral services were held at St. Paul's Lutheran Church in Muskego, Wisconsin. Notice circulated before the service stated that "Joshua went to meet Jesus on Monday, November 9, 2015 at the age of 36 . . . He was the beloved son of Richard and Ginger Braam."

For years the boy who had been beaten into oblivion had no fixed home, his impairments defeating the best intentions of caretakers; then the Braam's read about him. "We didn't pay a lot of attention to politics," Ginger Braam said, but Joshua's story drew them to him and they adopted him when he was twelve. "What we tried to do is provide Joshua with what he didn't have . . . a family and a home. We were content to have him a part of our family . . . He made a difference in our lives."

It rained the night before the funeral, but in the morning the sky was clear.

APPENDIX

DESHANEY V. WINNEBAGO COUNTY DEPARTMENT OF SOCIAL SERVICES, 489 U.S., 189 (1989)

Opinion

REHNQUIST, C.J., Opinion of the Court

CHIEF JUSTICE REHNQUIST delivered the opinion of the Court.

Petitioner is a boy who was beaten and permanently injured by his father, with whom he lived. Respondents are social workers and other local officials who received complaints that petitioner was being abused by his father and had reason to believe that this was the case, but nonetheless did not act to remove petitioner from his father's custody. Petitioner sued respondents claiming that their failure to act deprived him of his liberty in violation of the Due Process Clause of the Fourteenth Amendment to the United States Constitution. We hold that it did not.

I

The facts of this case are undeniably tragic. Petitioner Joshua DeShaney was born in 1979. In 1980, a Wyoming court granted his parents a divorce and awarded custody of Joshua to his father, Randy DeShaney. The father shortly thereafter moved to Neenah, a city located in Winnebago County, Wisconsin, taking the infant Joshua with him. There he entered into a second marriage, which also ended in divorce.

The Winnebago County authorities first learned that Joshua DeShaney might be a victim of child abuse in January, 1982, when his father's second wife complained to the police, at the time of their divorce, that he had previously "hit the boy, causing marks, and [was] a prime case for child abuse." App. 152–153. The Winnebago County Department of Social Services (DSS) interviewed the father, but he denied the accusations, and DSS did not pursue them further. In January, 1983, Joshua was admitted to a local hospital with multiple bruises and abrasions. The examining physician suspected child abuse and notified DSS, which immediately obtained an order from a Wisconsin juvenile court placing Joshua in the temporary custody of the hospital. Three days later, the county convened an *ad hoc* "Child Protection Team"—consisting of a pediatrician, a psychologist, a police detective, the county's lawyer, several DSS caseworkers, and various hospital personnel—to consider Joshua's situation. At this meeting, the Team decided that there was insufficient evidence of child abuse to retain Joshua in the custody of the court. The Team did, however, decide to recommend several measures to protect Joshua, including enrolling him in a preschool program, providing his father with certain counseling services, and encouraging his father's girlfriend to move out of the home. Randy DeShaney entered into a voluntary agreement with DSS in which he promised to cooperate with them in accomplishing these goals.

Based on the recommendation of the Child Protection Team, the juvenile court dismissed the child protection case and returned Joshua to the custody of his father. A month later, emergency room personnel called the DSS caseworker handling Joshua's case to report that he had once again been treated for suspicious injuries. The caseworker concluded that there was no basis for action. For the next six months, the caseworker made monthly visits to the DeShaney home, during which she observed a number of suspicious injuries on **[p193]** Joshua's head; she also noticed that he had not been enrolled in school, and that the girlfriend had not moved out. The caseworker dutifully recorded these incidents in her files, along with her continuing suspicions that someone in the DeShaney household was physically abusing Joshua, but she did nothing more. In November, 1983, the emergency room notified DSS that Joshua had been treated once again for injuries that they believed to be caused by child abuse. On the caseworker's next two visits to the DeShaney home, she was told that Joshua was too ill to see her. Still DSS took no action.

In March, 1984, Randy DeShaney beat 4-year-old Joshua so severely that he fell into a life-threatening coma. Emergency brain surgery revealed a series of hemorrhages caused by traumatic injuries to the head inflicted over a long period of time. Joshua did not die, but he suffered brain damage so severe that he is expected to spend the rest of his life confined to an institution for the profoundly retarded. Randy DeShaney was subsequently tried and convicted of child abuse.

Joshua and his mother brought this action under 42 U.S.C. § 1983 in the United States District Court for the Eastern District of Wisconsin against respondents Winnebago County, DSS, and various individual employees of DSS. The complaint alleged that respondents had deprived Joshua of his liberty without due process of law, in violation of his rights under the Fourteenth Amendment, by failing to intervene to protect him against a risk of violence at his father's hands of which they knew or should have known. The District Court granted summary judgment for respondents.

The Court of Appeals for the Seventh Circuit affirmed, 812 F.2d 298 (1987), holding that petitioners had not made out an actionable § 1983 claim for two alternative reasons. First, the court held that the Due Process Clause of the Fourteenth Amendment does not require a state or local governmental entity to protect its citizens from "private violence, or other mishaps not attributable to the conduct of its employees." *Id.* at 301. In so holding, the court specifically rejected the position endorsed by a divided panel of the Third Circuit in *Estate of Bailey by Oare v. County of York,* 768 F.2d 503, 510–511 (CA3 1985), and by dicta in *Jensen v. Conrad,* 747 F.2d 185, 190–194 (CA4 1984), *cert. denied,* 470 U.S. 1052 (1985), that, once the State learns that a particular child is in danger of abuse from third parties and actually undertakes to protect him from that danger, a "special relationship" arises between it and the child which imposes an affirmative constitutional duty to provide adequate protection. 812 F.2d at 303–304. Second, the court held, in reliance on our decision in *Martinez v. California,* 444 U.S. 277, 285 (1980), that the causal connection between respondents' conduct and Joshua's injuries was too attenuated to establish a deprivation of constitutional rights actionable under § 1983. 812 F.2d at 301–303. The court therefore found it unnecessary to reach the question whether respondents' conduct evinced the "state of mind" necessary to make out a due process claim after *Daniels v. Williams,* 474 U.S. 327 (1986), and *Davidson v. Cannon,* 474 U.S. 344 (1986). 812 F.2d at 302.

Because of the inconsistent approaches taken by the lower courts in determining when, if ever, the failure of a state or local governmental entity or its agents to provide an individual with adequate protective services constitutes a violation of the individual's due process rights, *see Archie v. Racine,* 847 F.2d 1211, 1220–1223, and n. 10 (CA7 1988) (en banc) (collecting cases), *cert. pending,* No. 88-576, and the importance of the issue to the administration of state and local governments, we granted certiorari. 485 U.S. 958 (1988). We now affirm.

II

The Due Process Clause of the Fourteenth Amendment provides that "[n]o State shall . . . deprive any person of life, liberty, or property, without due process of law." Petitioners contend that the State[n1] deprived Joshua of his liberty interest in "free[dom] from . . . unjustified intrusions on personal security," *see Ingraham v. Wright,* 430 U.S. 651, 673 (1977), by failing to provide him with adequate protection against his father's violence. The claim is one invoking the substantive, rather than the procedural, component of the Due Process Clause; petitioners do not claim that the State denied Joshua protection without according him appropriate procedural safeguards, *see Morrissey v. Brewer,* 408 U.S. 471, 481 (1972), but that it was categorically obligated to protect him in these circumstances, *see Youngberg v. Romeo,* 457 U.S. 307, 309 (1982).[n2]

But nothing in the language of the Due Process Clause itself requires the State to protect the life, liberty, and property of its citizens against invasion by private actors. The Clause is phrased as a limitation on the State's power to act, not as a guarantee of certain minimal levels of safety and security. It forbids the State itself to deprive individuals of life, liberty, or property without "due process of law," but its language cannot fairly be extended to impose an affirmative obligation on the State to ensure that those interests do not come to harm through other means. Nor does history support such an expansive reading of the constitutional text. Like its counterpart in the Fifth Amendment, the Due Process Clause of the Fourteenth Amendment was intended to prevent government "from abusing [its] power, or employing it as an instrument of oppression," *Davidson v. Cannon, supra*, at 348; *see also Daniels v. Williams, supra*, at 331 ("to secure the individual from the arbitrary exercise of the powers of government," and "to prevent governmental power from being 'used for purposes of oppression' ") (internal citations omitted); *Parratt v. Taylor*, 451 U.S. 527, 549 (1981) (Powell, J., concurring in result) (to prevent the "affirmative abuse of power"). Its purpose was to protect the people from the State, not to ensure that the State protected them from each other. The Framers were content to leave the extent of governmental obligation in the latter area to the democratic political processes.

Consistent with these principles, our cases have recognized that the Due Process Clauses generally confer no affirmative right to governmental aid, even where such aid may be necessary to secure life, liberty, or property interests of which the government itself may not deprive the individual. *See, e.g., Harris v. McRae*, 448 U.S. 297, 317–318 (1980) (no obligation to fund abortions or other medical services) (discussing Due Process Clause of Fifth Amendment); *Lindsey v. Normet*, 405 U.S. 56, 74 (1972) (no obligation to provide adequate housing) (discussing Due Process Clause of Fourteenth Amendment); *see also Youngberg v. Romeo, supra*, at 317 ("As a general matter, a State is under no constitutional duty to provide substantive services for those within its border"). As we said in *Harris v. McRae*:

Although the liberty protected by the Due Process Clause affords protection against unwarranted *government* interference, . . . it does not confer an entitlement to such [governmental aid] as may be necessary to realize all the advantages of that freedom.

448 U.S. at 317–318 (emphasis added). If the Due Process Clause does not require the State to provide its citizens with particular protective services, it follows that the State cannot be held liable under the Clause for injuries that could have been averted had it chosen to provide them.[n3] As a general matter, then, we conclude that a State's failure to protect an individual against private violence simply does not constitute a violation of the Due Process Clause.

Petitioners contend, however, that even if the Due Process Clause imposes no affirmative obligation on the State to provide the general public with adequate protective services, such a duty may arise out of certain "special relationships" created or assumed by the State with respect to particular individuals. Brief for Petitioners 13–18. Petitioners argue that such a "special relationship" existed here because the State knew that Joshua faced a special danger of abuse at his father's hands, and specifically proclaimed, by word and by deed, its intention to protect him against that danger. *Id.* at 18–20. Having actually undertaken to protect Joshua from this danger—which petitioners concede the State played no part in creating—the State acquired an affirmative "duty," enforceable through the Due Process Clause, to do so in a reasonably competent fashion. Its failure to discharge that duty, so the argument goes, was an abuse of governmental power that so "shocks the conscience," *Rochin v. California*, 342 U.S. 165, 172 (1952), as to constitute a substantive due process violation. Brief for Petitioners 20.[n4]

We reject this argument. It is true that, in certain limited circumstances, the Constitution imposes upon the State affirmative duties of care and protection with respect to particular individuals. In *Estelle v. Gamble*, 429 U.S. 97"] 429 U.S. 97 (1976), we recognized that the Eighth Amendment's prohibition against cruel and unusual punishment, made applicable to the States through the Fourteenth Amendment's Due Process Clause, 429 U.S. 97 (1976), we recognized that the Eighth Amendment's prohibition against cruel and unusual punishment, made applicable to the States through the Fourteenth Amendment's Due Process Clause, *Robinson v. California*, 370 U.S. 660 (1962), requires the State to provide adequate medical care to incarcerated prisoners. 429 U.S. at 103–104.[n5] We reasoned that, because the prisoner is unable " 'by reason of the deprivation of his liberty [to] care for himself,' " it is only " 'just' " that the State be required to care for him. Ibid., quoting *Spicer v. Williamson*, 191 N. C. 487, 490, 132 S.E. 291, 293 (1926).

In *Youngberg v. Romeo*, 457 U.S. 307 (1982), we extended this analysis beyond the Eighth Amendment setting,[n6] holding that the substantive component of the Fourteenth Amendment's Due Process Clause requires the State to provide involuntarily committed mental patients with such services as are necessary to ensure their "reasonable safety" from themselves and others. Id. at 314–325; see id. at 315, 324 (dicta indicating that the State is also obligated to provide such individuals with "adequate food, shelter, clothing, and medical care"). As we explained:

If it is cruel and unusual punishment to hold convicted criminals in unsafe conditions, it must be unconstitutional [under the Due Process Clause] to confine the involuntarily committed who may not be punished at all—in unsafe conditions.

Id. at 315–316; see also *Revere v. Massachusetts General Hospital*, 463 U.S. 239, 244 (1983) (holding that the Due Process Clause requires the responsible government or governmental agency to provide medical care to suspects in police custody who have been injured while being apprehended by the police).

But these cases afford petitioners no help. Taken together, they stand only for the proposition that, when the State takes a person into its custody and holds him there against his will, the Constitution imposes upon it a corresponding duty to assume some responsibility for his safety and general wellbeing. See *Youngberg v. Romeo*, supra, at 317 ("When a person is institutionalized—and wholly dependent on the State[,] . . . a duty to provide certain services and care does exist").[n7] The rationale for this principle is simple enough: when the State, by the affirmative exercise of its power, so restrains an individual's liberty that it renders him unable to care for himself, and at the same time fails to provide for his basic human needs—e.g., food, clothing, shelter, medical care, and reasonable safety—it transgresses the substantive limits on state action set by the Eighth Amendment and the Due Process Clause. See *Estelle v. Gamble*, supra, at 103–104; *Youngberg v. Romeo*, supra, at 315–316. The affirmative duty to protect arises not from the State's knowledge of the individual's predicament or from its expressions of intent to help him, but from the limitation which it has imposed on his freedom to act on his own behalf. See *Estelle v. Gamble*, supra, at 103 ("An inmate must rely on prison authorities to treat his medical needs; if the authorities fail to do so, those needs will not be met"). In the substantive due process analysis, it is the State's affirmative act of restraining the individual's freedom to act on his own behalf—through incarceration, institutionalization, or other similar restraint of personal liberty—which is the "deprivation of liberty" triggering the protections of the Due Process Clause, not its failure to act to protect his liberty interests against harms inflicted by other means.[n8]

The Estelle-Youngberg analysis simply has no applicability in the present case. Petitioners concede that the harms Joshua suffered did not occur while he was in the State's custody, but while he was in the custody of his natural father, who was in no sense a state actor.[n9] While the State may have been aware of the dangers that Joshua faced in the free world, it played no part in their creation, nor did it do anything to render him any more vulnerable to them. That the State once took temporary custody of Joshua does not alter the analysis, for, when it returned him to his father's custody, it placed him in no worse position than that in which he would have been had it not acted at all; the State does not become the permanent guarantor of an individual's safety by having once offered him shelter. Under these circumstances, the State had no constitutional duty to protect Joshua.

It may well be that, by voluntarily undertaking to protect Joshua against a danger it concededly played no part in creating, the State acquired a duty under state tort law to provide him with adequate protection against that danger. See Restatement (Second) of Torts § 323 (1965) (one who undertakes to render services to another may in some circumstances be held liable for doing so in a negligent fashion); see generally W. Keeton, D. Dobbs, R. Keeton, & D. Owen, Prosser and Keeton on the Law of Torts § 56 (5th ed.1984) (discussing "special relationships" which may give rise to affirmative duties to act under the common law of tort). But the claim here is based on the Due Process Clause of the Fourteenth Amendment, which, as we have said many times, does not transform every tort committed by a state actor into a constitutional violation. See *Daniels v. Williams*, 474 U.S. at 335–336; *Parratt v. Taylor*, 451 U.S. at 544; *Martinez v. California*, 444 U.S. 277, 285 (1980); *Baker v. McCollan*, 443 U.S. 137, 146 (1979); *Paul v. Davis*, 424 U.S. 693, 701 (1976). A State may, through its courts and legislatures, impose such affirmative duties of care and protection upon its agents as it wishes. But not "all common law duties owed by government actors were . . . constitutionalized by the Fourteenth Amendment." *Daniels v. Williams*, supra, at 335. Because, as explained above, the State had no constitutional duty to protect Joshua against his father's violence, its failure to do so—though calamitous in hindsight—simply does not constitute a violation of the Due Process Clause.[n10]

Judges and lawyers, like other humans, are moved by natural sympathy in a case like this to find a way for Joshua and his mother to receive adequate compensation for the grievous harm inflicted upon them. But before yielding to that impulse, it is well to remember once again that the harm was inflicted not by the State of Wisconsin, but by Joshua's father. The most that can be said of the state functionaries in this case is that they stood by and did nothing when suspicious circumstances dictated a more active role for them. In defense of them, it must also be said that, had they moved too soon to take custody of the son away from the father, they would likely have been met with charges of improperly intruding into the parent-child relationship, charges based on the same Due Process Clause that forms the basis for the present charge of failure to provide adequate protection.

The people of Wisconsin may well prefer a system of liability which would place upon the State and its officials the responsibility for failure to act in situations such as the present one. They may create such a system, if they do not have it already, by changing the tort law of the State in accordance with the regular lawmaking process. But they should not have it thrust upon them by this Court's expansion of the Due Process Clause of the Fourteenth Amendment.

Affirmed.

1.

As used here, the term "State" refers generically to state and local governmental entities and their agents.

2.

Petitioners also argue that the Wisconsin child protection statutes gave Joshua an "entitlement" to receive protective services in accordance with the terms of the statute, an entitlement which would enjoy due process protection against state deprivation under our decision in *Board of Regents of State Colleges v. Roth,* 408 U.S. 564 (1972). Brief for Petitioners 24–29. But this argument is made for the first time in petitioners' brief to this Court: it was not pleaded in the complaint, argued to the Court of Appeals as a ground for reversing the District Court, or raised in the petition for certiorari. We therefore decline to consider it here. See *Youngberg v. Romeo,* 457 U.S. at 316, n.19; *Dothard v. Rawlinson,* 433 U.S. 321, 323, n. 1 (1977); *Duignan v. United States,* 274 U.S. 195, 200 (1927); *Old Jordan Mining & Milling Co. v. Societe Anonyme des Mines,* 164 U.S. 261, 264–265 (1896).

3.

The State may not, of course, selectively deny its protective services to certain disfavored minorities without violating the Equal Protection Clause. See *Yick Wo v. Hopkins,* 118 U.S. 356 (1886). But no such argument has been made here.

4.

The genesis of this notion appears to lie in a statement in our opinion in *Martinez v. California*, 444 U.S. 277 (1980). In that case, we were asked to decide, inter alia, whether state officials could be held liable under the Due Process Clause of the Fourteenth Amendment for the death of a private citizen at the hands of a parolee. Rather than squarely confronting the question presented here—whether the Due Process Clause imposed upon the State an affirmative duty to protect—we affirmed the dismissal of the claim on the narrower ground that the causal connection between the state officials' decision to release the parolee from prison and the murder was too attenuated to establish a "deprivation" of constitutional rights within the meaning of § 1983. Id. at 284-285. But we went on to say:

[T]he parole board was not aware that appellants' decedent, as distinguished from the public at large, faced any special danger. We need not and do not decide that a parole officer could never be deemed to "deprive" someone of life by action taken in connection with the release of a prisoner on parole. But we do hold that, at least under the particular circumstances of this parole decision, appellants' decedent's death is too remote a consequence of the parole officers' action to hold them responsible under the federal civil rights law.

Id. at 285 (footnote omitted). Several of the Courts of Appeals have read this language as implying that, once the State learns that a third party poses a special danger to an identified victim, and indicates its willingness to protect the victim against that danger, a "special relationship" arises between State and victim, giving rise to an affirmative duty, enforceable through the Due Process Clause, to render adequate protection. See Estate of Bailey by *Oare v. County of York*, 768 F.2d 503, 510-511 (CA3 1985); *Jensen v. Conrad*, 747 F.2d 185, 190-194, and n. 11 (CA4 1984) (dicta), cert. denied, 470 U.S. 1052 (1985); *Balistreri v. Pacifica Police Dept.*, 855 F.2d 1421, 1425-1426 (CA9 1988). But see, in addition to the opinion of the Seventh Circuit below, *Estate of Gilmore v. Buckley*, 787 F.2d 714, 720-723 (CA1), cert. denied, 479 U.S. 882 (1986); *Harpole v. Arkansas Dept. of Human Services,* 820 F.2d 923, 926–927 (CA8 1987); *Wideman v. Shallowford Community Hospital Inc.,* 826 F.2d 1030, 1034–1037 (CA11 1987).

5.

To make out an Eighth Amendment claim based on the failure to provide adequate medical care, a prisoner must show that the state defendants exhibited "deliberate indifference" to his "serious" medical needs; the mere negligent or inadvertent failure to provide adequate care is not enough. *Estelle v. Gamble,* 429 U.S. at 429 U.S. 105"]105–106. In 105–106. In *Whitley v. Albers,* 475 U.S. 312 (1986), we suggested that a similar state of mind is required to make out a substantive due process claim in the prison setting. Id. at 326–327.

6.

The Eighth Amendment applies only after the State has complied with the constitutional guarantees traditionally associated with criminal prosecutions. . . . [T]he State does not acquire the power to punish with which the Eighth Amendment is concerned until after it has secured a formal adjudication of guilt in accordance with due process of law.

Ingraham v. Wright, 430 U.S. 651, 671–672, n. 40 (1977); see also *Revere v. Massachusetts General Hospital,* 463 U.S. 239, 244 (1983); *Bell v. Wolfish,* 441 U.S. 520, 535, n. 16 (1979).

7.

Even in this situation, we have recognized that the State "has considerable discretion in determining the nature and scope of its responsibilities." *Youngberg v. Romeo,* 457 U.S. at 317.

8.

Of course, the protections of the Due Process Clause, both substantive and procedural, may be triggered when the State, by the affirmative acts of its agents, subjects an involuntarily confined individual to deprivations of liberty which are not among those generally authorized by his confinement. See, e.g., *Whitley v. Albers*, supra, at 326–327 (shooting inmate); *Youngberg v. Romeo*, supra, at 316 (shackling involuntarily committed mental patient); *Hughes v. Rowe*, 449 U.S. 5, 11 (1980) (removing inmate from general prison population and confining him to administrative segregation); *Vitek v. Jones*, 445 U.S. 480, 491–494 (1980) (transferring inmate to mental health facility).

9. Complaint ¶ 16, App. 6 ("At relevant times to and until March 8, 1984, [the date of the final beating,] Joshua DeShaney was in the custody and control of Defendant Randy DeShaney"). Had the State, by the affirmative exercise of its power, removed Joshua from free society and placed him in a foster home operated by its agents, we might have a situation sufficiently analogous to incarceration or institutionalization to give rise to an affirmative duty to protect. Indeed, several Courts of Appeals have held, by analogy to Estelle and Youngberg, that the State may be held liable under the Due Process Clause for failing to protect children in foster homes from mistreatment at the hands of their foster parents. See *Doe v. New York City Dept. of Social Services*, 649 F.2d 134, 141–142 (CA2 1981), after remand, 709 F.2d 782, cert. denied sub nom. Catholic Home *Bureau v. Doe*, 464 U.S. 864 (1983); Taylor ex rel. *Walker v. Ledbetter*, 818 F.2d 791, 794–797 (CA11 1987) (en banc), cert. pending, *Ledbetter v. Taylor*, No. 87-521. We express no view on the validity of this analogy, however, as it is not =before us in the present case.

10. Because we conclude that the Due Process Clause did not require the State to protect Joshua from his father, we need not address respondents' alternative argument that the individual state actors lacked the requisite "state of mind" to make out a due process violation. See *Daniels v. Williams*, 474 U.S. at 334, n. 3. Similarly, we have no occasion to consider whether the individual respondents might be entitled to a qualified immunity defense, see *Anderson v. Creighton*, 483 U.S. 635 (1987), or whether the allegations in the complaint are sufficient to

support a § 1983 claim against the county and DSS under *Monell v. New York City Dept. of Social Services*, 436 U.S. 658 (1978), and its progeny.

BRENNAN, J., Dissenting Opinion

JUSTICE BRENNAN, with whom JUSTICE MARSHALL and JUSTICE BLACKMUN join, dissenting.

"The most that can be said of the state functionaries in this case," the Court today concludes, "is that they stood by and did nothing when suspicious circumstances dictated a more active role for them." Ante, this page. Because I believe that this description of respondents' conduct tells only part of the story, and that, accordingly, the Constitution itself "dictated a more active role" for respondents in the circumstances presented here, I cannot agree that respondents had no constitutional duty to help Joshua DeShaney.

It may well be, as the Court decides, ante at 194–197, that the Due Process Clause, as construed by our prior cases, creates no general right to basic governmental services. That, however, is not the question presented here; indeed, that question was not raised in the complaint, urged on appeal, presented in the petition for certiorari, or addressed in the briefs on the merits. No one, in short, has asked the Court to proclaim that, as a general matter, the Constitution safeguards positive as well as negative liberties.

This is more than a quibble over dicta; it is a point about perspective, having substantive ramifications. In a constitutional setting that distinguishes sharply between action and inaction, one's characterization of the misconduct alleged under § 1983 may effectively decide the case. Thus, by leading off with a discussion (and rejection) of the idea that the Constitution imposes on the States an affirmative duty to take basic care of their citizens, the Court foreshadows—perhaps even preordains—its conclusion that no duty existed even on the specific facts before us. This initial discussion establishes the baseline from which the Court assesses the DeShaneys' claim that, when a State has—"by word and by deed," ante at 197—announced an intention to protect a certain class of citizens, and has before it facts that would trigger that protection under the applicable state law, the Constitution imposes upon the State an affirmative duty of protection.

The Court's baseline is the absence of positive rights in the Constitution and a concomitant suspicion of any claim that seems to depend on such rights. From this perspective, the DeShaneys' claim is first and foremost about inaction (the failure, here, of respondents to take steps to protect Joshua), and only tangentially about action (the establishment of a state program specifically designed to help children like Joshua). And from this perspective, holding these Wisconsin officials liable—where the only difference between this case and one involving a general claim to protective services is Wisconsin's establishment and operation of a program to protect children—would seem to punish an effort that we should seek to promote.

I would begin from the opposite direction. I would focus first on the action that Wisconsin has taken with respect to Joshua and children like him, rather than on the actions that the State failed to take. Such a method is not new to this Court. Both *Estelle v. Gamble*, 429 U.S. 97"] 429 U.S. 97 (1976), and 429 U.S. 97 (1976), and *Youngberg v. Romeo*, 457 U.S. 307 (1982), began by emphasizing that the States had confined J. W. Gamble to prison and Nicholas Romeo to a psychiatric hospital. This initial action rendered these people helpless to help themselves or to seek help from persons unconnected to the government. See Estelle, supra, at 104 ("[I]t is but just that the public be required to care for the prisoner, who cannot, by reason of the deprivation of his liberty, care for himself"); Youngberg, supra, at 317 ("When a person is institutionalized—and wholly dependent on the State—it is conceded by petitioners that a duty to provide certain services and care does exist"). Cases from the lower courts also recognize that a State's actions can be decisive in assessing the constitutional significance of subsequent inaction. For these purposes, moreover, actual physical restraint is not the only state action that has been considered relevant. See, e.g., *White v. Rochford,* 592 F.2d 381 (CA7 1979) (police officers violated due process when, after arresting the guardian of three young children, they abandoned the children on a busy stretch of highway at night).

Because of the Court's initial fixation on the general principle that the Constitution does not establish positive rights, it is unable to appreciate our recognition in Estelle and Youngberg that this principle does not hold true in all circumstances. Thus, in the Court's view, Youngberg can be explained (and dismissed) in the following way:

In the substantive due process analysis, it is the State's affirmative act of restraining the individual's freedom to act on his own behalf—through incarceration, institutionalization, or other similar restraint of personal liberty—which is the "deprivation of liberty" triggering the protections of the Due Process Clause, not its failure to act to protect his liberty interests against harms inflicted by other means.

Ante at 200. This restatement of Youngberg's holding should come as a surprise when one recalls our explicit observation in that case that Romeo did not challenge his commitment to the hospital, but instead argue[d] that he ha[d] a constitutionally protected liberty interest in safety, freedom of movement, and training within the institution; and that petitioners infringed these rights by failing to provide constitutionally required conditions of confinement.

457 U.S. at 315 (emphasis added). I do not mean to suggest that "the State's affirmative act of restraining the individual's freedom to act on his own behalf," ante at 200, was irrelevant in Youngberg; rather, I emphasize that this conduct would have led to no injury, and consequently no cause of action under § 1983, unless the State then had failed to take steps to protect Romeo from himself and from others. In addition, the Court's exclusive attention to state-imposed restraints of "the individual's freedom to act on his own behalf," ante at 200, suggests that it was the State that rendered Romeo unable to care for himself, whereas in fact—with an I.Q. of between

8 and 10, and the mental capacity of an 18-month-old child, 457 U.S. at 309—he had been quite incapable of taking care of himself long before the State stepped into his life. Thus, the fact of hospitalization was critical in Youngberg not because it rendered Romeo helpless to help himself, but because it separated him from other sources of aid that, we held, the State was obligated to replace. Unlike the Court, therefore, I am unable to see in Youngberg a neat and decisive divide between action and inaction.

Moreover, to the Court, the only fact that seems to count as an "affirmative act of restraining the individual's freedom to act on his own behalf" is direct physical control. Ante at 200 (listing only "incarceration, institutionalization, [and] other similar restraint of personal liberty" in describing relevant "affirmative acts"). I would not, however, give Youngberg and Estelle such a stingy scope. I would recognize, as the Court apparently cannot, that "the State's knowledge of [an] individual's predicament [and] its expressions of intent to help him" can amount to a "limitation of his freedom to act on his own behalf" or to obtain help from others. Ante at 200. Thus, I would read Youngberg and Estelle to stand for the much more generous proposition that, if a State cuts off private sources of aid and then refuses aid itself, it cannot wash its hands of the harm that results from its inaction.

Youngberg and Estelle are not alone in sounding this theme. In striking down a filing fee as applied to divorce cases brought by indigents, see *Boddie v. Connecticut*, 401 U.S. 371 (1971), and in deciding that a local government could not entirely foreclose the opportunity to speak in a public forum, see, e.g., *Schneider v. State*, 308 U.S. 147 (1939); *Hague v. Committee for Industrial Organization*, 307 U.S. 496 (1939); *United States v. Grace*, 461 U.S. 171 (1983), we have acknowledged that a State's actions—such as the monopolization of a particular path of relief—may impose upon the State certain positive duties. Similarly, *Shelley v. Kraemer*, 334 U.S. 1 (1948), and *Burton v. Wilmington Parking Authority*, 365 U.S. 715 (1961), suggest that a State may be found complicit in an injury even if it did not create the situation that caused the harm.

Arising as they do from constitutional contexts different from the one involved here, cases like Boddie and Burton are instructive, rather than decisive, in the case before us. But they set a tone equally well established in precedent as, and contradictory to, the one the Court sets by situating the DeShaneys' complaint within the class of cases epitomized by the Court's decision in *Harris v. McRae*, 448 U.S. 297"] 448 U.S. 297 (1980). The cases that I have cited tell us that 448 U.S. 297 (1980). The cases that I have cited tell us that *Goldberg v. Kelly*, 397 U.S. 254] 397 U.S. 254 (1970) (recognizing entitlement to welfare under state laws) can stand side by side with 397 U.S. 254 (1970) (recognizing entitlement to welfare under state laws) can stand side by side with *Dandridge v. Williams*, 397 U.S. 471"] 397 U.S. 471, 484 (1970) (implicitly rejecting idea that welfare is a fundamental right), and that *Goss v. Lopez*, 419 U.S. 565, 573 (1975) (entitlement to public education under state law), is perfectly consistent with 397 U.S. 471, 484 (1970) (implicitly rejecting idea that welfare is a fundamental right), and that *Goss v. Lopez*, 419 U.S. 565, 573 (1975) (entitlement to public education under state law), is perfectly consistent with San Antonio Independent School *Dist. v. Rodriguez*, 411 U.S. 1, 29–39 (1973) (no fundamental right to education). To put the point more directly, these cases signal that a State's prior actions may be decisive in analyzing the constitutional significance of its inaction. I thus would locate the DeShaneys' claims within the framework of cases like Youngberg and Estelle, and more generally, Boddie and Schneider, by considering the actions that Wisconsin took with respect to Joshua.

Wisconsin has established a child welfare system specifically designed to help children like Joshua. Wisconsin law places upon the local departments of social services such as respondent (DSS or Department) a duty to investigate reported instances of child abuse. See Wis.Stat. § 48.981(3) (1987–1988). While other governmental bodies and private persons are largely responsible for the reporting of possible cases of child abuse, see § 48.981(2), Wisconsin law channels all such reports to the local departments of social services for evaluation and, if necessary, further action. § 48.981(3). Even when it is the sheriff's office or police department that receives a report of suspected child abuse, that report is referred to local social services departments for action, see § 48.981(3)(a); the only exception to this occurs when the reporter fears for the child's immediate safety. § 48.981(3)(b). In this way, Wisconsin law invites—indeed, directs—citizens and other governmental entities to depend on local departments of social services such as respondent to protect children from abuse.

The specific facts before us bear out this view of Wisconsin's system of protecting children. Each time someone voiced a suspicion that Joshua was being abused, that information was relayed to the Department for investigation and possible action. When Randy DeShaney's second wife told the police that he had "hit the boy causing marks and [was] a prime case for child abuse," the police referred her complaint to DSS. Ante at 192. When, on three separate occasions, emergency room personnel noticed suspicious injuries on Joshua's body, they went to DSS with this information. Ante at 192–193. When neighbors informed the police that they had seen or heard Joshua's father or his father's lover beating or otherwise abusing Joshua, the police brought these reports to the attention of DSS. App. 144–145. And when respondent Kemmeter, through these reports and through her own observations in the course of nearly 20 visits to the DeShaney home, id. at 104, compiled growing evidence that Joshua was being abused, that information stayed within the Department—chronicled by the social worker in detail that seems almost eerie in light of her failure to act upon it. (As to the extent of the social worker's involvement in, and knowledge of, Joshua's predicament, her reaction to the news of Joshua's last and most devastating injuries is illuminating: "I just knew the phone would ring some day and Joshua would be dead." 812 F.2d 298, 300 (CA7 1987).)

Even more telling than these examples is the Department's control over the decision whether to take steps to protect a particular child from suspected abuse. While many different people contributed information and advice to this decision, it was up to the people at DSS to make the ultimate decision (subject to the approval of the local government's corporation counsel) whether to disturb the family's current arrangements. App. 41, 58. When Joshua first appeared at a local hospital with injuries signaling physical abuse, for example, it was DSS that made the decision to take him into temporary custody for the purpose of studying his situation—and it was DSS, acting in conjunction with the corporation counsel, that returned him to his father. Ante at 192. Unfortunately for Joshua DeShaney, the buck effectively stopped with the Department.

In these circumstances, a private citizen, or even a person working in a government agency other than DSS, would doubtless feel that her job was done as soon as she had reported her suspicions of child abuse to DSS. Through its child welfare program, in other words, the State of Wisconsin has relieved ordinary citizens and governmental bodies other than the Department of any sense of obligation to do anything more than report their suspicions of child abuse to DSS. If DSS ignores or dismisses these suspicions, no one will step in to fill the gap. Wisconsin's child protection program thus effectively confined Joshua DeShaney within the walls of Randy DeShaney's violent home until such time as DSS took action to remove him. Conceivably, then, children like Joshua are made worse off by the existence of this program when the persons and entities charged with carrying it out fail to do their jobs.

It simply belies reality, therefore, to contend that the State "stood by and did nothing" with respect to Joshua. Ante at 203. Through its child protection program, the State actively intervened in Joshua's life and, by virtue of this intervention, acquired ever more certain knowledge that Joshua was in grave danger. These circumstances, in my view, plant this case solidly within the tradition of cases like Youngberg and Estelle.

It will be meager comfort to Joshua and his mother to know that, if the State had "selectively den[ied] its protective services" to them because they were "disfavored minorities," ante at 197, n. 3, their § 1983 suit might have stood on sturdier ground. Because of the posture of this case, we do not know why respondents did not take steps to protect Joshua; the Court, however, tells us that their reason is irrelevant, so long as their inaction was not the product of invidious discrimination. Presumably, then, if respondents decided not to help Joshua because his name began with a "J," or because he was born in the spring, or because they did not care enough about him even to formulate an intent to discriminate against him based on an arbitrary reason, respondents would not be liable to the DeShaneys because they were not the ones who dealt the blows that destroyed Joshua's life.

I do not suggest that such irrationality was at work in this case; I emphasize only that we do not know whether or not it was. I would allow Joshua and his mother the opportunity to show that respondents' failure to help him arose, not out of the sound exercise of professional judgment that we recognized in Youngberg as sufficient to preclude liability, see 457 U.S. at 322–323, but from the kind of arbitrariness that we have in the past condemned. See, e.g., *Daniels v. Williams,* 474 U.S. 327, 331 (1986) (purpose of Due Process Clause was "to secure the individual from the arbitrary exercise of the powers of government" (citations omitted)); *West Coast Hotel Co. v. Parrish,* 300 U.S. 379, 399 (1937) (to sustain state action, the Court need only decide that it is not "arbitrary or capricious"); *Euclid v. Ambler Realty Co.,* 272 U.S. 365, 389 (1926) (state action invalid where it "passes the bounds of reason and assumes the character of a merely arbitrary fiat," quoting *Purity Extract & Tonic Co. v. Lynch,* 226 U.S. 192, 204 (1912)).

Youngberg's deference to a decisionmaker's professional judgment ensures that, once a caseworker has decided, on the basis of her professional training and experience, that one course of protection is preferable for a given child, or even that no special protection is required, she will not be found liable for the harm that follows. (In this way, Youngberg's vision of substantive due process serves a purpose similar to that served by adherence to procedural norms, namely, requiring that a state actor stop and think before she acts in a way that may lead to a loss of liberty.) Moreover, that the Due Process Clause is not violated by merely negligent conduct, see Daniels, supra, and *Davidson v. Cannon,* 474 U.S. 344 (1986), means that a social worker who simply makes a mistake of judgment under what are admittedly complex and difficult conditions will not find herself liable in damages under § 1983.

As the Court today reminds us, the Due Process Clause of the Fourteenth Amendment was intended to prevent government "from abusing [its] power, or employing it as an instrument of oppression."

Ante at 196, quoting Davidson, 474 U.S. at 348. My disagreement with the Court arises from its failure to see that inaction can be every bit as abusive of power as action, that oppression can result when a State undertakes a vital duty and then ignores it. Today's opinion construes the Due Process Clause to permit a State to displace private sources of protection and then, at the critical moment, to shrug its shoulders and turn away from the harm that it has promised to try to prevent. Because I cannot agree that our Constitution is indifferent to such indifference, I respectfully dissent.

JUSTICE BLACKMUN, dissenting.

Today, the Court purports to be the dispassionate oracle of the law, unmoved by "natural sympathy." Ante at 202. But, in this pretense, the Court itself retreats into a sterile formalism which prevents it from recognizing either the facts of the case before it or the legal norms that should apply to those facts. As JUSTICE BRENNAN demonstrates, the facts here involve not mere passivity, but active state intervention in the life of Joshua DeShaney—intervention that triggered a fundamental duty to aid the boy once the State learned of the severe danger to which he was exposed.

The Court fails to recognize this duty because it attempts to draw a sharp and rigid line between action and inaction. But such formalistic reasoning has no place in the interpretation of the broad and stirring Clauses of the Fourteenth Amendment. Indeed, I submit that these Clauses were designed, at least in part, to undo the formalistic legal reasoning that infected antebellum jurisprudence, which the late Professor Robert

Cover analyzed so effectively in his significant work entitled Justice Accused (1975).

Like the antebellum judges who denied relief to fugitive slaves, see id. at 119–121, the Court today claims that its decision, however harsh, is compelled by existing legal doctrine. On the contrary, the question presented by this case is an open one, and our Fourteenth Amendment precedents may be read more broadly or narrowly depending upon how one chooses to read them. Faced with the choice, I would adopt a "sympathetic" reading, one which comports with dictates of fundamental justice and recognizes that compassion need not be exiled from the province of judging. Cf. A. Stone, Law, Psychiatry, and Morality 262 (1984) ("We will make mistakes if we go forward, but doing nothing can be the worst mistake. What is required of us is moral ambition. Until our composite sketch becomes a true portrait of humanity, we must live with our uncertainty; we will grope, we will struggle, and our compassion may be our only guide and comfort").

Poor Joshua! Victim of repeated attacks by an irresponsible, bullying, cowardly, and intemperate father, and abandoned by respondents, who placed him in a dangerous predicament and who knew or learned what was going on, and yet did essentially nothing except, as the Court revealingly observes, ante at 193, "dutifully recorded these incidents in [their] files." It is a sad commentary upon American life, and constitutional principles—so full of late of patriotic fervor and proud proclamations about "liberty and justice for all," that this child, Joshua DeShaney, now is assigned to live out the remainder of his life profoundly retarded. Joshua and his mother, as petitioners here, deserve—but now are denied by this Court—the opportunity to have the facts of their case considered in the light of the constitutional protection that 42 U.S.C. § 1983 is meant to provide.

NOTES

Chapter One

1. The account of what transpired on January 23, 1983, when Joshua was brought into the emergency room at Theda Clark comes from deposition of the various parties in deposition testimony contained in the *Joint Appendix* to the record submitted to United States Supreme Court.

2. The account of Thomas Hoare's movements and views are taken from his deposition testimony found in the Joint Appendix, pp. 42–63 and from local newspaper stories regarding the Department of Social Services.

3. Keith Nelson gave his account of his involvement in deposition testimony. See the Joint Appendix, pp. 64–72.

4. The almost happenstance involvement of Anne Kemmeter's initial involvement in the story is taken from deposition testimony found in the Joint Appendix, p. 35.

5. The Oshkosh and Milwaukee public libraries contain extensive histories and documents on the Fox River valley, its towns and cities, and the fascinating people whose lives and adventures form the region's story.

6. The observations regarding Randy and Marie's parenting skills are found in Memo to Juvenile Court Intake, January 27, 1983, p. 2.

Chapter Two

1. The "Little Mary Ellen" story is found in the *New York Times*, December 24, 1873, p. 6; December 25, 1873, pp. 3 and 8; April 10, 1874, p. 8; December 5, 1920, p. 16; and December 12, 1921, p. 15.

2. The New York Society for the Prevention of Cruelty to Children, 44th Annual Report, December 31, 1918.

3. For a discussion of the evolution of the public response to the private abuse of children, see "The Rediscovery of Child Abuse," Stephen Antler, in *The Social Context of Child Abuse and Neglect*, ed. Leroy H. Pelton (New York: Human Science Press, 1981).

4. *The Social Work Yearbook: 1929*, Fred S. Hall, editor, Russell Sage Foundation, New York, 1930, p. 66.

5. For a review of circumstances attending the rediscovery of child abuse see, *The Battered Child*, ed. Ray Holfer and C. Henry Kempe (Chicago and London: University of Chicago Press, 1974).

6. The *New York Times* estimates were similar to those appearing in many publications.

7. The *Time* magazine piece appeared on July 20, 1962, and the *Saturday Evening Post* article on October 6, 1962.

8. Despite the reporting laws, some doctors were reluctant to report abuse, the *New York Times*, February 19, 1965, p. 37. See also Richard Light, "Abused and Neglected Children in America: A Study of Alternative Policies," *Harvard Educational Review* 43 (1973), pp. 556–98.

9. For a brief comment on some of the social work studies on removal published in the 1980s, see "Child Protection: With Liberty and Justice for All," Marion Huxtable, *Social Work* 39, no. 1, January 1994, pp. 60–66.

10. See also "Resocializing Abusive Parents," Margot Breton, *Social Work* 26, no. 2 (March 1981): 119–24.

11. The account of the Team Meeting is taken from accounts given by various parties as set forth in the Joint Appendix.

12. This memo is identified as Attachment I in the case file. It contains the name of the dispatcher and a complaint number. Alternatively, see Court Referral-Juvenile, FS-17576-CW.

Chapter Three

1. The record of this visit is taken from the Joint Appendix submitted as part of the United States Supreme Court filing. Statements regarding other visits can be found in other filings in the Intervening Narrative, FS-17560-CW, pp. 12, 13, and 14.

2. The review of Anne Kemmeter's background is taken from the Joint Appendix.

3. See, for example, James Tracy and Elizabeth Clark, *Social Work*, "Treatment of Child Abusers" (May 1974): 338–42, and other works previously cited.

4. The record of contacts between the Social Service Department and Randy is drawn from the Joint Appendix, pp. 116–21.

5. The account of Melody's circumstance on surrendering Joshua is taken from the Joint Appendix, pp. 73–77.

6. For a sense of the emotional impact of cascading events on Melody see the *New York Times Magazine* profile, October 2, 1988.

7. See Michael Lesy, *Wisconsin Death Trip* (New York: Knopf Doubleday, 1976). This work provides a sense of the terror lurking just below the surface of the normal, the unseen madness poised to lunge at the innocent passerby.

8. The record of the visits in May and June of 1983 is taken from the Joint Appendix, pp. 108, 116, and 129.

9. The Service Plan Review can be found in the Joint Appendix, pp. 115–17.

10. See the Joint Appendix, p. 91.

11. See the Joint Appendix throughout and the Service Plan Review for the record of contacts between the Social Service Department and Randy. See also the Intervening Narrative, FS-17576.

12. See the Joint Appendix, p. 120.

13. See the Joint Appendix, p. 145.

14. An account of the last visit can be found in the Joint Appendix, pp. 130–31.

15. See the Joint Appendix, p. 129.

16. See the Joint Appendix, p. 131.

Chapter Four

1. See the Joint Appendix, pp. 120–30 for an account of what transpired at the hospital the night of Joshua's operation.

Chapter Five

1. The evens in the period immediately following Joshua's operation, including the first contact with Melody, are recounted in the Joint Appendix, pp. 120–30.

2. Both Melody and her mother gave deposition testimony claiming that Kemmeter told them the she feared picking up the phone one day and hearing that Joshua was dead, the Joint Appendix, pp. 107–08; Kemmeter denied in deposition testimony and in the local newspaper that she made such a statement.

3. The circumstances attending Melody's surrender of Joshua and her strained relationship with him and her in-laws afterward are recounted in the Joint Appendix and a *New York Times Magazine* profile, October 2, 1988.

4. There are summaries of Joshua's medical condition in the Joint Appendix, pp. 131–35.

5. The legal proceedings against Randy are recounted in the Joint Appendix, pp. 135–36. See also the *State of Wisconsin v. Randy E. DeShaney*. See "Menasha Man Faces Abuse Charge," in the *Northwestern*, June 20, 1984, for a summary of the testimony by Letellier and Kerali and Thomas Fink's defense of Randy.

6. *DeShaney* was both a series of events and a mood, a tone, a mournful refrain on the human condition. That mood, tone, and refrain link the events Michael Lesy recounts in *Wisconsin Death Trip* and the events that transpired eighty years later in the same towns and valleys.

7. Don Sullivan was interviewed in September of 2001. All references to his observations and comments come from that interview.

8. Curry First was interviewed in 1999 and 2001. All references to his observations and comments come from those interviews.

9. The Eli Creekmore story appeared in the *New York Times*, December 31, 1988. The tragedy led to the building of a center in Seattle for abused children.

Chapter Six

1. The Complaint, the Answer, and various other documents can be found in the Seventh Circuit District Court of Appeals case file.

2. The abstracts relative to those similarly situated can be found in the *Northwestern* newspaper, November 18, 1984.

3. See the *New York Times*, April 14, 1988, p. 33.

4. See the *New York Times*, February 4, 1989, p. 6.

5. The account of the whistle-blower punished for bringing childcare failures to public attention appears in the *New York Times*, April 25, 1984.

6. The low cap was cited by Sullivan and First in various documents relative to the inadequacy of a state remedy.

7. Don Sullivan commented on his impression of Kemmeter in a 2001 interview.

8. See p. 109 of the Joint Appendix relative to testimony about the joint visits to the DeShaney household.

9. The bitterness seeping through can be inferred from comments in the transcripts of deposition testimony from the main parties. For Hoar's entire deposition, see the Joint Appendix, pp. 42–64.

10. Thomas Hoare, the reference with regard to Randy's interaction with Joshua appears on p. 55 of the Joint Appendix.

11. For Keith Nelson's entire deposition, see the Joint Appendix, pp. 64–72.

12. See the Joint Appendix, Exhibit F, regarding Gehringer's testimony.

13. See the Joint Appendix, Exhibit G, regarding this testimony.

14. Melody's entire deposition can be found in the Joint Appendix, pp. 73–84.

15. The Brief in Support of Motion to Dismiss can be found in the District Court file.

16. See the Brief in Support of the Motion to Dismiss.

Chapter Seven

1. Curry First's answer to the Motion to Dismiss provides an excellent recapitulation of the case that would be put before a jury on behalf of Joshua and Melody.

2. The essential posture of both sides had been established by this point. The tension lied in getting a firm trial date and in waiting for Judge Reynolds's response to the motion to dismiss.

3. The Defendant's Proposed Jury Instructions can be found in the District Court case file.

4. John Reynolds's Decision and Order started the case on the way to the United States Supreme Court.

5. See the Decision and Order, throughout.

6. The Bill of Cost, Docket No. 85-C-0310, seeks compensation for the costs attending taking depositions, photocopying, and what were termed "witness and service fees."

7. There is a voluminous body of writing by and on Richard Posner, including "Judging the Judges," a review of Posner's *Divergent Paths: The Academy and the Judiciary, New York Times Book Review*, January 31, 2016.

8. See "Free Market Jurist," *Newsweek*, June 10, 1985, p. 93, for a brief description of Posner's office and working habits.

9. Posner's decision appears in 812 F2d 298 (1987).

Chapter Eight

1. The *New York Times*, February 22, 1987, ran a two-page story on the Lazarovich tragedy. Multiple agencies were involved, none of which seemed to be in touch with any of the others.

2. State of Bailey v. Oare, 768 Fd2d 503 (1985).

3. The Elena Kagan story received attention at the time of her confirmation hearings for a seat on the Supreme Court. Some of her critics claimed it showed she would be influenced by emotion rather than the dictates of the law.

4. The *New York Times*, "High Court to Decide on Liability of Local Officials in Child Abuse," March 22, 1987, p. A21.

5. The *New York Times* ran the Stewart story on March 29, 1988. At last report Wayne was in good condition in Bronx Lebanon Hospital.

6. The Easter egg hunt is an annual event sponsored by the Oshkosh Jaycees and various local businesses.

7. The file on the *DeShaney* case in the Supreme Court library has the exchange of correspondences between the parties regarding extensions of time and other matters.

8. This is drawn from the interview with Sullivan in October of 2001.

9. Copies of Melody's letter to Judge Williams can be found in the case file for *DeShaney* in the Supreme Court library.

10. The account of the call to Judge Williams was offered by Curry First in interviews conducted in 1999 and 2001.

11. Don Sullivan recounted his impression of Melody on the eve of the Supreme Court battle in my interview with him in the fall of 2001.

12. Biographical material on Chief Justice Rehnquist is plentiful, for an account of the changes in judicial philosophy in the years that saw Rehnquist's rise to the chief justice position see David Savage, *Turning Right: The Making of the Rehnquist Court* (New York: John Wiley and Sons, 1992).

13. For an account of Blackmun's life and times see Linda Greenhouse, *Becoming Justice Blackmun* (New York: Henry Holt and Company, 2005).

14. A tape of the oral argument before the Supreme Court was obtained from the National Archives.

15. See Joan Biskupic, *Sandra Day O'Connor* (New York: Harper Collins, 2005).

16. An account of Scalia's life and times can be found in Joan Biskupic's *American Original: The Life and Constitution of Supreme Court Justice Antonin Scalia* (New York: Farrar, Straus and Giroux, 2009).

17. Among the other entities filing Friend of the Court briefs in support of Winnebago County were the National Association of Counties and allied bodies, including the United States Conference of Mayors, the National Conference of State Legislatures, the U.S. Conference of Mayors, the National League of Cities, and the International City Management Association.

18. The Michael Anthony Baker tragedy was reported in the *New York Times*, January 20, 1989.

19. The notes the justices exchanged were reproduced from the Manuscript Division of the Library of Congress, Washington, DC.

20. The Jessica Cortez story, "Court Did Not Get Report of Neglect," appeared in the *New York Times*, December 20, 1988, pp. 1 and 4, Sections A and B, and on January 21, 1989, pp. 29–30, Section Two.

21. There are several books on the career of Thurgood Marshall; for an account of his views in his own words see *Thurgood Marshall*, ed. Mark Tushnet (Chicago: Lawrence Hill Books, 2001).

22. The opinion is *DeShaney v. Winnebago County Department of Social Services*, 489 U.S. 189 (1989).

23. Brennan's dissent in *DeShaney v. Winnebago County Department of Social Services*, 489 U.S. 189 (1989), for a biographical account of Brennan see Kim Isaak Eisler, *A Justice for All* (New York: Simon and Shuster, 1993).

24. For an excellent exposition on Blackmun's philosophy, see David Savage, "Often in Dissent, Blackmun Was 'Voice for the Outsider,'" *Los Angeles Times*, April 7, 1994, p. 1. See also Blackman's dissent in *DeShaney v. Winnebago County Department of Social Services*, 489 U.S. 189 (1989) in terms of his distinctive voice.

25. See Linda Greenhouse, "At a Shrine of American Documents, Pathos, Poetry and Blackmun's Rosebud," *New York Times*, March 7, 2004, p. 7.

26. The comments of nationally syndicated columnist Ellen Goodman in support of the majority decision appeared in the February 26, 1989 edition of the *Post Crescent*, the local Oshkosh-area newspaper.

27. See "Where Reverence for the Family Must End," the *Chicago Sun Times*, March 27, 1988, p. 15.

28. Debbie Ratterman, No Constitutional Right to Protection," *Off Our Backs: A Womens' News Journal* 19, no. 6 (June 30, 1989): 8.

29. See Jim Fain, "Does Blind Justice Shed Tears for Joshua?" the *Austin American Statesman*, March 1, 1989, p. A 14.

30. Laurence Tribe, "My Most Famous Students: President Obama and Justice Roberts," *Newsweek* online, www.Newsweek, July 9, 2012, and "Constitional Physics," New York Times, May 12, 1989, p. B11.

31. See the Oshkosh *Northwestern*, February 23, 1989, for a strong editorial defense of the majority decision. For Anne Kemmeter's reaction to the Supreme Court decision, see "DeShaney Case Worker Ends Silence" in the *Post-Crescent*, February 24, 1989, and "Five Year Ordeal for Social Worker," in the Oshkosh *Northwestern*, 1989, p. 28 n, February 24, 1989, pp. 1 and 2.

32. In general, the Social Work profession has been conflicted over the years about *DeShaney*. Some see it as lifting a burden; others see it as creating a risk structure that favors inaction.

33. Years later when contacted, Melody still found these chapters in her life too painful to relive.

34. Don Sullivan's comment appeared in the *Post-Crescent*, February 23, 1989, p. 2.

Chapter Nine

1. The Christian Cisneros story was chronicled by Dan Wilson in a series of articles in the *Post-Crescent* newspapers: "A Lonely Death: Toddler's Short Life Marred by Alleged Abuse," "Child Abuse Cases Pose Challenge as Social Workers Make Decisions," and "Reports Show a History of Injuries in Life of Christian Cisneros," all posted, March 9, 2003, and "Review Urges New Methods in Abuse Cases," posted April 10, 2003.

2. The director of the Menasha district office of the Children's Service Society of Wisconsin was quoted to this effect in the *Post-Crescent*, February 23, 1989.

3. See Powell v. Georgia Department of Human Resources, 114 F3rd 1074 (11th Cir. 1997).

4. Simpson v. Masten Childers, 71 F.3d 1182 (6th Cir. 1995).

5. See White v. Chambliss, 112 F3d 731 (4th Cir. 1997).

6. The Larry and Gary Bass holding can be obtained by accessing the 8th Circuit Court of Appeals site. Their mother and her line-in-partner were responsible for the horrific occurrences.

7. Pinder, Carol v. Johnson, Donald, 54 F.3d 1169 (CA4 1995).

8. Balistreri v. Pacific Police Dept., 901 F2d 696 (9th Cir. 1990).

9. See Flor Maria Soto v. Carlos Flores, et al., No. 96-1024, United States Court of Appeals for the First Circuit.

10. Jane Doe v. Covington County School District, United States Court of Appeals, 5th Circuit, filed March 23, 2012, p. 31.

11. D.R. v. Middle Bucks Area Vocational Technical School, 972 E.2d 1364 (3 Cir. 1992).

12. Brum v. Town of Dartmouth, 690 NE2d 844 (Mass. App. Ct. 1998).

13. Niziol v. Pasco Count School Board, 2002 WL31063883 (M.D. Florida, August 9, 2002).

14. See Estate of Montana Lance v. Lewisville Ind. School District, 5th Circ. Court of Appeals, No 12-41139, decided February 28, 2014, and references other relevant *DeShaney* cases.

15. LaGuardia v. Ross Township (Middle District, Pa., November 10, 2016).

16. Estate of Jimm Pal Peat, et al. v. Rodriguez, United States Court of Appeals, 10th Circuit, August 12, 2016, p. 12.

17. See NASW brief submitted in City of New York v. Sonny Southerland available on NASW website along with NASW briefs submitted in other cases.

18. See David Murley, "Private Enforcement of the Social Contract: *DeShaney* and the Second Amendment Right to Own Firearms," *Duquesne Law Review*, Summer 1998, p. 827.

19. GunsSaveLives.Net, "Supreme Court Ruling: Police Have No Duty to Protect the General Public," January 28, 2013.

20. National Clearinghouse on Child Abuse and Neglect Information, "Child Maltreatment 2002: Summary of Key Findings" and Department of Health and Human Services data, 2010.

21. David Olinger published a series of articles in the *Denver Post*: "The Loss of Innocents," "Child-Protection Failings Detailed" and "Little Girl's Fate Leaves a Trail of Accusations," January 18, 2004, and "Neglect Abuse Warnings Led to 12 Deaths in El Paso," January 19, 2004.

22. The *Philadelphia News + Opinion*, May 25, 2016.

23. David Olinger, the Denver Post, "Little Girls Fate Leaves Trail of Accusations," June 7, 2005.

24. See the *New York Daily News*, "Dad Left Myls Dobson, 4, in Care of Girlfriend . . . ," January 10, 2014.

25. For the Zymire Perkins story see the *New York Times*, September 29, 2016, October 6, 2016, and December 14, 2016.

26. James Kilpatrick, "The Case of the Schoolyard Bully," the *Tulsa World*, July 16, 2001.

27. Dale Margolin Cecka, "It's Time For the 4th Circuit to Rethink DeShaney," *South Carolina Law Review* 67, no. 679 (2016).

28. Linda Greenhouse, the *New York Times*, Opinion pages, June 17, 2010.

Chapter Ten

1. "Cries for Help for Jeanette Maples Got No Answer," Susan Goldsmith, the *Oregonian*, January 2, 2010.

2. Kelli M. Mulder-Westrate, "Waiting for the Justice League: Motivating Child Welfare Agencies to Save Children," *Notre Dame Law Review* 88, no. 532 (2012).

3. Aviam Soifer, "Moral Ambition, Formalism and the 'Free World' of DeShaney," *George Washington Law Review* 57, no. 1513 (1989).

4. Peter Edelman, "Boy Abused by Father Becomes Another Victim of High Court's Callousness," *The Manhattan Lawyer*, March 28, 1989, p. 14.

5. Anita Binayifaal, "Reexamining School Liability and the Viability of a Special Relationship Claim in the Aftermath of *DeShaney v. Winnebago County Department of Social Services*," *St. John's Law Review* 87, no. 4 (2015): 1092.

6. Montgomery v. City of Ames, 8th Circuit Court of Appeals, No. 13-2111, decided, April 10, 2014.

7. An array of decisions were offered against Warren, Brennan and other members of the Court as evidence of their dangerous radicalism including those having to do with the rights of the criminally accused and decisions supporting minority rights.

8. Jeff Shesol, "Opening the Door to a Conservative Court," the *New York Times*, June 22, 2016, in a review of *The Burger Court and the Rise of the Judicial Right*, by Michael Graetz and Linda Greenhouse.

9. See John Howard, *The Shifting Wind: The Supreme Court and Civil Rights from Reconstruction to Brown* (Albany: SUNY Press, 1999); in his early decades on the Court Holmes differed little from those of the justices who supported segregation, but in the 1920s in Nixon v. Herndon and in *Dempsey v. Moore* his jurisprudence showed a greater understanding of the savage realities inherent in racial segregation. See also John Robert's majority opinion, *Foster v. Chatman*, 578 U.S. (2016).

10. Erwin Chermerinsky makes the same point in "Government Duty to Protect: Post DeShaney Developments," *Touro Law Review* 19, no. 3 (2015), 679–705.

11. Thomas Eaton and Michael Wells, "Government Inaction as a Constitutional Tort," *Washington Law Review* 66 (1991): 119.

12. Liliya Abramchayev, "A Social Contract Argument for the State's Duty to Protect from Private Violence," *Journal of Civil Rights and Economic Development* 18, no. 3 (2004): 867.

13. Eaton and Wells, *Washington Law Review*, 119.

14. Laura Rae Dove, "A Constitutional Right to Police Protection and Classical Liberal Theory: Complement, Not Conflict," *Akron Journal of Constitutional Law and Policy* 4, no. 37 (2012), quoting Professor Oren.

15. Dove, *ConLawNow: An Online Journal of Constitutional Issues* (2012–2013): 55, quoting Professor Oren.

16. There is extensive discussion in the law review literature, including Kay Kindred, "God Bless the Child: Poor Children, *Parens Patriae*, and a State Obligation to Provide Assistance," Scholarly Works, Paper 52, http: scholars.lawunlv.edu/facpub/52.

17. Aileen Bigelow, "In the Ghetto: The State's Duty to Protect Inner-City Children from Violence," 7 *Notre Dame Journal of Law, Ethics and Public Policy*: 567.

18. Schall v. Martin, 467 *U.S.* 253, 365 (1984).

19. John Howard, "Rearguing DeShaney," *Thomas M. Cooley Law Review* 18, no. 3 (2001).

20. Akhil Amar and Daniel Widawsky, "Child Abuse as Slavery: A Thirteenth Amendment Response to DeShaney," *Harvard Law Review* 105: 1359, 1376.

21. Kristin Davenport, "Due Process—Claims of Abused Children against State Protective Agencies—The State's Responsibility after *DeShaney v. Winnebago*

Count Dep't of Soc. Serv., 489 U.S. 189 (1989)," *Florida State University Law Review* (1991): 243, 246.

22. Breaden Douthett, "The Death of Constitutional Duty: The Court Reacts to the Expansion of Section 1983 Liability in *DeShaney v. Winnebago County Dep't of Soc. Serv.*," *Ohio State Law Journal* 52 (1991): 643.

23. Rudolph Alexander, "The Legal Liability of Social Workers after *DeShaney*," *Social Work* 38, no. 1: 64. It is unlikely that states will increase the damage amount that could be sought under state law, there being little probability they will increase their own potential financial exposure.

24. Kelli Mulder-Westrate, "Waiting for the Justice League: Motivating Child Welfare Agencies to Save Children," *Notre Dame Law Review* 88 (2012): 536.

25. Kelli Mulder-Westrate, Waiting for the Justice League: Motivating Child Welfare Agencies to Save Children," *Notre Dame Law Review* 88 (2012): 550.

26. Kelli Mulder-Westrare, "Waiting for the Justice League: Motivating Agencies to Save Children," *Notre Dame Law Review* 88 (2012).

27. Lynne Curry, *The* DeShaney *Case: Child Abuse, Family Rights, and the Dilemma of State Intervention* (University Press of Kansas, 2007, Lawrence, Kansas).

28. At its heart the *DeShaney* case goes to the purposes of law and the Constitution. Was Rehnquist's jurisprudence, presented as a sober and dispassionate reading of the Constitution, simply an arcane rationalization for and justification of prevailing, inequitable distributions of status and power? Within this framework "law" has no necessary relationship to "justice." Many sense that there is something fundamentally wrong with the *DeShaney* decision on many levels. A *DeShaney* community would address this case and much more.

BIBLIOGRAPHY

Books, Journals, and Newspapers

Abramchayev, Liliya. "A Social Contract Argument for the State's Duty to Protect from Private Violence." *Journal of Civil Rights and Economic Development* 18, no. 3 (2004).

Adederin, Atinuke. "The State-Created Danger Doctrine in Domestic Violence Cases: Do We Have a Solution in Okin v. Village of Cornwall-on-Hudson Police Department?" *Columbia Journal of Gender and Law* 20, no. 1 (2011): 1.

Alexander, Ralph. "The Liability of Social Workers after *DeShaney*." *Social Work* 38, no. 1 (1993): 64–68.

Amar, Akhil Reed, and Daniel Widawsky. "Child Abuse as Slavery: A Thirteenth Amendment Response to DeShaney." *Harvard Law Review* 105 (1992): 1359.

Antler, Stephen. "The Rediscovery of Child Abuse." In *The Social Context of Child Abuse and Neglect*, edited by Leroy H. Pelton. New York: Human Science Press, 1981.

Bethel, Alison. "Keeping Schools Safe: Why Schools Should Have an Affirmative Duty to Protect Students from Harm by Other Students." *Pierce Law Review* 183 (2004). http://scholars.unh.edu/unh_lr/vol2/iss2/7.

Bigelow, Aileen M. "In the Ghetto: The State's Duty to Protect Inner-City Children from Violence." *Notre Dame Journal of Law, Ethics & Public Policy* 7 (1993): 533.

Binayifaal, Anita. "Reexamining School Liability and the Viability of a Special Relationship Claim in the Aftermath of *DeShaney v. Winnebago County Department of Social Services*." *St. John's Law Review* 87, no. 4 (2015): 1092.

Biskupic, Joan. *Sandra Day O'Connor.* New York: Harper Collins, 2005.

———. *American Original: The Life and Constitution of Supreme Court Justice Antonin Scalia.* New York: Farrar, Straus, and Giroux, 2009.

Breton, Margot. "Resocializing Abusive Parents." *Social Work* 26, no. 2 (1981): 119–24.

Cecka, Dan Margolin. "It's Time for the Fourth Circuit to Rethink DeShaney." *South Carolina Law Review* 67, no. 4 (2016).

Chemerinsky, Erwin. "Government Duty to Protect: Post-DeShaney Developments." *Touro Law Review* 19, no. 3 (2015).

Corry, John, "A Somber Daily Round of Child Abuse Cases, *New York Times*, February 12, 1985.

Curry, Lynne. *The* DeShaney *Case: Child Abuse, Family Rights, and the Dilemma of State Intervention.* University Press of Kansas, Lawrence, Kansas, 2007.

Davenport, Kristin. "Due Process—*Claims of Abused Children against State Protective Agencies—The State's Responsibility after DeShaney v. Winnebago County Department of Social Services,* 489 U.S. 189 (1989)." *Florida State University Law Review* 19 (1991): 243, 246.

Diner, Hasia R. *Service and Scholarship: Seventy-Five Years of the School of Social Service Administration of the University of Chicago, 1908–1983.* Chicago: University of Chicago, 1985.

Douthett, Breaden. "The Death of Constitutional Duty: The Court Reacts to the Expansion of Section 1983 Liability in DeShaney v. Winnebago County Departmentt of Social. Services." *Ohio State Law Journal* 52 (1991): 643.

Dove, Laura Rae. "A Constitutional Right to Police Protection and Classical Liberal Theory: Complement, Not Conflict." *Akron Journal of Constitutional Law and Policy* 4 (2013): 37.

Eaton, Thomas, and Michael Wells. "Government Inaction as a Constitutional Tort." *Washington Law Review* 66 (1991): 119.

Edelman, Peter. "Boy Abused by Father Becomes Another Victim of High Court's Callousness." *Manhattan Lawyer* 14 (March 18, 1989).

Egan, Timothy, "Child Abuse Cses Draw New Attention," *New York Times,* January 1, 1988.

Eisler, Kim Isaak. *A Justice for All.* New York: Simon and Shuster, 1993.

The Encyclopedia of Social Work, New York, National Association of Social Workers, 16th ed., vol. 2, 1971, Robert Mulford, "Protective Services for Children."

Fox Cities: Your Guide to Activities in Wisconsin's Fox Cities. Fall/Winter 1997. Fox Cities Convention and Visitors Bureau. Appleton, Wisconsin.

Gil, David G. *Violence against Children: Physical Child Abuse in the United States.* Cambridge: Mass.: Harvard University Press, 1970.

Greenhouse, Linda. *Becoming Justice Blackmun.* New York: Henry Holt and Company, 2005.

———."Correspondence/The Blackmun Papers: At a Shrine of American Documents, Pathos, Poetry and Blackmun's 'Rosebud,' " March 4, 2004.

———. "Justices Rule Police Do Not Have a Constitutional Duty to Protect Someone." *New York Times,* June 28, 2005.

———. "A Second Chance for Joshua." *New York Times,* June 17, 2010.

———. "The Supreme Court and a Life Barely Lived." *New York Times,* January 7, 2016.

Kilpatrick, James. "The Case of the Schoolyard Bully." *Tulsa World,* July 16, 2001.

Hall, Fred. S., ed. *The Social Work Yearbook.* New York, Russell Sage Foundation, 1929.

Harris Cohn, Ann. "Effective Treatment of Child Abuse and Neglect." *Social Work* 24, no. 6 (1979): 513–19.

Hofler, Raye, and C. Henry Kempe, *The Battered Child.* Chicago and London: University of Chicago Press, 1974.

Howard, John. "Rearguing DeShaney," *Thomas M. Cooley Law Review* 18, no. 3 (2001).

Hovland, Lindsey. "Due Process—Fifth Circuit Incorrectly Holds School Lacks DeShaney Special Relationship with Students."*Southern Methodist University Law Review* 66 (2013): 385.

Huxtable, Marion. "Child Protection: With Liberty and Justice for All." *Social Work* 39, no. 1 (1994).

Kearney, Mary Kate. "DeShaney's Legacy in Foster Care and Public School Settings." *Washburn Law Journal* (2002): 275–97.

Kindred, Kay P. "God Bless the Child: Poor Children, Parens Patriae, and a State Obligation to Provide Assistance." (1996.) Scholarly Works paper 52, http://scholars.lawunlv.edu/facpub/52.

Kurtz, Russell H., ed. *Social Work Yearbook 1954: A Description of Organized Activities in Social Work and Related Fields*, 12th ed. New York: American Association of Social Workers, 1954.

LeMoyne, James, "Inquiry Faults City Agencies in Child Abuse Cases," *New York Times*, April 24, 1984.

Lesy, Michael. *Wisconsin Death Trip*. New York: Knopf Doubleday, 1973.

Levin, Michael. "A Revolution in Liability for State-Created Danger." *Pennsylvania School Board Association Bulletin* (2000): 33–40.

Light, Richard. "Abused and Neglected Children in America: A Study of Alternative Policies." *Harvard Educational Review* 43 (1973).

MacNaughton, James. "Positive Rights in Constitutional Law: No Need to Graft, Best Not to Prune." *University of Pennsylvania Journal of Constitutional Law* 3 (2001): 750.

Mulder-Westrate, Kelli. "Waiting for the Justice League: Motivating Child Welfare Agencies to Save Children." *Notre Dame Law Review* 88 (2012): 532.

Murley, David. "Private Enforcement of the Social Contract: DeShaney and the Second Amendment Right to Own Firearms." *Duquesne Law Review* (Summer1998): 827.

New York City Health and Hospitals Corporation. *Suspected Child Abuse and Neglect: Protocol for Identification, Reporting, and Treatment*. Author, 1991. The New York Society for the Prevention of Cruelty to Children, 44th Annual Report, December 31, 1918.

New York Times. "Christmas Week." December 24, 1873, p. 6.

———. "Work of the St. John's Guild." December 25, 1873, p. 3.

———. "Charitable Institutions." December 25, 1873, p. 8.

———. "Mr. Bergh Enlarging the Sphere of Usefulness." April 10, 1874, p. 8.

———. "Little Mary Ellen Finally Disposed of." December 12, 1874.

———. "Protection for Children." December 17, 1874.

———. "Caring for Children." January 27, 1880, p. 1.

———. "First Rescued Girl Facilitates S.P.C.C." December 5, 1920, p. 16.

———. "Mrs. E.A. Wheeler, Child Rescuer, Dies." December 12, 1921, p. 15.

———. "City Finds Doctors Reluctant to Report Child Abuse Cases." February 19, 1965, p. 37.

———. "2-Year-Old's Skull Fracture Is Traced to Bureaucratic Errors." March 15, 1987.

———. "High Court to Decide on Liability of Local Officials in Child Abuse." March 22, 1987, p. A21.

———. "Mother Held in Second Child Abuse Case." March 29, 1988.

———. "Ex-Case Workers Indicted in Deaths of Infants." April 14, 1988, p. 33.

———. "Determined to be Heard." October 2, November 13, 1988.

———. "Philadelphia Agency for Young Loses Permit." February 4, 1989, p. 6.

———. "The Supreme Court: Statements on Retirement of Blackmun from Court." April 7, 1994.

The Northwestern. "Menasha Man Faces Abuse Charge." June 20, 1984.

Olinger, David. *Denver Post*, "Neglect Abuse Warnings Led to 12 Deaths in El Paso." January 19, 2004.

———. *Denver Post*. "Mom Sues Agency in Drowning." May 13, 2005.

Oren, Laura E. "The State's Failure to Protect Children and Substantive Due Process: DeShaney in Context." *North Carolina Law Review* 68 (1990): 659.

Roosevelt, Kermit. "Judging the Judges." A review of Posner's *Divergent Paths: The Academy and the Judiciary. New York Times*, January 31, 2016, p. BR 13.
Savage, David. *Turning Right: The Making of the Rehnquist Court.* New York: John Wiley and Sons, 1992.
———. "Often in Dissent, Blackmun Was 'Voice of the Outsider,' *Los Angeles Times*, April 7, 1994.
Shesol, Jeff. "Opening the Door to a Conservative Court." *New York Times*, June 22, 2016.
Snead, Lisa, "Domestic Violence Litigation in the Wake of DeShaney and Castle Rock." *Texas Journal of Women and the Law*. 18, no. 2 (Spring 2009): 305.
Sofier, Aviam. "Moral Ambition, Formalism and the 'Free World' of DeShaney." *George Washington Law Review* 57 (1989): 1513.
Tracy, James, and Clark, Elizabeth. "Treatment of Child Abusers, *Social Work* (May 1974): 338–42.
Tribe, Laurence, Constitutional Physics," *New York Times*, May 12, 1989, p. B11.
Tushnet, Mark, ed. *Thurgood Marshall*. Chicago: Lawrence Hill Books, 2001.
Zietz, Dorothy. *Child Welfare: Principles and Methods*. New York: John Wiley & Sons. 1959.

Cases and Court Records

Balistreri v. Pacific Police Dept., 901 F.2d 696 (9th Cir. 1990).
Brum v. Town of Dartmouth, 690 NE.2d 844 (Mass. App. Ct.1998).
DeShaney v. Winnebago County Department of Social Services, 489 U.S. 189 (1989).
DeShaney v. Winnebago County Department of Social Services, 812 F.2d 298 (1987)
DeShaney v. Winnebago County Department of Social Services, Decision and Order, United States District Court, Eastern District of Wisconsin (1986).
D.R. v. Middle Bucks Area Vocational Technical School, 972 E.2d 1364 (3rd Cir. 1992).
Estate of Bailey v. Oare, 768 Fd.2d 503 (1985).
Estate of B.I.C. v. Gillen, 702 F.3d 1182 (10th Cir. 2012).
Estate of Jimma Pal Reat v. Rodriguez, 824 F.3d 960 (10th Cir. 2016).
Estate of Montana Lance v. Lewisville Ind. School District, 743 F.3d 982 (5th Cir. 2014).
Flor Maria Soto v. Carlos Flores, 103 F.3d 1056 (1st Cir. 1997).
Forrester v. Dixon, 397 F.3rd 1047 (8th Cir. 2005).
Foster v. Chatman, 587 U.S. (2016).
Jensen v. Anderson County Department of Social Services, 304 S.C. 195, 403 S.E.2d 615 (1991).
Horridge v. St. Mary's Count, 854 A.2d 1232 (MD Ct. App. 2004).
Joint Appendix: The Supreme Court of the United States, October Term 1987, DeShaney v. Winnebago Count Department of Social Services, no. 87-154.
LaGuardia v. Ross Township, Civil Action, 3:15-01475 (Pennsylvania Middle District Court 2016).
Lance v. Lewisville Independent School District, F.3d WL 805452 (5th Circ. 2014).
Magee v. Covington School District, 675 F.3d 849 (5th Cir. 2012).
Montgomery v. City of Ames, 829 F.3d 968 (8th Cir. 2016).

Niziol v. Pasco County School Board, 240 F. Supp. 2d 1194 (U.S. District Court, Middle District, Florida 2002).
Pinder, Carol v. Johnson, Donald, 54 F.3d 1169 (4th Cir. 1995).
Powell v. Georgia Department of Human Resources, 114 F.3d 1074 (11th Cir. 1997).
Schall v. Martin, 467 U.S. 253, 365 (1984).
Simpson v. Masten Childers, 71 F.3d 1182 (6th Cir. 1995).
White v. Chambliss, 112 F.3d 731 (4th Cir. 1997).
Wood v. Ostrander, 879 F.2d 583 (9th Cir. 1989).

INDEX

Note: Family relationships with Joshua DeShaney are indicated in parentheses after names; e.g., (father), (mother)

Adoption Assistance and Child Welfare Act of 1980, 17
Alexander, Rudolph, 149, 150
Amar, Akhil, 140
American Civil Liberties Union (ACLU), 61
American Humane Association, 16
appeals courts. *See* United States Court of Appeals for the Seventh Circuit (Chicago); United States Supreme Court
Armbruster, Mary, 22
Austin American, 121
Ayers, Donald, 115

Bailey, Aleta (case), 86–87, 89–90, 96, 99–101
Bailey, Cameron, 100
Baker, Michael Anthony (case), 115, 150
Balisteri, Jena (case), 132
Barbara S. (case), 69
Bass, Larry and Gary (case), 131
Battered Child, The (Kempe), 16
"battered child syndrome," 15–16, 20
battered women, 132–33
Bergh, Henry, 12–13
Billy Budd (Melville), 90
Birch, Tom, 124
Blackmun, Harry, 101; background, 107–8, 143–44; dissenting opinion in *DeShaney* case, 117, 119–21, 123, 125, 148, 157; "Poor Joshua!," 120–21, 122; retirement in 1994, 157
Bodnar, John, 19, 22–23, 47, 63
Bork, Robert, 92
Bowers, T. L., 37, 67
Braam, Ginger, 157–58
Braam, Richard, 157–58
Brennan, William, 93, 101; background, 118, 143, 144; dissenting opinion in *DeShaney* case, 111–12, 117, 118–19, 145
Bridgewater, Myrna (grandmother), 50–51, 74
"bright line test," 89
Brown, Nixzmary (case), 138
Brown v. Board of Education, 91, 106, 108, 117, 137
bullying, 134, 138–39
Burger, Warren, 94, 106, 108–9, 143–44
Bush, George H. W., 144
Bush, George W., 144

California, *Martinez v. California,* 82
Campbell, Jonathan (case), 70
Carter, Robert, 137
Carter, William, 55
Cathleen ni Houlihan (Yeats), 118
Central Wisconsin Center for the Developmentally Disabled, 53–54
Charen, Mona, 121

Cheyenne, Wyoming. *See also* Sullivan, Donald: described, 57, 59–60; mother's claim for custody of Joshua in, 56–57, 59, 60
Chicago, Jonathan Campbell (case), 70
child abuse (generally), 11–18; "battered child syndrome," 15–16, 20; child abuse hotlines, 136–37; denials of, 6–7, 34, 37; errors in reporting, 150–51; evidence of, 4–9, 10, 13, 15, 16, 17; federal child protection laws, 16–17; legacy of *DeShaney* case, 127–39, 153–54, 155–57; media coverage of, 13, 15–16, 17, 28, 35, 130, 136, 139; medical research literature, 15–16, 34; pilot programs to increase awareness, 8; rescue and remove/family support dilemma, 10, 11, 14, 17–18, 34, 37–38, 148–52; rise of social work profession, 14–15; "shock the conscience" standard, 69, 112, 142; state reporting requirements, 16; temporary custody orders, 4–5, 6; Wisconsin state laws regarding, 9–10, 35
Child Abuse and Neglect, 17
child abuse cases. *See also* DeShaney, Joshua: Aleta Bailey, 86–87, 89–90, 96, 99–101; Michael Anthony Baker, 115, 150; Barbara S., 69; Larry and Gary Bass, 131; Nixzmary Brown, 138; Jonathan Campbell, 70; Christian Cisneros, 127–30; Jessica and Nicholas Cortez, 116, 150; Eli Creekmore, 62; Dean H., 69; Myls Dobson, 137–38; Donald O., 69; Amanda Gallegos, 137; Eliza Izquierdo, 138; "Little Mary Ellen," 11–13; Jeanette Maples, 141; Zymire Perkins, 138; Carole Pinder, 131–32; Bruce James Powell, Jr., 130–31; Simpson brothers, 131; Alex Stevenson, 138–39; Thelma Steward, 102; Keena White, 131
Child Abuse Prevention and Treatment Act of 1974, 16–17
Child Abuse Prevention Month (Wisconsin), 53
Child Protection Team (Theda Clark Medical Center), 18–24. *See also* Kemmeter, Ann; background, 16–18; dismissal of temporary court protective order, 23–24, 27, 28, 34, 38; first meeting (January 26, 1983), 18–24, 28, 47; follow-up activities, 28–29; formation for Joshua (January, 1983), 9–10; nature of, 9; participants, 18–19; rescue and remove/family support dilemma, 10, 17–18; temporary protective order for Joshua, 4–5, 6, 51, 90, 147–48
Children's Bureau, 16
Child Welfare, 15, 17
choice of error problem, 150–51
Christian Century, 15
Circuit Court of Appeals, 92–93. *See also* United States Court of Appeals for the Seventh Circuit (Chicago)
Cisneros, Christian (case), 127–30
City Bar Association of New York, 122
Clinton, Bill, 144, 157
compensatory damages, 68, 79
compulsory school attendance laws, 133–34
Connolly, Mary, 12–13
Constitution. *See* United States Constitution
Cortez, Jessica (case), 116, 150
Cortez, Nicholas (case), 116, 120
Creekmore, Eli (case), 62
Curry, Lynne, 155
Curtis, George, 56–57

Davenport, Kristin, 148
Davis, Ruth, 35–36

Dean H. (case), 69
Death in the Afternoon (Hemingway), 97
Demorest, Dr., 76
Denver Post, 136
depositions: defined, 71; for *DeShaney* District Court case, 71–80
DeRozier, Dr., 18–19, 21–22, 29
DeShaney, Christine (stepmother), 8, 25, 51, 67
DeShaney, Joshua: adoption, 157–58; birth in 1979, 29; brain injury and surgery, 41–46, 52–54; Child Protection Team and (*See* Child Protection Team [Theda Clark Medical Center]); consultation with Dr. DeRozier (January, 1983), 21–22; death in 2015, 157–58; due process of law rights, 68; equal protection of the law rights, 68; evidence of child abuse, 4–10, 18–24; guardians ad litem, 52, 63, 92; Head Start and, 32–33, 35–36; injuries and emergency room visits, 3–7, 8–10, 20, 28–34, 36–37, 38, 41–46, 51, 52, 55, 67, 73–75; inner world of the child and, 34–35; legal cases (See *DeShaney v. Winnebago County Department of Social Services* [1989]); mother's claim to assume custody of, 56–57, 59, 60–61, 67–68; parental expectations for, 32–33, 36–37; permanent order of protection/foster care placement options, 24; placement at Central Wisconsin Center for the Developmentally Disabled, 53–54; placement at Gillette Rehabilitation Center (St. Paul), 54; placement in foster care facility after further surgery, 75; post-surgery at Mercy Medical Center, 47–51, 52–54; rescue and remove/family support dilemma, 18–24, 37–38, 148–50; separation anxiety issues, 21–22, 29; social worker home visits, 27–28, 29, 30–32, 34–35, 37, 38–39, 44, 48–49, 63; temporary custody order decision (January, 1983), 4–5, 6, 9–10, 18–24, 27, 28, 51
DeShaney, Kim (aunt), 50
DeShaney, Marie: advised of Miranda rights, 46; expectations for Joshua, 32–33, 36–37; family move to Oshkosh (1983), 32; interview with Thomas Hoare (January, 1983), 8; interview with Keith Nelson (January, 1983), 6–7, 20–21; Joshua's brain injury and surgery, 41–46; Joshua's injuries and emergency room visits, 3–7, 8–10, 20, 28–34, 36–37, 38, 41–46, 52; Mercy Medical Center visitation procedures, 47–48, 49, 50; parenting skills, 8–9, 31, 35–38; recommendation to leave Joshua's household, 22, 23, 28, 29–30, 32; social worker home visits, 27–28, 29, 30–32, 34–35, 37, 38–39, 44, 48–49; son, Rusty, 8, 30, 36, 38–39, 41, 43–44, 46, 48, 50
DeShaney, Melody (mother), 49–52, 54–60; arrival in Wisconsin, 50–51; birth of Joshua in 1979, 29; deposition testimony for *DeShaney* District Court case, 74, 79–80; files claim to assume custody of Joshua, 56–57, 59, 60–61, 67–68; fires legal team, 104–5; gives up custody of Joshua, 8, 22, 29–30, 51, 79–80; hires George Curtis in Wisconsin, 56–57; legal team (*See* First, Curry; Sullivan, Donald); Supreme Court decision in *DeShaney,* 124, 156; survivor's guilt, 30, 52, 57; trial track for *DeShaney* District Court case, 72, 74–75, 79–80; visitation rights

DeShaney, Melody (mother) *(continued)* and child support, 29-30, 51-52, 67-68, 79-80
DeShaney, Randy (father): agreement with Winnebago County Department of Social Services (January, 1983), 23, 27-28, 29, 31-32; arrest and arraignment procedures, 46, 55-56, 57, 60, 70; background, 9, 22, 29; custody of Joshua, 8, 22, 27-28, 29-30; expectations for Joshua, 32-33, 36-37; family move to Oshkosh (1983), 32; interview with Thomas Hoare (January, 1983), 8; interview with Keith Nelson (January, 1983), 6-7, 20-21; Joshua's brain injury and surgery, 41-46; Joshua's injuries and emergency room visits, 3-7, 8-10, 20, 28-34, 36-37, 38, 41-46, 51, 52, 55, 67, 73-75; Joshua's temporary custody order decision (January, 1983), 4-5, 6, 9-10, 18-24, 27, 28, 51; marital history, 8, 29-30; Mercy Medical Center visitation procedures, 47-48, 49, 50; as named party in *DeShaney,* 63; parenting skills, 8-9, 23, 24, 27-28, 29-30, 35-38; Police Complaint report (1982), 24-25; social worker home visits, 27-28, 29, 30-32, 34-35, 37, 38-39, 44, 48-49
DeShaney, Tom (grandfather), 50
DeShaney v. Winnebago County Department of Social Services (1989), 159-81 (text); broader implications of case, 68-71, 91, 96; call for Supreme Court to return to, 124-25, 138-39, 141-52; and *DeShaney* community, 154-55; impact of potential Supreme Court reversal, 152-54; initial establishment of case, 60-61; legacy of, 127-39, 153-54, 155-57; media coverage, 101-2, 105, 120-25, 141-42; named parties, 63; Notices of Appearance for Sullivan and First, 63; status of children under the law, 147-48; and United States Court of Appeals for the Seventh Circuit, 90-98, 99-102, 117-18; and United States District Court for the Eastern District of Wisconsin, 62-63, 67-91; and United States Supreme Court, 99-125, 138-39, 141-52
Dewey, Thomas, 142
Dickman, Lori, 75
discovery: defined, 71; for *DeShaney* District Court case, 71-80
District Court. *See* United States District Court for the Eastern District of Wisconsin
Dobson, Myls (case), 137-38
Doe v. New York City Department of Social Services, 82
Donald O. (case), 69
Douglas, Elsie, 107
Douthett, Breaden, 148
D.R. (case), 133
due process clause, Fourteenth Amendment, 68, 80-81, 86, 87, 91, 95, 97, 102, 110, 117-18, 120, 132, 133, 135, 145-48, 157
Dyer, Dee, 43

Eaton, Thomas, 151-52
Economic Analysis of Law (Posner), 93-94
Edelman, Peter, 142
Eisenhower, Dwight, 92, 118, 142-43
equal protection under the law, 68, 117, 119
Estate of Bailey v. County of York, 86-87, 89-90, 96, 99-101

Fain, Jim, 121

Farr, Gladys, 46
Federal Code, Section 1983, 80–81, 86, 95
First, Curry, 60–63; appeal of *DeShaney* to Seventh Circuit Court of Appeals, 90–98; background and training, 61; claim preparation for *DeShaney,* 62–63; *DeShaney* Supreme Court pretrial period, 103–5; dismissal track for *DeShaney* District Court case, 80–81, 85–87; establishment of *DeShaney* case, 60–61; fired by Melody DeShaney, 104–5; as guardian ad litem for Joshua DeShaney, 63, 92; oral arguments in *DeShaney* Supreme Court case, 108–15; petition for *DeShaney* writ of certiorari, 97–98, 99–102; Supreme Court decision in *DeShaney,* 124; trial track for *DeShaney* District Court case, 71–80, 87–88
foster care: Joshua DeShaney and, 24, 75; *Doe v. New York City Department of Social Services,* 82; problems of, 24, 131; Keena White (case), 131
Foster v. Chatman, 144
Fourteenth Amendment, due process clause, 68, 80–81, 86, 87, 91, 95, 97, 102, 110, 117–18, 120, 132, 133, 135, 145–48, 157
Friendship, Wisconsin, Donald O. (case), 69

Gallegos, Amanda (case), 137
Gehringer, Robert: and Child Protection Team, 18–19, 24, 29, 31; deposition testimony for *DeShaney* District Court case, 76–78; Joshua's emergency room visits, 3–4; third-party complaint in *DeShaney* District Court case, 78
George Washington Law Review, 142
Gerry, Elbridge, 13
Gillette Rehabilitation Center (St. Paul), 54
Goldwater, Barry, 106
Goodman, Ellen, 121
Great Depression, 14, 16
Greenberg, Jack, 137
Greenhouse, Linda, 120–21, 139
gross negligence claims, 69, 74–75, 88, 89, 111, 112, 115, 132, 142, 156
guardian ad litem, 52, 63, 92
guns, 134–36

Haase, Robert, 55
Hake, Larry, 86
Harlan, John Marshall, 120
Harvard Educational Review, 15
Harvard Law Review, 148
Hein, Sister Joanne, 41
Hentoff, Nat, 118, 121
Hoare, Thomas: background, 4; Child Protection Team and, 9–10, 18–24, 74–75; deposition testimony for *DeShaney* District Court case, 76; interviews Joshua's family members (January, 1983), 8; Joshua's emergency room visits, 4–6, 8, 28–30; as medical social worker at Theda Clark, 4
Hobart, Wisconsin, Christian Cisneros (case), 127–30
Holmes, Oliver Wendell, 144
homosexual conduct, 107
How the Other Half Lives (Riis), 13
Hudak, Brenda, 137
Humphrey, Hubert, 16, 143

Illinois: Chicago, Jonathan Campbell (case), 70; Joliet, *Jackson v. City of Joliet,* 81–82
Industrial Workers of the World, 92
Izquierdo, Eliza (case), 138

Jackson, Robert, 106, 107
Jackson v. City of Joliet, 81–82
Johnson, Lyndon, 16, 143
Johnson v. Santa Clara County, 106
Joliet, Illinois, *Jackson v. City of Joliet,* 81–82
Joshua. *See* DeShaney, Joshua
Journal of the American Medical Association, 15
Juknialis, John, 47, 50

Kagan, Elena, 101
Kayali, Basher, 55
Kemmeter, Ann. *See also* Child Protection Team (Theda Clark Medical Center): assists Winnebago County Juvenile Court, 47; background and training, 28; Child Abuse Prevention Month, 53; and Child Protection Team, 19, 24, 27; *DeShaney* District Court case, 72, 73–75, 88; DeShaney home visits, 27–28, 29, 30–32, 34–35, 37, 38–39, 44, 48–49; *DeShaney* Supreme Court decision, 115–16, 123–24, 156; interviews Joshua's family members (January, 1983), 6–7, 8, 21; Joshua's brain injury and surgery, 41–43, 46; Joshua's injuries and emergency room visits, 5–7, 8, 28–30, 31, 33–34, 37, 41–43; as named party in *DeShaney,* 63; post-surgery activities, 47–49, 50–51; Service Plan reviews, 32–33, 36–38; as social worker at Winnebago County Department of Social Services, 5–6, 24, 74–75
Kempe, C. Henry, 15–16
Kennedy, Anthony, 114
Kennedy, John F., 16, 92, 143
Keyes, Tommy (case), 133
Kilpatrick, James, 122, 138–39
Kimberly-Clark Corporation, 7
Klan Acts, 146
Kronenwetter, Officer, 43, 46

LaGuardia, Frances, 134–35
LaGuardia, James (case), 134–35
Langtry, Lilly, 59
Letellier, Dr., 46, 52–53, 55
"Little Mary Ellen" (case), 11–13
Los Angeles Times, 120

Manhattan Lawyer, 142
Maples, Jeanette (case), 141
Marshall, Ann, 47–48, 50
Marshall, Thurgood, 101, 117, 137, 143
Martin, Gregory (case), 147–48
Martinez v. California, 82
Medford, Wisconsin, Dean H. (case), 69
Meese, Edwin, 93
Melville, Herman, 90
Mercy Medical Center (Oshkosh): background and history, 50; Joshua's brain injury and surgery, 41–46; Joshua's emergency room visits, 33–34, 36–37, 41–46, 63; Joshua's post-surgery period, 47–51, 52–54
Milwaukee, Wisconsin, Barbara S. (case), 69
Mingo, Mark: background and training, 71; *DeShaney* Supreme Court pretrial period, 103–4; dismissal track for *DeShaney* District Court case, 72, 80–83, 85–87, 100; oral arguments in *DeShaney* Supreme Court case, 113–15; trial track for *DeShaney* District Court case, 71–80, 88, 100
Missouri, Larry and Gary Bass (case), 131
Montgomery v. City of Ames, 142
Moore, Michelle, 136
Moschella, Steven, 134
Mueller, John, 124
Murley, David, 135–36

National Association of Social Workers, 15, 135–36
National Center for Child Abuse and Neglect, 16–17
National Child Abuse Coalition, 124
Neenah, Wisconsin. *See also entries beginning with* "Winnebago County": background and description, 7–8, 27–28, 30–31; Police Department (*See* Neenah Police Department); Theda Clark Medical Center (*See* Theda Clark Medical Center [Neenah])
Neenah Boot and Shoe, 7
Neenah Police Department: and Joshua DeShaney case (*See* Nelson, Keith); Police Complaint report on Randy DeShaney (1982), 24–25
"negative rights," of Constitution, 101, 122, 145–47, 148–49
Nelson, Keith: deposition testimony for *DeShaney* District Court case, 76; interviews DeShaney neighbors (January, 1983), 21, 38; interviews Joshua's family members (January, 1983), 6–7, 20–21; Joshua's emergency room visits, 5–7; as Neenah Police Department investigator, 6–7, 13, 20–21, 38
Nelson, Sandy, 103, 104
New Deal, 16
Newell, Rockne, 134–35
New England Journal of Medicine, 15
New York City: Michael Anthony Baker (case), 115, 150; Nixzmary Brown (case), 138; Jessica and Nicholas Cortez (case), 116, 150; Myls Dobson (case), 137–38; *Doe v. New York City Department of Social Services,* 82; Eliza Izquierdo (case), 138; "Little Mary Ellen" (case), 11–13; Mayor's Task Force investigations of child protective system, 69–70; Zymire Perkins (case), 138; Thelma Steward (case), 102
New York Civil Liberties Union, 61
New York Times, 13, 15, 17, 101–2, 105, 120–21, 122–23, 139
Nicolet Clinic (Neenah), 7, 29, 31
Nixon, Richard, 93, 106, 107, 143–44
Niziol, Ted (case), 134
North Carolina, Alex Stevenson (case), 138–39
Northwestern, 123
Notre Dame Law Review, 141, 149
Novotny, Detective, 43, 46, 50

Obama, Barack, 122, 144
O'Connor, Sandra Day, 110–11, 116, 149, 150
Off Our Backs, 121
Olinger, David, 136
Oregon, Eugene, Jeanette Maples (case), 141
originalism, 113
Oshkosh, Wisconsin, 7. *See also entries beginning with* "Winnebago County"; described, 102–3; DeShaney family move in 1983, 32; Mercy Medical Center (*See* Mercy Medical Center [Oshkosh]); Police Department (*See* Oshkosh Police Department)
Oshkosh Police Department: DeShaney family and, 34, 35, 36–37, 43, 45–46; investigation of Joshua's case, 53; third party complaint in *DeShaney* District Court case, 79

parens patriae doctrine, 147–48
Pennsylvania: *Estate of Bailey v. County of York,* 86–87, 89–90, 96, 99–101; Philadelphia Human Services Department loses license, 70
Perkins, Zymire (case), 138
Peters, Theda Clark, 7–8

Philadelphia, Human Resource Department loses license, 70
Pinder, Carole (case), 131–32
Pittman, Don, 131–32
Plessy, Homer, 120
Plessy v. Ferguson, 91, 106–7, 120, 137
Plueddeman, Dr., 42
Posner, Richard A., 90–98; appointment to Court of Appeals, 93; background, 93; *DeShaney* decision for United States Court of Appeals for the Seventh Circuit (Chicago), 95–98, 99–102, 117–18, 150; law and economics mode of analysis, 93–94, 97–98; razor's edge decisions, 150
Post-Crescent newspaper, 123, 130
Powell, Bruce, 130–31
Powell, Bruce James, Jr. (case), 130–31
Powell, Lewis F., Jr., 144
privacy, 107, 108
Psychological Bulletin, 15
punitive damages, 68, 79

"qualified immunity" doctrine, 82–83, 87
Quam, Mark, 123

Ratteman, Debbie, 121
razor's edge decisions, 148–52
Readers Guide to Periodical Literature, 15
Reagan, Ronald, 92–94, 106, 109, 115
Reat, James Pal, 135
Reat, Ran Pal (case), 135
Regents of University of California v. Bakke, 106
Rehnquist, William, 94, 105; background, 106–7, 143–44; majority opinion in *DeShaney,* 116, 117–18, 119–20, 121–25, 142, 145, 154; oral arguments in *DeShaney* Supreme Court case, 108–15; *parens patriae* doctrine, 147–48
Reynolds, John, 67–91; and appeal of decision on *DeShaney* District Court case, 90–98; background, 83; conferences for *DeShaney* District Court case, 72–73; decision and order for *DeShaney* District Court case, 88–91; dismissal track for *DeShaney* District Court case, 72, 80–83, 85–87, 88–91; razor's edge decisions, 149, 150; trial track for *DeShaney* District Court case, 71–80, 87–88
Riis, Jacob, 13
Roberson (case), 133–34
Robinson, Spottswood, 137
Rodriguez, Angel, 132–33
Roe v. Wade, 106, 107, 109
Rusty (Marie DeShaney's son), 8, 30, 36, 38–39, 41, 43–44, 46, 48, 50

Saturday Evening Post, 15
Savage, David, 120
Scalia, Antonin, 94, 112–14, 116, 118
Schall v. Martin, 147–48
schools, 133–34, 138–39
Second Amendment, 135–36
Section 1983, Federal Code, 80–81, 86, 95
Seventh Circuit Court of Appeals. *See* United States Court of Appeals for the Seventh Circuit (Chicago)
"shock the conscience" standard, 69, 112, 142
Simarski and Stack, 67–68
Simpson brothers (case), 131
Sisters of the Sorrowful Mother, 50
Sixth Amendment, right to counsel, 145
Smith, Rysheim, 138
social work: and *DeShaney* community, 154–55; impact of reversal of *DeShaney,* 152–54; legacy of *DeShaney,* 135–36, 153–54, 155–57; razor's edge decisions,

148–52; rescue and remove/family support dilemma of child abuse, 10, 11, 14, 17–18, 34, 37–38, 148–52; rise of profession, 14–15; state reporting requirements for child abuse, 16
Social Work, 15, 17, 28, 149
Social Work Yearbook, 14
Society for the Prevention of Cruelty to Animals, 12, 13
Society for the Prevention of Cruelty to Children, 13–14, 16–17, 22
Sofier, Avian, 142
Soto, Flor Maria (case), 132–33
South Carolina, Keena White (case), 131
South Carolina Law Review, 139
Spaniol, Joseph, 103, 104, 105
"special relationship" claims, 81–82, 86–87, 89–90, 96, 133–34, 142, 147
St. John's Law Review, 142
"state-created danger" doctrine, 135, 142
Stelse, Cheryl: Child Abuse Prevention Month, 53; and Child Protection Team, 19; *DeShaney* District Court case, 72, 88; as named party in *DeShaney,* 63; as supervisor of Ann Kemmeter, 19, 33, 35, 43, 46, 53, 63, 72, 88
Stevens, John Paul, 112, 116
Stevenson, Alex (case), 138–39
Steward, Thelma (case), 102
"strict constructionists," 93
Suebert, Patrick, 52
Sullivan, Donald: appeal of *DeShaney* to Seventh Circuit Court of Appeals, 90–98; background and training, 58, 61; claim preparation for *DeShaney,* 62–63; *DeShaney* Supreme Court pretrial period, 103–5; dismissal track for *DeShaney* District Court case, 80–81, 85–87; establishment of *DeShaney* case, 60–61; fired by Melody DeShaney, 104–5; oral arguments in *DeShaney* Supreme Court case, 108–15, 149; petition for *DeShaney* writ of certiorari, 97–98, 99–102; reasons not to accept *DeShaney* case, 59; Supreme Court decision in *DeShaney* case, 117–21, 124–25, 155–56; trial track for *DeShaney* District Court case, 71–80, 87–88; and Wyoming Trial Lawyers Association, 58
Sunstein, Cass, 122
Supreme Court. *See* United States Supreme Court

Taylor, Sandra, 125
temporary custody orders: Child Protection Team role in, 9–10, 18–24; and Joshua's emergency room visits, 4–5, 6, 18–24, 27, 28, 51; procedures for obtaining, 4–5, 6
Theda Clark Medical Center (Neenah): background and description, 7–8; Child Protection Team (*See* Child Protection Team [Theda Clark Medical Center]); Joshua's emergency room visits, 3–7, 8–10, 25, 28–30, 31, 32, 52
third-party complaints, 78–79
Thirteenth Amendment, 148
Time magazine, 15
Today's Health, 15
Tourgee, Albion, 137
Tribe, Laurence, 122
type-one errors, 150–51
type-two errors, 150–51

United States Attorney General, 115
United States Constitution: Second Amendment gun rights, 135–36; Sixth Amendment right to counsel, 145; Thirteenth Amendment abolition of slavery, 148; Fourteenth Amendment due process clause, 68, 80–81, 86, 87, 91, 95, 97, 102, 110,

United States Constitution *(continued)* 117–18, 120, 132, 133, 135, 145–48, 157; "negative rights," 101, 122, 145–47, 148–49
United States Court of Appeals for the Seventh Circuit (Chicago), 90–98; appeal of *DeShaney*l filed with District Court, 90–98; Richard Posner as presiding judge, 92, 93, 94; Richard Posner decision, 95–98, 99–102, 117–18, 150
United States Department of Health and Human Services (HHS), 136
United States District Court for the Eastern District of Wisconsin, 67–91; allegations and recitations, 67–68; appeal of *DeShaney,* 90–98; bill of costs for *DeShaney,* 92; complaint filed, 62–63, 67–68; damage claims, 68, 79; decision and order on motion to dismiss, 88–91; depositions and discovery, 71–80; dismissal track for *DeShaney,* 72, 80–83, 85–87, 88–91; general denial of complaint, 71; John Reynolds as presiding judge (*See* Reynolds, John); third-party complaints, 78–79; trial track for *DeShaney,* 71–80, 87–88
United States Supreme Court, 99–125; *amicus*/Friend of the Court briefs in *DeShaney* case, 115; call for return to *DeShaney,* 124–25, 138–39, 141–52; changes in composition and direction, 93, 94, 106, 108–9, 142–44; circuit court judges as appointees, 92–93; deliberations in *DeShaney* case, 115–17; dissenting opinion in *DeShaney* case, 111–12, 117, 118–21, 123, 125, 145, 148, 152, 156, 157; impact of potential reversal of *DeShaney,* 152–54; majority opinion in *DeShaney* case, 116, 117–18, 119–20, 121–25, 142, 145, 154, 156; oral arguments in *DeShaney* case, 104, 108–15, 149; petition for *DeShaney* writ of certiorari, 97–98, 99–102; pretrial activities for *DeShaney* case, 102–8; split decision on *DeShaney* case, 117–25

Venne, Dan, 6

Warren, Earl, 93, 108–9, 142–44
Washington state, Eli Creekmore (case), 62
Wells, Michael, 151–52
Wheeler, Etta Angell, 11–13
White, Byron, 101, 114, 116
White, Keena (case), 131
White v. Rockford, 86
Widawsky, Daniel, 148
Williams, Thomas, 104–5
Wilson, Dan, 130
Winnebago County Board of Supervisors, 56–57
Winnebago County Circuit Court, temporary custody order procedures, 4–5, 6, 18–24, 27, 28, 51
Winnebago County Department of Social Services. *See also* Kemmeter, Ann: agreement with Randy DeShaney on parenting duties, 23, 27–28, 29, 31–32; Child Abuse Prevention Month, 53; Child Protective Unit supervisor, 19, 33, 35, 43, 46, 53, 63, 72, 88; dismissal of temporary court protective order, 23–24, 27, 28; federal civil rights case against, 62–63 (See also *DeShaney v. Winnebago County Department of Social Services* [1989]); gross negligence claims, 74–75; Joshua's brain injury and surgery, 41–43, 46; Joshua's injuries and emergency room visits, 5–7, 8–10, 28–30, 31, 32, 33–34, 37; legal defense team (*See* Mingo, Mark;

Yankala, Wayne); mother's claim to assume custody of Joshua, 56–57, 59, 60–61; Police Complaint report on Randy DeShaney (1982), 24–25; state review of child abuse/neglect procedures, 85; Supreme Court decision in *DeShaney*, 123–24, 155–56
Winnebago County Juvenile Court: authorizes temporary custody of Joshua DeShaney, 46, 47–49; initial dismissal of DeShaney temporary custody orders, 6, 23–24, 27, 28, 38
Wisconsin: child abuse laws, 9–10, 35; Child Abuse Prevention Month, 53; Friendship, Donald O. (case), 69; Hobart, Christian Cisneros (case), 127–30; Medford, Dean H. (case), 69; Milwaukee, Barbara S. (case), 69; Neenah (*See* Neenah, Wisconsin); Oshkosh (*See* Oshkosh, Wisconsin); Winnebago County (*See entries beginning with* "Winnebago County")
Wisconsin Department of Health and Human Services, 129
Wisconsin Supreme Court, ruling on search warrants in child abuse cases, 35
World War II, 14
writ of certiorari, 97–98, 99–102
Wyoming Trial Lawyers Association, 58

Yankala, Wayne, 71; dismissal track for *DeShaney* District Court case, 72, 80–83, 85–87; trial track for *DeShaney* District Court case, 71–80, 88
Yeats, William Butler, 118